Miseducating for the Global Economy

MISEDUCATING

for the

GLOBAL ECONOMY

How Corporate Power Damages Education and

Subverts Students' Futures

by GERALD COLES

MONTHLY REVIEW PRESS

New York

Library of Congress Cataloging-in-Publication Data:
available from the publisher

ISBN: 978-158367-6912 paper
ISBN: 978-158367-6936 cloth

Typeset in Minion Pro

Monthly Review Press, New York
monthlyreview.org

5 4 3 2 1

Contents

To Maria, my love and comrade these many years,
"I carry your heart in my heart"

Acknowledgments

My thanks to Maria Iannacome Coles, John Marciano and Jon Garlock for reading and contributing to the crafting of this book. Michael Yates provided valuable editing advice, but also deserves a deep acknowledgment for his admirable, unflagging scholarly and activist work for a better world. I appreciate Erin Claremont's helpful copy editing.

As I wrote this book, my thoughts constantly drifted back to the many educators who have worked and mostly failed, from the 1960s onward, to create a thoughtful, caring, democratic education. Nonetheless, this struggle continues, as exemplified by the educators associated in myriad ways to the *Rethinking Schools* project. To these educators, past, present and future, I offer gratitude.

Introduction

In the late 1960s, I taught basic literacy classes in an adult education program in Watts, Los Angeles in the midst of what many people have called the "Watts Riots" but others, including myself, have called the "Watts Uprisings." Uprisings in black communities throughout the nation had been a reaction to decades of severe poverty, housing segregation, unemployment, police brutality, and other abhorrent expressions of racial and class discrimination. In response to these revolts and the civil rights activism that preceded and accompanied them, the federal government funded various community development projects, with educational programs serving as the policy centerpiece that would lead black communities to a better future. A chief program in the Lyndon Johnson administration's "War on Poverty" was the Job Corps, which provided education and job training for young people. I knew that program well, having taught at the Breckenridge Job Corps Center in Morganfield, Kentucky, before teaching in a War on Poverty program in Watts.

Around the time I worked in Watts, a popular song was Curtis Mayfield's "Choice of Colors," whose lyrics struck me as encapsulating the chief explanation and answer in the legislative response to heartless, oppressive suffering. Mayfield sang about the way that more education and greater love of the nation would create a better society.[1]

The lyrics could be interpreted as meaning that if all Americans were better educated about equality and justice, and truly dedicated to creating a country that embodied these values, the United States would become a better nation. Yet the song also included lines that seemed to be speaking not to "our nation" but primarily and critically to black people, asking how long they've hated their white teachers and why "some of us" would prefer to "cuss" and "fuss."

The lyrics would appeal to many white listeners who blamed black people for causing their own problems and perhaps contributed to the song rising to the top of *Billboard*'s rhythm and blues chart. Given the social issues that the educational programs I worked in were intended to address, I felt that the lyrics expressed, consciously or not, the ideology that the chief cause of the miseries of African-American communities was insufficient schooling, rather than class and racial oppression, and that "more education" was the primary answer for black people.

While working in these War on Poverty programs, the insufficiencies of this policy direction became apparent to me. At Breckenridge, the students had "rioted" after they frustratingly concluded that the Job Corps was more about removing black youth from urban areas to a remote part of Kentucky, and less about providing occupational training that would help them obtain work and attain better futures. In Watts, "more education" similarly reflected a minimal policy response. Certainly the community had educational needs, but the "skills center" in which I taught, run by a for-profit trade school, was considered a pilot program for educating adults, purportedly intended to see "what works" in Watts and similar black communities. As such, the skills center provided education for only a small fraction of the many adults in Watts who wanted to enroll in the program.

Personally and professionally, my teaching was satisfying. I helped non-literate adults learn to read and write and moderately literate adults to advance their literacy. By creating instructional materials with rich content, even at basic literacy levels, I was able to evoke classroom conversations drawn from students' adult experiences and sophisticated understandings, thereby enabling them to feel intellectually capable, rather than embarrassed by their rudimentary literacy competence. Nonetheless, with respect to the skills center as a whole, I recognized that it drew attention away from the answers needed for Watts and similar communities.

Particularly disappointing to the students were the narrow boundaries of the vocational curriculum. The students thought they would obtain extensive job training but discovered that the Watts Skills Center provided no more than basic vocational skills. Consequently, students who went on to obtain jobs in manufacturing companies in the Los Angeles area would get entry-level jobs in which they would have difficulty advancing. An entry-level job was better than no job, but the adult students concluded that the skills center was wholly deficient in addressing individual and community employment issues.

From these teaching experiences I saw how schooling can serve as an ideological device to deflect understanding of the source of social problems, particularly occupational and income problems. I also learned that no matter how satisfying classroom teaching can be for a teacher, "schools" as institutions can be used to create misunderstandings of and deficient answers to problems generated by an inequitable economic system.

IN RECENT YEARS, MANY AMERICANS have been unemployed or underemployed because of company closings and relocations, technology replacing human labor, an increase in individual workload to reduce the number of employees needed, and more use of part-time workers. Vast numbers of workers earn unlivable wages, receive deficient benefits, and cobble together earnings through several part-time jobs. Why has this been happening?

A dominant answer for corporations and their political surrogates has been that U.S. public schools are primarily to blame because they have failed potential employees in the face of the twenty-first-century global economy. Though many new kinds of jobs requiring science, technology, engineering, and math (STEM) skills have been created, schools are criticized for not teaching these skills to enough students.

Consequently, thanks to bad schooling, the new economy's plethora of skilled, good-paying jobs have remained unfilled, handicapping both U.S. businesses and workers.

National educational policy has been crafted on behalf of this claim, starting at the beginning of the twenty-first century with George W. Bush's No Child Left Behind (NCLB) legislation. NCLB's educational policies were introduced as research-proven answers for teaching and learning that would lead to academic success in later coursework and, consequently, future job attainment. For example, Reading First, formulated as the bedrock schooling policy for NCLB, supposedly was "scientifically based reading instruction." In fact, it was of no value at all, as research later revealed that reading scores across the nation had remained flat a decade after the instruction had been introduced into the nation's classrooms.[2] In 2000, I wrote a book reviewing and debunking the entire body of research garnered to justify Reading First teaching, showing that the evidence did not support the policy conclusions. Not surprisingly, however, politics trumped science and education was identified as the chief answer to the well-being of Americans, especially those living in poverty.[3]

With the failure of NCLB to achieve its projected results, President Barack Obama's answer for a national educational policy that would lead to better occupational outcomes was Common Core State Standards, whose mission statement was to have youth leave school with the skills to compete in the twenty-first-century global economy. Because of an array of criticisms of the legislation, the policy was reconfigured as the Every Child Succeeds Act, which transferred policy power from the federal government to the states, but retained the goal of strengthening STEM education for work in the global economy. In the words of Minnesota Democratic Senator Amy Klobuchar, who helped introduce provisions into the legislation to promote STEM education and training, these "STEM initiatives ensure that our students have the skills and education they need to be competitive today and into the future . . . to give our students the skills they need to be successful in high-tech, high-wage jobs."[4] Reinforcing these governmental educational policies has been a sequence of books and national reports arguing that schools are failing the future occupational opportunities of students by failing to educate them for the new global economy. Shortly after Donald Trump became president and Betsy DeVos was selected to head the Department of Education, Vince M. Bertram, CEO of the corporate-led educational organization, Project Lead the Way, and author of *One Nation Under-Taught: Solving America's Science, Technology, Engineering and Math Crisis*, urged the new administration to "set a clear vision of what we're preparing [students] for." He explained that STEM employment has continued to grow and the future job market will have an "exponential demand for qualified STEM employees." Therefore, the administration's most important task must be to "to cast a vision for what education can be for our next generation to meet the demands of a global economy."[5]

Similarly, the STEM Education Coalition, an "alliance of more than 600 business, professional, and education organizations," stated:

> In today's economy every student needs to have a strong foundation in the STEM subjects in order to land and succeed in virtually any job—from the shop floor to the research lab to the boardroom. Further, the best, most highly paying jobs are nearly all in the STEM fields. If we are going to enable our students to compete in the global economy we must maintain a strong federal commitment to improve teaching and learning in the STEM fields.[6]

DeVos assured the coalition of her awareness that "STEM is an important part of education, no matter a student's background," because "most jobs today require a much higher degree of technical competence than even five years ago." She pledged to "prioritize STEM education," underscoring that "a strong pipeline of students interested in pursuing STEM careers . . . is important to our nation's success."[7]

THE EXTENT TO WHICH THE EMPLOYMENT and income problems of Americans are fundamentally a consequence of the nation's schools failing to provide the needed education for the new economy will be addressed in the pages ahead, beginning with a discussion of the actual constitution of the so-called global economy. Is Silicon Valley's high-tech labor a microcosm of the work that is transforming the U.S. and global economy, or is the opening scene of *Manufactured Landscapes*, a 2006 documentary that begins with photographer Edward Burtynsky's 8-minute tracking shot inside a Chinese factory, about two-thirds of a mile long, where 23,000 workers sit or stand in row after row, producing and assembling clothes irons, piece by piece, a more accurate image of that economy?[8] And where does other factory work in China, Bangladesh, Vietnam, Mexico, etc., fit into the image of the global economy for which U.S. schools are faulted for failing to prepare students? In the United States, will the twenty-first-century STEM jobs soon replace employment in retail sales, fast food production, internet order filling, office cleaning, home health care, and security workers? For STEM-skilled workers, what is the effect of employment obtained through "crowdsourcing," a process through which skilled workers bid against one another for jobs, mostly short-term, awarded to the lowest bidder, with no benefits and no future? And within the new global economy how will many high-skilled U.S. workers fare when fighting for jobs against foreign workers who compete at lower pay, fewer benefits, and for limited time periods?

Not surprisingly, for all the discussion and clamoring about education and the global economy, very little about that economy is studied in the schools. Portrayed in largely cheerful terms, the economy is conceptualized as one that emerged around 1492 and ever since has extended and deepened global connections, benefited from new technologies, and expanded the movement and consumption of goods. As for the twenty-first-century curriculum delivered through twenty-first-century digital means, even though it has creative features for engaging students and is available to them any time, an examination of its content reveals that it remains within boundaries that ensure minimal understanding of and critical thinking about the global economy.

HOW BADLY ARE THE U.S. SCHOOLS doing in preparing workers for the national economy? Are they really failing businesses and their employee needs? Or are they doing a splendid job serving an economy in which the value of work has consistently remained stratified, with STEM work comprising, as it has for many decades, just a relatively small portion of work? I will argue that corporations are leading criticism of schools for doing exactly what schools have always done and continue to do well: that is, provide a portion of Americans with the educational abilities to obtain work in the upper-level occupations of the economy, and in a multi-tiered educational system, providing an array of lesser abilities to other students, who will meet the stratified labor needs that constitute the vast portion of the stratified economy. These outcomes are not what many educators want to achieve, but given the pedagogical constraints on teachers, the social-class hardships imposed on many youngsters, and the unequal resources in a stratified system of education, these outcomes are very much in sync with the needs of the economy's actual workforce. Overall, schools do "quite well" in meeting business needs. Moreover, given the association between the economy's actual needs and the success of schools in fulfilling those needs, the worst outcome for those holding dominant power in the U.S. profit-driven economy would be if schools produced a vast number of STEM-educated adults, who would then confront and appraise the reality of that economy and those who dominate it.

To ensure that schools focus education on occupational goals and not on how the economy really works, corporations have intruded into schooling in various ways, such as financing STEM education, providing STEM curricula, and creating other curricula aimed at nurturing uncritical acceptance of the dominant economic-political order. These corporate funding levels, though hardly commensurate with the vast wealth behind them, have been sufficient to help ensure that schools shrink key areas of the curriculum, narrow students' understandings and critical thinking, and promote classroom silence and confusion about the contemporary global economy and its impact on humanity.

Many educational reformers have sought to improve school conditions and educational outcomes in numerous ways, such as demanding smaller classroom size and improving the well-being of poor children. Achieving these and related goals certainly would contribute to the educational success of many students. However, a major impediment to these reforms, which their advocates must confront, is that the reforms will *never* be achieved in the currently constituted economy because improved educational outcomes for students would, in turn, expose the fundamental impossibility of the current economic system to provide good jobs, incomes, and benefits in a purported twenty-first-century global economy filled with STEM work. For those at the top of the economy and their political helpers who need to explain the increasing financial divide between them and everyone else, what better strategy to use than to blame schools and what better way to do that than by obstructing the reforms that educational organizations propose?   Consequently, those working for reforms for schools and students must face the fact that these reforms cannot be achieved within the economic system as currently constructed. This is because the well-being of those at the top of the economy is dependent on preventing the implementation of reform. *Miseducating for the Global Economy* focuses largely on schooling and the damaging corporate-dominated contemporary economy, but in the final chapter I offer some ideas on how educators, parents, and activists can fight back.

1. Education for the Global Economy

The prevailing story about schooling in the twenty-first century goes something like this: The chief educational imperative of the century is to prepare students to compete successfully in the global economy for jobs that increasingly require advanced technical skills, far beyond those required of workers in the past. This century also brings another challenge to workers. Due to enormous changes in communication technology, much work can be done by skilled laborers around the globe, thereby reducing the advantage of locality formerly possessed by workers in advanced economies. And if these challenges weren't enough for twenty-first-century employees, there is the added problem of ever-advancing technologies requiring constant upgrading of skills, making jobs obsolescent at a pace never before seen. To meet these challenges, look to the schools as the key institution for providing future workers with the education needed for twenty-first-century jobs and business needs.

So goes the story of leaders in politics, corporations, universities, teachers unions, and social policy institutes. In the words of President Barack Obama:

The source of America's prosperity has never been merely how ably we accumulate wealth, but how well we educate our people. This has never been more true than it is today. In a twenty-first-century world where jobs can be shipped wherever there's an Internet connection, where a child born in Dallas is now competing with a child in New Delhi, where your best job qualification is not what you do, but what you know—education is no longer just a pathway to opportunity and success, it's a prerequisite for success.[1]

As John McCain and Mitt Romney, Obama's respective Republican opponents in the 2008 and 2012 presidential elections made clear, the view is bipartisan. For McCain, "Education is the key to building a strong and competitive workforce in a global economy."[2] One of Romney's chief education points focused on providing students "with the skills they need to compete in the global economy."[3] On the same wavelength, Betsy DeVos, secretary of education in the Trump administration, emphasized: "Every child deserves access to a world class education. This is not merely an aspirational goal, but a necessary policy objective if our children are to compete successfully in a global economy."[4]

Within this formulation, the global economy is comprised of an array of businesses, workers, and consumers. Businesses and their employees, now often called "associates," create products and services that compete with similar products and services that consumers purchase and use. To maximize profits, businesses go where production- and service-work, such as telephone technical support and various customer services, are least costly, a perpetual problem for those moving across the globe seeking employment or trying to hold on to jobs in their home nations. Hence, the starting point is the claim that workers need to obtain the right kind of education—have the best skills sets—to obtain one of the good jobs in this global economy. Along with the formulation that each person must stand on his own feet, but nonetheless might, despite one's best efforts, totter, tumble, and fall, is the assumption that a person's well-being should not be tethered to businesses, and businesses are not expected to provide a lifeline for individuals whose services they no longer require.

Where is government in this economy? As geographer and social theorist David Harvey writes, for the citizenry, government's role is to help create the social order in which the individual has the opportunity to obtain occupational skills for making choices in the free market. However, "while personal and individual freedom in the marketplace is guaranteed, each individual nevertheless is held responsible and accountable for his or her own actions and well-being."[5] Individual success or failure rests on the individual; and the outcome is a consequence of an individual's personal preparation and actions. Choice has to be limited to how "I," not "we," find a place and sustenance in the global economy.

The extent to which this model and mission has been widely absorbed among educators is evident in the assertion of Randi Weingarten, president of the American Federation of Teachers, that "today's public school teachers are on the front lines of our collective efforts to compete in a global economy."[6] Similarly, U.S. Chamber of Commerce senior vice-president Arthur Rothkopf affirmed: "The Chamber has always emphasized that a first-class education system is the only way for America to compete and succeed in the global economy."[7]

Within this formulation of "we're all in it together," schools are the essential institution, with the determination of the value of its curriculum content lying in the answer to a question that was asked in an *Education Week* article on school reform: "How Can I Use This in the Real World?"[8] Does the academic program serve a utilitarian purpose? Does it pay off in the global economy? Unfortunately, according to opinion from atop this economy, the answers are largely negative: schools are not doing a good job providing a payoff. For example, mega-billionaire Bill Gates, expressing concern about the state of U.S. education, lamented that "we must demand strong [high-tech] schools so that young Americans enter the workforce with the math, science and problem-solving skills they need to succeed in the knowledge economy. . . . To remain competitive in the global economy, we must build on the success of such schools."[9]

With those at the top of the global economy pronouncing that many students are facing a tough time in that economy, it is not surprising that the mission statement of the major national educational policy initiative, the Common Core State Standards, created by the Obama administration, explains that the policy was devised "to ensure that students are equipped with the necessary knowledge and skills to be globally competitive."[10] Obtaining jobs and serving business—that's what schooling should be predominantly about.

"Compete," "Competing," "Competitiveness," "Competition"

In the global economy, ideology, "dog eat dog," is a reigning necessity for individuals, businesses, and nations, with school defined as an institution critical for providing the new advanced skills that will determine which dog will prevail. An example of this view is *Innovate America*, a 2005 report of the Council on Competitiveness.[11] Written by a committee composed of CEOs of major corporations and presidents of leading research universities, *Innovate America* proposed that future American generations will require that the nation not merely cooperate with, but lead other nations to create "a new era of prosperity at home and abroad." The "fierce competition" and "relentless pressure" in the world confronts us all, the Council asserts. "American businesses, government, workers and universities" and "we" must choose how "we" will "handle this geopolitical reality." In a global version of "stand your ground," self-defense by-any-means-necessary laws, the Council contended that this new era of competition requires that "we" not "retreat."

Schooling provides armaments in this equation because global competition puts "an increasing premium on skills and education" that will enable America's workers to "be better prepared to engage more productively in the global economy." In the global skills race, it is skills and education (not a more equitable distribution of wealth) that will provide the possible means within the competitive "geopolitical reality" for acquiring the "price of admission to the middle class."[12] Because competition is the guiding force in the global economy, defeat and loss both for individuals and businesses are always around the corner, but unfortunately that is how global economic competition works.

Echoing these prospects and laments is a coalition of major business and technology organizations calling itself Tapping America's Potential (TAP). Included in TAP are the Council on Competitiveness, the National Association of Manufacturers, the National Defense Industrial Association, and the U.S. Chamber of Commerce.[13] Worrying about the nation's economic leadership, TAP's 2008 report, *Gaining Momentum, Losing Ground*, maintained that it expressed the "consensus in the business community that the United States must address its competitiveness challenges" because economic life for businesses and individuals means constant battles. To help win these battles, "TAP aims to formulate policy solutions for helping to strengthen the U.S. workforce for the 21st century economy."[14] And what is fundamental for gaining momentum and not losing ground? Schools, of course, in educating the future workforce in "the critical fields of science, technology, engineering and mathematics (STEM)."

In the report, a pull-quote from Anne Mulcahy, CEO of the Xerox Corporation, highlighted the essential role of schools in a world of perpetual competition: "The race to stay ahead in the brain race is critical to our future world leadership, and we need our government, our education system and the private sector to step up to the challenge." To which Joseph M. Tucci, CEO of the computer technology company EMC, echoed: "To sustain our economic leadership in the world" *we* will need "highly skilled workers, trained in science, technology, engineering and mathematics," those who will be "the ones who generate breakthrough innovations, new products and processes, even whole new industries that lead to productivity gains, economic growth . . . high-wage employment . . . and a higher standard of living for all Americans." TAP warned,[15] however, that economic combat will not be easy, particularly because schools are failing to contribute, as they should, to the "competitiveness challenges." Among their concerns were the following:

- "Although U.S. fourth graders score well against international competition, they fall near the bottom or dead last by 12th grade in mathematics and science, respectively."
- "This generation now faces an entirely new challenge, both at home and abroad. Any number of countries in Asia and Europe are educating and training their citizens and competing with—and, in several cases, beginning to surpass—the United States for talent to develop new technologies, new cures, new frontiers."
- "To sustain American competitiveness in science and engineering, we need a focused, long-term, comprehensive initiative by the public and private sectors."
- "The United States is in a fierce contest with other nations to remain the world's scientific leader. Education is central in determining who will win, but other countries are demonstrating a greater commitment to building their brainpower."

When framing the education needed for this "fierce contest," TAP, as similar corporate groups, is silent on the issue of what students should learn *about* the global economy—how it really works; its impact on humanity and the earth; its morality; how it shapes human beings; the contending views of that economy; and whether we should seek to create an alternative economy, one grounded in cooperation and dedicated to the sustenance and support of all global life. No, the economy's troops are to be trained to fight, but not think about the "fierce contest" itself.

The Learning Society

Guided by these assumptions, the meaning of school "learning" has increasingly narrowed, as illustrated by the central premise in Nobel economist Joseph Stiglitz and fellow-economist Bruce Greenwald's *Creating a Learning Society*.[16] Though Stiglitz has been critical of capitalist inequities, his conception of learning is confined to thinking that fosters invention and innovation within the global market, because, he explains, the leading "learning societies," created around

1800 in Western capitalist economies, and more recently in Asia, have had a major positive impact on social well-being. For example, with the creation of the Industrial Revolution and the market economy, and spurred by technological and productive innovation, per capita income continuously soared, interrupted only by depressions and other economic setbacks. Wholly omitted from this explanation of the learning society is any discussion of the toll on those who did the work: backbreaking work in mills and mines; harsh child labor, 12 to 14 hours a day; deplorable, dangerous working conditions; the high mortality rate of workers; the workhouses for paupers unable to find employment in these horrific conditions.

The historical focus of Stiglitz and Greenwald's portrayal of the learning society is on making and producing things better, with knowledge building upon knowledge. To advance these goals, a nation's economic policy must include education programs that promote the ability and incentives to learn. Generated by a learning society, the economy—that is, businesses and various sectors of the economy that serve businesses—will be more productive and, in turn, people's standards of living will increase.

We see in this version of the needs of the current economic system Stiglitz and Greenwald's use of the prevailing, attenuated definition of learning. Absent is any critical examination of the economy, such as the human concerns and values that formulate its aims, and the extent to which the learning process accords with the standards and responsibilities of a democracy and people's needs. Learning and innovating appear to be value-free.

Stiglitz and Greenwald's conceptions are light years from those of philosopher Cornel West, who insists that questions about what it means to be human and to engage in a virtuous life must be fundamental in education. What "kind of sensitivity, what kind of compassion, what conceptions of justice" are embedded in and should be cultivated in our studies? What should education teach us about "the centrality of love and empathy"?[17] Similarly, the conception of the learning society does not include examination of how that learning is related to the basic needs of all people around the globe and how best to fulfill them; how to create and sustain an economy dedicated to the good of all who are living today and to the sustenance of future generations; how to measure all aspects of material life against standards of caring for and preserving the earth. Fundamental questions such as these are so far from the projected educational content of the learning society, as to sound like an indecipherable foreign language. Nor does this content include education in art, music, literature, history, or social studies. The majority in the learning society serve as functionaries for "growth, development, and social progress," goals defined solely in market terms.

Aiding Our Businesses in Global Economic Competition

In the name of defending U.S. economic interests in the global economy and defeating economic alternatives, overwhelming military power has protected and advanced U.S. business interests around the globe. Whether in El Salvador, Nicaragua, Vietnam, Cuba, Iran, Iraq, Angola, and numerous other countries, U.S. military intervention has been framed as protecting a God-given right for U.S. businesses to plant themselves wherever they want. As Chilean poet Pablo Neruda's poem, "United Fruit Company," explains, Coca Cola, Anaconda, Ford Motors and similar corporations have acted as though God parceled out the earth to them.[18]

The details of buttressing the competitive edge of these entities have been amply documented by foreign policy analyst William Blum. Branding oppositional groups and liberation movements as communists, leftists, terrorists, nationalists, and just plain "enemies," U.S. military intervention has saved the day for U.S. business control across the globe, especially when an economy other than a capitalist one has been envisioned. Wherever U.S. business interests have been threatened or where liberation movements have sought to create nationalist or socialist alternatives to foreign capitalist control, the U.S. military has been there to destroy these attempted changes. As part of these interventions, the U.S. has bombed people in more than thirty countries since the Second World War.[19] Journalist Garry Leech observes:

> Washington's global political dominance manifests itself
> through military and economic support to allied governments
> regardless of how corrupt, undemocratic and violent they may
> be in order to defend U.S. interests. . . . When governments do
> come to power and challenge U.S. interests then Washington
> inevitably responds with economic sanctions, support for a
> military coup and, if necessary, direct military intervention.
> The objective is to ensure that the capitalist model is the domi-
> nant social model throughout the world.[20]

Military intervention on behalf of U.S. business competition has,
in turn, required the allocation of a huge portion of the public treasury, with military spending exceeding all other areas of spending.
For example, of the 2015 U.S. discretionary spending budget of $1.16
trillion, the military budget represented 55.2 percent ($640 billion).
Compare this 55.2 percent to the 6.2 percent of the federal budget for
education, not exactly the kind of proportionate spending suggesting
a strong national commitment to educating youth to compete in the
global economy. The 2016 U.S. military budget, like those before it,
continues to dwarf the military spending of all other nations.[21]

Given the militarism that is a major part of the U.S. participation
in the global economy, any thorough curriculum on that economy
should (1) include study of the extent to which this economy is not a
benign process of production, invention, employment, and consumption, but one with a military dimension that has been essential to the
deployment, functioning, expansion, and dominance of U.S. corporate interests; 2) note that the cost of this militarism is directly related
to the issue of work in the global economy because were these funds
put to civilian, rather than military, use, they would create many more
jobs. For example, the Political Economic Research Institute states in
their study of domestic versus military jobs:

> Our conclusion . . . is straightforward: $1 billion spent on each
> of the domestic spending priorities will create substantially
> more jobs within the U.S. economy than would the same $1

billion spent on the military. . . . Investments in clean energy, health care and education create a much larger number of jobs across all pay ranges, including mid-range jobs (paying between $32,000 and $64,000) and high-paying jobs (paying over $64,000). Channeling funds into [these job categories would] therefore create significantly greater opportunities for decent employment throughout the U.S. economy than spending the same amount of funds with the military.[22]

The Global Economy and the Destruction of Earth

Education about, not simply for, the benefit of the global economy must also include the impact of that economy on the environment and the sustenance of Earth. As I write this, the carbon dioxide level (CO_2) in the atmosphere is at 400 parts per million (ppm), considerably above the 350 ppm scientists say is the safe limit for humanity. This dangerous threshold is well-known, yet government agreements to establish a maximum level threshold for carbon pollution have failed year after year because corporations dominating the global economy and their advocates among elected officials have prevented any adequate environmental constraints on their ability to make profits. With the Trump administration's environmental policies based on the view that global warming is a hoax and on dismantling the relatively mild climate policies of the Obama administration,[23] the dangers worsen.

As Naomi Klein and others have concluded, global warming is a direct consequence of the global capitalist economy. We are facing a crisis because "our economic system and our planetary system are now at war."[24] For example, the transportation of goods now traveling by "carbon-spewing container ships, jumbo jets and trucks" has increased "nearly 400 percent over the last 20 years" and further "shipping emissions are set to double or even triple by 2050."[25] Yet the "indiscriminate economic growth," of which this transportation of goods is a manifestation, is wholly omitted from any educational, business, or political conception of the "global economy" and how students should be educated for it. Klein grimly observes:

Our economy is at war with many forms of life on earth, including human life. What the climate needs to avoid collapse is a contraction in humanity's use of resources; what our economic model demands to avoid collapse is unfettered expansion. Only one of these sets of rules can be changed, and it's not the laws of nature.[26]

Yet nowhere in the dominant conceptions of "education for the global economy" is there a hint of this disastrous contradiction.

Why Not Call Capitalism "Capitalism"?

Why is the global economic system primarily called the "global economy" rather than "capitalism," its more accurately descriptive name, and one readily used even by conservative policy institutes that relish and defend the economic system? The American Enterprise Institute (AEI), for example, discusses without euphemism the "moral superiority of dynamic capitalism"[27] and argues that "profits and capitalism have improved the human condition."[28] Similarly, Edwin J. Feulner, founder and former president of the Heritage Foundation, glowingly explained that while "capitalism's carping critics" have attacked it "so fiercely, so falsely and so foolishly," the reality is "that capitalism has done more good for more people than any other economic arrangement ever devised by man." Capitalist nations, such as the United States, "are prosperous, growing and expansive, creating opportunities and wealth for ever-increasing numbers of people." Unlike other economic systems, "the free-market capitalist system in the United States presents opportunities for every individual to improve his life." Its extensive benefits help "explain why capitalism has outlasted all of its challengers over the past century."[29]

Along with capitalist booster organizations like Heritage and AEI, there is the Center for Advancing Capitalism, a project of the Competitive Enterprise Institute funded by various right-wing foundations, such as the Koch family foundations, and major corporations such as ExxonMobil, Ford Motor Company, Philip Morris, and

Texaco. For the 2015 Valentine's Day, the Center published a cuddly "Valentine for Capitalism," which asked that we "celebrate capitalism not only for the prosperity it creates, but for the many ways in which it fosters and validates friendships, enriching the vast array of connections that bind us together in civil society."[30]

Also not shy about using the term freely and adoringly is Bill Gates. No vanilla term like "global economy" for him. Why? As Gates explained at the World Economic Forum, "The genius of capitalism lies in its ability to make self-interest serve the wider interest."[31] As such, he asserted at the Forbes 400 Summit on Philanthropy, "I am a true believer in the power of capitalism to improve lives."[32] Capitalism, for Gates, is "agile and creative."[33] Capitalism is a "wonderful thing."[34] Capitalism is a "phenomenal system."[35]

Given these laudatory accomplishments, shouldn't a deep, extensive exploration of *capitalism* guide the discussions of the aims of education and the curriculum? Moreover, following Gates's lead, would not such discussions openly address criticisms of global capitalism, as has the Heritage Foundation in answering "capitalism's carping critics"?

Gates sets an example of not only answering criticism but expressing criticisms of capitalism. While he assures us that "the world is better off" because of this system, he nonetheless acknowledges that "*capitalism has shortfalls*"[36] (my emphasis): it has neglected the world's poor, done too little to eliminate diseases, and underfunded innovation. At the global level, Gates recognizes that capitalism has created a hierarchical sorting of humankind that has produced many riches for those at the top but has done little, if anything, for the "bottom billion" of humanity. And yes, Gates readily admits, much of this problem is due to the hierarchy that is intrinsic to capitalism, a ranking that, by definition, cannot fully eliminate the unequal distribution of wealth. Extending his criticism, he points to certain capitalist practices that have "aggravated the inequities in the world." Moreover, capitalism's priorities can be misdirected, as when, for example, investment in male baldness research exceeds research funding for finding a malaria vaccine, which is (unfortunately for bald men) "in humanist terms the biggest need."[37] This misdirection of priorities, Gates notes, is an example of how capitalism can be too shaped by "marketplace imperatives."[38]

Nonetheless, for anyone worrying about the radical sound of his frankness, Gates assures us that his criticism is about shortfalls, not illustrations of anything intrinsically immoral in capitalism. These flaws can be offset; they certainly do not require asking "whether capitalism is wrong." The good has to be balanced with the bad, and when doing so it is clear, Gates concludes, that capitalism is one of the "great advances in the world." He reminds us that while one can be critical of capitalism, it "has improved the lives of billions of people," no other economic system has "improved humanity to the same degree," and in the years ahead "creative capitalism" will continue to work to improve the "lives of those who don't fully benefit from today's market forces."[39] Capitalism will make "more people better off" and make the world "a lot better." Gates recognizes these achievements will not come without difficulty because "we have to find a way to make the aspects of capitalism that serve wealthier people serve poorer people as well."

Since leading conservative policy organizations and the richest man in the world easily use the C-word, one would think that this forthright term, rather than the amorphous, lackluster phrase "global economy," would describe the economic system that is supposed to be the overarching framework of educational policy and curricula. Yet, in educational discourse, "capitalism" remains the-name-that-shall-not-be-named, and, regardless of its other appellations, also remains the-economic-system-that-shall-not-be-studied.

"Global Economy" — A Perfect Name

Consider the problem of legitimizing an economic system that is a disaster for billions of people worldwide. What are those who sit atop the "global economy" to do? Well, first, rename the economy chiefly responsible for these disparities and miseries: start by not calling it "capitalism," a word associated with Marx and socialism, and which contains too many historical and contemporary negative connotations and interpretations. A simple illustration of the importance of using the right name is evident in an Internet search of alternative terms for the economic system. For example, a search for quotes expressing various observations about capitalism will likely find the "Brainy Quotes" website at the top of the search engine list. There, among the entry quotes are many positive definitions and observations, such as Ralph Waldo Emerson's: "Doing well is the result of doing good. That's what capitalism is all about." Overall, however, the definitions are more critical than laudatory: for example, the John Maynard Keynes quote explains: "Capitalism is the astounding belief that the most wickedest of men will do the most wickedest of things for the greatest good of everyone." Or, Bertrand Russell's conclusion: "Advocates of capitalism are very apt to appeal to the sacred principles of liberty, which are embodied in one maxim: The fortunate must not be restrained in the exercise of tyranny over the unfortunate." Or, Michael Moore's summary: "Capitalism and democracy are the opposite of each other. Capitalism is a system that guarantees that a few are going to do very well, and everybody else is going to serve the few. Democracy means everybody has a seat at the table. Everybody."[40]

To help deflect these negative views that call attention to and criticize those at the top, better to call capitalism something else—say, the "global economy." As these "Brainy Quotes" help illustrate, it's a preferable alternative because it stresses legitimate individual competition in that economy and the necessity of attaining sufficient education for its necessary competition.

A further Internet search suggests how the purposes of schooling must be contrived to focus on "working in," not on an "understanding of" the global economy. A search of "preparing students to *compete* in the global economy" (my emphasis) yielded nearly 45 million results with similar perspectives. Illustrative of the common perspective is a Texas school district dedicated to preparing its students for the "global challenge" by providing them with "the edge they need to compete in a global marketplace when they graduate."[41] Or, in Minnesota, the state's Department of Education highlights its goal of improving "student achievement/prepare students to compete in a global economy . . . taking our students from nation-leading to world competing."[42]

In contrast to these nearly 45 million results, a search of "preparing students for the global economy," that is, one that omits the pugilistic word *compete*, produces about 10 million results. Here, too, the educational scope is constrained by an emphasis on *work in*, not thinking about or understanding, the global economy. Typical of results for this search is the recommendation of the National Education Association (NEA), advising a "4Cs" education: three of the C's are "communication, collaboration, and creativity" to "prepare this next generation for new careers for this new global society." The fourth "C" is "critical thinking," but it is thinking that is narrowly contained within career preparation. Absent in the NEA advice is any recommendation that critical thinking should include any ideas critical of either "this new global society" or the "new careers" it generates (or does not generate).[43]

A search of "education for the global economy" yields over 3 million results, with most of them focused on the dominant theme of preparing students for work in that economy.

In contrast to all these, with a change to the search words "education *about* the global economy," the results drop to four citations!

Education For *or* About *the Global Economy?*

The global economy school curriculum veers far from even a relatively moderate assessment of capitalism, and woe to the teacher who decides to ask students to discuss, as Bill Gates has, the morality of an economic system that invests more in male baldness research than in finding a malaria vaccine. And, woe also to the Gates-supported charter and other privatized schools whose curricula delve into the consequences for humanity of global capitalism's skewed hierarchy, market imperatives, ignored human needs, and other "shortfalls" that Gates himself recognizes.

More woe is likely to befall any teacher who introduces into the classroom the more critical view of the global economy that is held by the majority of people in the world. According to a 2012 twenty-two nation poll, conducted for BBC World Service, 25 percent of people globally believe that capitalism is *"fatally flawed and needs to be replaced,"* up two points from the same survey done in 2009 (my emphasis).   Furthermore, while 61 percent of people in eighteen countries tracked in both years (2009 and 2012) do not hold to the "fatally flawed" view, they believe that the distribution of economic benefits and burdens is unfairly shared in their country. In the United States, 58 percent held this view.[44]

Given the attitudes expressed in these global surveys, clearly the best positive statement that can be made about humanity's view of the value of capitalism is that it is contentious. A quarter of those in the BBC poll felt that capitalism needs to be replaced, and even in the six nations where the accrued wealth of the rich is admired, a significant minority of people, around 40 percent, had a negative view of the rich deserving their wealth.

These figures help explain why the wealthy and those who serve them have created a call for education *for*, not *about*, the global economy. The omission in educational policy discussions of capitalism's qualities and benefits reflects an increasingly dominating policy power that excludes alternative views from the curriculum, even when those alternative views are held by a large proportion of members of the society. How can teachers begin classroom dialogues about various views of capitalism, including the one held by 25 percent of people globally, that capitalism is fatally flawed and needs to be replaced? These critical views are, of course, all the more reason why, from the perspective of those who hold economic power and can shape educational policy, the scope of the curriculum must be constrained, why study "about" capitalism must be excluded from curricula aimed at preparing students for working and living in the global economy.

It is not as if there were no curricula materials for comprehensively studying alternative views of capitalism/the global economy. For example, the teacher organization Rethinking Schools publishes a curriculum volume titled *Rethinking Globalization* that includes a variety of instructional materials on inequality, poverty, world wealth, the World Bank, the IMF, the World Trade Organization, free trade, the debt crisis, global sweatshops, attacks on trade union organizers, child labor, world hunger, global warming, and ecological destruction. Are these curricular materials biased and partisan? The authors address the question, explaining the distinction between "biased" and "partisan." Teaching is biased when it ignores multiple perspectives and does not allow interrogation of its own assumptions and propositions. Partisan teaching, on the other hand, invites diversity of opinion but does not lose sight of the aim of the curriculum: to alert students to global injustice, to seek explanations, and to encourage activism. This is the kind of teaching we hope *Rethinking Globalization* will encourage. For Rethinking Schools educators, fundamental in the educational process fostering students' critical abilities is the opportunity to question all they are taught and are being asked to do.[45]

Creating Competitors for the Global Economy

How must students prepare to compete in the global economy? What state of mind should they have? The prevailing answer to these questions was captured by Amanda Ripley, who looked at "the smartest kids in the world," with "smart" defined largely by high test scores on the Programme for International Student Assessment (PISA) test of mathematics, reading and science, administered to fifteen-year-old students in nations worldwide.[46] Presumably, the highest scorers would be best prepared to compete and achieve in the global economy, and the best students would embody the clearest understanding of the occupational goals that hard work in school can achieve.

While Ripley went around the world to find the "smartest kids," she failed to see that she didn't have to leave the United States. Is there really a problem of U.S. public school students scoring worse on math and science tests than students in other nations? No, because when social class is factored into analyses of scores on international tests such as PISA and TIMSS (Trends in Mathematics and Science Study), economic inequality is recognized as the chief correlate with

score outcomes. Hence, not surprisingly, students from more affluent homes score better than do students from poorer homes. With
respect to the science and mathematics scores of U.S. students in the
top quartile, performance is very strong compared with students elsewhere. Not so for U.S. students in the lower quartile.

Nonetheless, Ripley was convinced that she needed to travel the
earth to understand what accounts for score differences. In this quest,
she describes a U.S. high school student, Kim, who was studying in
Finland, where students score high on the PISA test. "What makes
you work so hard in school?" Kim asked fellow Finnish students. The
"girls looked baffled, as if Kim had just asked them why they insisted
on breathing so much." One of the students answered: "How else will
I graduate and go to university and get a good job?" This, for Ripley,
was the right answer, one not shared by U.S. students. Ripley observed
that they tend not to "take education very seriously," even though "for
them, too, getting a good education was the only way to go to college
and get a good job."[47]

In other words, the predominant reason for going to school and
doing well academically must be consonant with Ripley's definition
of the dominant purpose of education: to obtain the skills and knowledge for finding a job in the global economy. Education is not about
understanding the world and its economy, not about deepening one's
understanding of and involvement in culture, not about addressing
the world's problems, not about strengthening community. No, as
Ripley underscores, school is the vehicle for work in an economy
where competition for work, and winners and losers in that competition, are the accepted givens. What's a good student? One who is
aware of the nature of today's global economy and, therefore, understands the "need to be driven [and] how to adapt, since they would be
doing it all their lives." Schools, in turn, need to embody a culture of
"rigor," a predominant characteristic of superior teaching and learning, Ripley underscores.[48]

She recognizes that sometimes "rigor" can go too far. In South
Korea, for example, Ripley is disturbed by that nation's "hamster
wheel" school learning (incessant, excessive, exhausting, joyless),

but given how the contemporary global economy is constructed, this kind of learning felt more honest to her than schooling elsewhere (for example, the United States) because "kids in hamster-wheel countries knew what it felt like to grapple with complex ideas and think outside their comfort zone; they understood the value of persistence. They knew what it felt like to fail, work harder, and do better." Thus, the "hamster wheel" lives of these students might not be pretty, but by adhering to focus, values, and a constricted meaning of "education," they will be "prepared for the modern world."[49]

Above all, education must be attuned to the "real world" that does "not always give second and third chances." Learning is a "currency" that brings "freedom" and "happiness." Why? Because of the equation: "Education increases income, and income increases happiness." In the "World Happiness Report," compiled by a group of economists from several countries, the Finns ranked high because their incomes were high.[50] Consequently, in a world where happiness is associated with good-paying jobs that are in limited supply, schools are central mechanisms for satisfying a skill=good jobs=high incomes=happiness equation.

How Much Education Does the Global Economy Require?

Putting aside for the moment the extent to which schools exclude learning about global capitalism, there is the issue of the extent to which education *for* the global economy can provide students the means for occupational success in that economy. In other words, if the young do attain advanced education in STEM occupations, how much will this attainment provide a secure material life?

One answer comes from a study by the United Nations' International Labour Organization, which reports that unemployment rates among young people cannot be explained primarily by their insufficient educational achievement. In most advanced economies, despite a high portion of well-educated young people, their unemployment rates were already high, and have worsened "substantially with the onset of the [2008 economic] crisis and have not been resolved since then."[51] Nearly 40 percent of college-educated young people in Spain and 30 percent in Greece are unemployed. In India one in three graduates up to the age of twenty-nine is unemployed.[52] In Turkey, unemployment among college graduates between the ages of eighteen and twenty-four is approximately 30 percent.[53] In other nations, such as Sweden, the United Kingdom, and Portugal, youth unemployment among college graduates has also worsened. As a consequence, a large percentage of the graduates accept jobs for which they are overqualified—if they can get a job.[54] For example, approximately 44 percent of college graduates in 2014, that is, those ages twenty-two to twenty-seven with a B.A. or higher, had jobs that did not require a bachelor's degree. By 2017, "degree inflation" continued to advance, causing the Harvard Business School to worry that this was "undermining U.S. competitiveness and hurting America's middle class." Hence, though a college degree remains valuable for young people obtaining a job and a relatively better salary because employers hire applicants who are college graduates, the degree itself has been useful primarily for obtaining, not *doing* a job, and though salaries for these jobs are relatively better, they are lower than in the past.[55] As business correspondent Jordan Weissman explained, "Close to half of those [college graduates] who land work won't immediately find a job that requires their degree, and for those stuck in that situation, there are fewer 'good' jobs to go around."[56]

This view is backed by job projections of the U.S. Bureau of Labor Statistics. Currently, approximately two-thirds of current occupations do not require post-secondary education. Although jobs not requiring post-secondary education will decline in the years ahead, by 2022, they will still comprise *more than half of all new jobs that are expected to be created*. Furthermore, of the thirty occupations with the largest projected employment increase by 2022, two-thirds—such as jobs in personal health care aides, home health care aides, retail salespersons, food preparation and service workers (which includes fast-food workers), janitors and cleaners, medical secretaries, insulation workers, and construction assistants—will typically not require post-secondary education.[57]

Have U.S schools failed to provide adequate STEM education for young people for work in the new global economy, thereby ruining their chances to obtain good jobs and live satisfactory, happy lives? Are businesses suffering because they are unable to fill job openings with workers who possess the necessary job skills? Reviewing these various alarms, labor and workforce researcher Michael Teitelbaum cites various studies that fail to "find credible evidence" that there are insufficient "numbers or quality of scientists and engineers being produced by U.S. higher education." Nor are there "shortages of scientists and engineers in the U.S workforce." Moreover, one study found that "U.S. higher education routinely awards more degrees in science and engineering than can be employed in science and engineering occupations."[58]

The Global Economy and Its Minimally Educated Workforce

International and U.S. figures reveal that within global capitalism as a whole, the actual work contradicts the insistence that education to compete in the global economy is a sufficient occupational and life answer for those in advanced capitalist countries. Even worse for measuring the accuracy of this mantra is the overall extent to which global capitalism relies on labor with minimal education.

For example, Nike, which employs over a million workers worldwide, largely in Indonesia, Vietnam, and China, has a long history of low-wage jobs and labor abuse. Approximate weekly wages in Bangladesh are $9; in Vietnam $19; in India $20; in South Africa $8; in Mexico $40; in Thailand $65.[59] Nike's unblinking focus on their bottom line was evident in Indonesia, where Nike factory workers earn about 50 cents an hour.[60] For Nike, however, this wage cut too far into its profits, so it applied for an exemption in which a worker would earn $3.70/day, which, after rent and transportation costs, left only enough money to afford a single meal. When workers objected to this exemption, Nike hired military personnel to coerce workers into signing a document supporting Nike's request.[61]

Similar conditions exist for global workers who make products for an array of U.S. retailers, such as Macy's and Walmart, and product manufacturers, such as Calvin Klein and the Gap.[62] Comparable working conditions and circumstances exist for high-tech commodities. The iPhone is assembled in China, for example, by workers earning less than half the monthly wages necessary to live at minimal standards. Thousands of these are underage and students, doing the same work as adults.[63]

These low-wage, hard work manufacturing jobs—jobs not requiring college degrees—make up much of the "global economy" and reveal the extent to which the projection of the twenty-first-century high-skills and education workforce is a reality or mirage. Certainly, there is considerable work requiring STEM education, but overall the global economy is one in which most of the work does not require an advanced degree, and for countless manufacturing workers around the globe, minimal education is all that is necessary to learn to do a job in a sweatshop.

The capitalist-created mirage blames schools and teachers for the hardships of workers in a global economy that maximizes profit for a few, is indifferent to the needs of the many, and eschews supporting any education about the real workings and morality of this economy. If only schools and teachers would provide the occupational equipment for competing in the global economy. Yet at the same time corporations and politicians rail against the public schools and work to destroy these schools so that public money can be channeled through charter schools into private hands. Upon assuming the presidency, Donald Trump proposed legislation to cut the Department of Education budget by "$9.2 billion—or 13.5 percent—a dramatic downsizing that would reduce or eliminate grants for teacher training, after-school programs and aid to low-income and first-generation college students." Simultaneously, $1.4 billion would be shifted to "expanding charter schools, private-school vouchers and other alternatives to traditional public schools."[64]

Who are the unemployed, underemployed, underpaid, overworked, in debt, suffering day after day to blame, as they look on helplessly as their children struggle to find a rewarding place in the global economy? Simple. From billionaire high-rises across the globe, the explanation is clear. Blame yourselves, blame the schools, but don't blame us or our global economy.

Education for Idiot Savants

At its best, education to compete in the global economy creates a form of idiot savantism in which a student could be very competent in a technical skill but understand virtually nothing about the context of that skill, namely, the global economy. Schools can nibble around the edges of capitalism. They can teach various languages, cultures, religions, literature, and history. Excluded in this education, however, is the opportunity to transcend these circumscribed areas and help students think fully and critically about that economy and their places in it. Hence, key curriculum imperatives are these:

1) Schools must teach about the global economy as if it were a natural phenomenon within which human beings must act to meet their needs and promote their well-being. Doing so, schools must focus solely on providing students with the skills, creativity, and innovative abilities necessary for successful employment within this natural global economy that will, in turn, provide for their needs and well-being.

2) Schools must be silent about the hierarchical structure that is the fundamental essence of the global economy, that is, the minute number of the rich who are at the top, the relatively small portion of the upper part that is composed of elite workers who are paid well, and the huge bottom portion of the structure that contains the rest of humanity.

    With respect to this pyramid, students must not think about facts like those in 2016, when the anti-poverty organization Oxfam reported that the richest 1 percent of adults in the global economy owned 48 percent of the planet's wealth, with sixty-two people having as much wealth as the world's 3.6 billion poorest. As I wrote this book, the division of wealth continued to increase and by January 2017 Oxfam's newest data calculated that just "eight men owned the same wealth as the 3.6 billion people who make up the poorest half of humanity."[65]

These and similar numbers of inequality in the global economy are staggering to contemplate and in any thoughtful curriculum would provide content for math and social studies courses. However, as "education for the global economy" is framed, students must concern themselves with securing as high a place as possible in the hierarchy, not thinking about its morality. Students must not think about whether a different, more equitable structure and distribution of global wealth should enfold humanity.

3) Schools must never identify or call the global economy a "human-created" global economy or a "class-created" global economy because those terms imply that the very nature of the global economy is open to students' critical inquiry, which could include unacceptable questions about the extent to which that human- or class-created economy serves the needs of humanity, fosters equality and inequality, damages Earth, promotes wars, creates real and false needs, and so forth.

4) The curriculum must assume there have to be winners and losers among workers in the global economy, and the job of students is to acquire an education that will enable them to become winners. Students must not think about whether there could be an alternative global economy that would not be composed of winners and losers. Nor can students think about how educational winners can still become occupational losers, as evident in the currently high percentage of unemployed college graduates. In learning to compete and win in the global economy, students must not be encouraged to reflect about feelings of indifference or even their callousness toward the well-being of the losers. The curriculum works to obliterate any concern for the human community. Instead, schooling encourages a self-centered, indifferent disconnection to and responsibility within that community.

5) Schooling must proceed on the assumption that, within the global economy, it is legitimate for businesses to pay people as little as

possible and thereby drive a "race to the bottom" within humanity.

6) Schools must not teach about the harmful effects of the global economy on the earth and its ecology, and how a different global economy could transform the planet's ecology and promote the survival of life. Students must not think about how and why the earth's resources are used, about, for example: "the 12 percent of the world's population that lives in North America and Western Europe [and] accounts for 60 percent of private consumption spending, while the one-third living in South Asia and sub-Saharan Africa accounts for only 3.2 percent."[66] Similarly, students must not think about the United Nations calculation of per capita "material footprint," an indicator of consumption and resource use that found North America's average was 25 tons, with the amount of consumption paralleling levels of wealth, while Africa's material footprint was below 3 tons. Beyond this inequitable distribution, students should not think about the excessive use and consumption of resources that portends a future, reached perhaps by the middle of this century, when much of the world's resources will have been exhausted.[67]

These matters are not important for educating students to work in the global economy. The perfect fulfillment of this educational mission would be an employee such as the one aptly described in singer/satirist Tom Lehrer's song about a value-free scientist, Wernher von Braun, who made deadly rockets, but once they were up in the air, where they came down wasn't his concern.[68]

2. The Flat World and the Education Needed for It

E very adult American [must] possess the knowledge and skills necessary to compete in a global economy," asserts *America 2000: An Education Strategy,*[1] a 1991 federal report that heralded the linkage that has become inseparable in political and educational rhetoric. With the advancement of international trade agreements, global communication technologies, international production of products and services, financially feasible global transportation, and the transfer (outsourcing) of Internet-related work across the globe (for example, medical testing evaluations, legal services, call centers for travel, accounting transactions, data entry, graphic design, and engineering tasks), the context of work has increasingly been conceived as a single word: the "21stcenturyglobaleconomy." In turn, as noted in chapter 1, "education for the global economy" has become the concept defining the chief aim of education and for grounding individual and national well-being.

Describing the work and survival challenges for Americans in a global economy, *New York Times* columnist Thomas Friedman lamented in his book *The World Is Flat*: "What can happen is a decline in our standard of living if more Americans are not empowered and educated to participate in a world where all the knowledge centers are being connected."[2] Friedman describes the experience in India that evoked the insight encapsulated in the book's title. Visiting Infosys, an Indian technology company, he was shown a conference room that was this global company's "ground zero." On the wall was the largest flatscreen TV Friedman had ever seen, one that could be used to hold a virtual meeting with techies from across the globe. The screen, for Friedman, represented the extensive technology that facilitated work on a global scale and the ability of "countries like India . . . to compete for global knowledge work as never before—and that America had better get ready for this." Added to this experience was a conversation with Infosys's CEO, Nandan Nilekani, who remarked, "Tom, the playing field is being leveled."[3] From this, Friedman arrived at the staggering conclusion that globalization is flat.

The concept of a "flat" playing field has captured the imagination of many educators, who have woven it into educational policy recommendations. "Flat" means that well-educated workers from around the world collaborate and compete to make, distribute, and sell the best products and services and, in turn, make profits for the companies that employ them. Worker competition occurs within a global democracy. Workers with the best education, regardless of where they live around the globe, merely have to be "connected" to do various kinds of work that contributes to the global economic process. Similarly, businesses, regardless of where they are situated, have increasingly equal opportunities to achieve success.

Within this new economy, schools are critical because of the skills they teach and the future employees they create. Unfortunately for young Americans, Friedman concludes, the education American schools provide their students contributes to a bleak future for the nation's workers. Friedman quotes Bill Gates, who puts the problem squarely: "In the international competition to have the biggest and best supply of knowledge workers, America is falling behind." To which Friedman adds a familial homily:

There is no sugar-coating this: in a flat world, every individual is going to have to run a little faster if he or she wants to advance his or her standard of living. When I was growing up, my parents used to say to me, "Tom, finish your dinner—people in China are starving." But after sailing to the edges of the flat world for a year, I am now telling my own daughters, "Girls, finish your homework—people in China and India are starving for your jobs."[4]

Some parents would find this flat world conception disturbing because it abandons nurturing a sense of sympathetic concern for others whose basic needs are not met. Nonetheless, any compassion that was fostered in the earlier lesson conveyed to Young Tom is obliterated in Parent Tom's dog-eat-dog admonition to his daughters: It's you or them; that job goes to you or to Chinese workers; don't let them get those jobs; that's what this world of work is all about! Parent Tom's admonition offers no nurturing of thought about creating an economy that could transcend the dog-eat-dog flat world economy. The world is what it is, kids.

India's Flat World

Friedman's parenting picture, echoing a fundamental assumption in educational policy, is disturbing both because of its callous morality and its misleading characterization of the global economy, which is decidedly *not* flat. Consider the episode that initiated Friedman's epiphany. Who told him that globalization is increasingly "level"? Why, it was the billionaire owner of Infosys, Nandan Nilekani. True, Nilekani might think a lot about "leveling" because he is not a big billionaire as far billionaires go. On the *Forbes* list, he had a relatively modest $1.59 billion in 2017, which put him at number 1,121 among billionaires worldwide and at 80th place among India's billionaires in 2016.[5] Yet, the verticality of Nilekani and the globe's other 1,810 billionaires who have gained their riches within global capitalism has no place in Friedman's flat world tapestry.

Unlike Friedman, this verticality would not be lost on the workers who inhabited Infosys's ground zero conference room, for were they to leave that room, travel over to Mumbai, and look upward, they would see a building, estimated to cost over $1 billion, extending 27 stories, that has three helipads, nine lifts, hanging gardens, ballrooms, weather rooms, gymnasiums, six floors of parking, and six hundred servants. This is "home" to a single person, India's richest man, Mukesh Ambani, worth $34.8 billion in 2017 (up from $20 billion in 2015), and number 33rd on *Forbes*'s "richest" 2017 list.[6] His residence sits within a city in which "roughly 62 percent of the population lives in slums," "including one of Asia's biggest, Dharavi, which houses more than one million people."[7]

If Nilekani's riches and Ambani's "home" were not enough to undercut a conception of a flat world, a broad set of figures from India might also help: the nation's 100 richest people, in a nation of 1.2 billion, "own assets equivalent to one-fourth" of the country's GDP. As writer Arundhati Roy, who has described much of India's wealth distribution, observed, "Trickle-down" hasn't worked, "but Gush-Up certainly has."[8]

Similarly, were "21stcenturyglobaleconomy" workers in Manhattan to exit their workplaces, go to 57th Street and look up, they would see a stretch of billionaire high-rises, some extending to ninety floors above the flat world. Here, as well as in other parts of Manhattan, such as Park Avenue, Central Park South, and 53rd Street, the rich of the vertical world often want these apartments, not to live in, but to stash money. As one real estate CEO observed, "These properties are the world's most expensive safety deposit boxes. People buy them and put their possessions in them and maybe visit them a couple times a year."[9] Comparable high-rises abound in London, Monaco, Hong Kong, and Singapore.[10]

Infosys's workers, walking elsewhere outside their workplace, would find an even more disturbing consequence of the new global economy, such as the suicides of 300,000 Indian farmers since 1995. This abomination has been called "GM genocide" to describe the link of the deaths to the use and failures of genetically modified (GM) seed, a major product of the new flat earth, high-tech global economy.

GM companies and government officials promised Indian farmers that these were "magic seeds" that would produce better crops free from parasites and insects. Beguiled by the prospect of unheard-of harvests and income, the farmers stopped using traditional seeds and borrowed money for these GM seeds, which cost about $15 for 100 grams, compared with less than that price for 1,000 times more traditional seeds. Behind this conjured-up magic were biotech giant companies, such as Monsanto, the leading GM seed manufacturer, that were aided by the International Monetary Fund, which provided loans to India on condition that these seed manufacturers have access to the Indian market.[11]

Rather than being "pest-proof," however, the GM seeds have been destroyed by parasites and required double the amount of water as traditional seeds; and unlike traditional seeds, which could be saved for planting in the following year, GM seeds contain a "terminator technology" that prevents the resulting crops from producing viable seeds of their own. As a result, although farmers have had to buy new seeds, they could not afford them.

Making the suicidal horror worse, the debt borne by these farmers was transmitted to their widows and often resulted in the remaining family losing its land and becoming part of the hordes of roadside beggars. Even if the family were able to maintain the farm and pay the debt, the children would be necessary for working the farm and could not attend school. In his investigation of the suicides, British journalist Andrew Malone concluded, "Cruelly, it's the young who are suffering most from the GM—the very generation supposed to be lifted out of a life of hardship and misery by these 'magic' seeds."[12]

OK, The World Isn't So Flat

If readers get to page 373 in *The World Is Flat*, they discover that Friedman confesses: "I know that the world is not flat." Yes, he acknowledges, "there are hundreds of millions of people on this planet who have been left behind by the flattening process." Nonetheless, this confession is not particularly heartrending because, for Friedman,

the plight of the billions of poor and impoverished is not a consequence of the global economy's wealth distribution but of the "new
economy" that has left behind large numbers of people who lack the
education and talent for life in the new, flat world.

Of course, many of those "who have been left behind" do not
see their problem exactly as Friedman explains it. For example, in
May 2015, the Zapatistas, an armed social movement in Chiapas,
Mexico, held "A Seminar of Critical Thought versus the Capitalist
Hydra." Throughout the presentations, the Spanish word *despojo* was
repeatedly used. Roughly equivalent in English to "dispossession," its
meaning stands in sharp contrast to the passive, apolitical economic
explanation of those "left out" of the new flat world economy. *Despojo*
is an active word conveying agency, class, and power, a word synony-
mous with "to be stripped violently of everything that sustains you."
The term, explained activist Christy Rodgers, who attended the seminar, embodies the "key experience of capitalism's innumerable losers:
the mass of humans without power or privilege."[13]

An example of *despojo* related to education and the global economy was the seminar's remembrance of Jose Luis Solís López, a teacher
in the Zapatistas' elementary Little School (*La Escuelita*), who was
targeted and murdered in May 2014 by paramilitary groups representing right-wing political parties. For them, criticism of their power
and that of their economic paymasters and allies has no place in any
school. Also part of the *despojo* remembrances was the "disappear-
ance"—that is, the murder and burial in a mass grave—of forty-three
students enrolled in a Mexican teachers' college.[14] According to the
Associated Press, the teachers' college "was known for its radical
political stance and some of the students had been involved in demonstrations." What was the crime of these students and the college?
"The students hailed from farm families and attended a college that
trained teachers to give classes in impoverished pockets of Guerrero
state, which is located to the south of Mexico City and includes some
of the country's most marginalized municipalities."[15]

Unfortunately for the students, those who killed them indu-
bitably had not read Friedman and thereby attained an accurate

understanding of the thinking and aspirations of the poor. Otherwise, the economic and politically powerful who hired the murderers would have understood, as Friedman explains, that despite the many forms of *despojo*, "The world's poor do not resent the rich anywhere nearly as much as the left-wing parties in the developed world imagine. What they resent is not having any pathway to get rich and to join the flat world."[16]

Education Policy and the Flat World

The "flat" and "flattening" model has captured the imagination of many contemporary educational policymakers. For example, educator Vivian Stewart of the Asia Society, an organization devoted to promoting "compassionate capitalism," advocates for the educational preparedness of American youth now required in a "transformed" world.[17] Toward that end, she opens her book on a "world-class education" by citing Friedman's conception of "the world transformed": "We used to think that people who thought the Earth was flat were uneducated. But Thomas Friedman's best-selling book, *The World Is Flat*, helped us to understand that if the world is not exactly flat, then it is deeply interconnected as never before."[18]

She then praises the glories of twenty-first-century capitalism: the free trade treaties that "introduced 3 billion people, previously locked into their own national economies, into the global economy, the wiring of the world [and the] economic liberalization of India, which jump-started that country's tremendous growth. . . . While the living standards of the world are still highly uneven, 400 million people have moved out of extreme poverty since 1980—more than at any other time in human history."[19] With these changes have come the need for the United States to create a world-class educational system whose graduates can compete effectively in the "global talent pool."[20]

Similar is prominent Stanford University education professor Linda Darling-Hammond's use of Friedman's term and analysis in her book, *The Flat World and Education: How America's Commitment to Equity Will Determine Our Future*.[21] She underscores that "the world is changing, and as Tom Friedman has demonstrated, it is increasingly flat. Globalization is changing everything. Employers can distribute their activities around the entire globe."[22] Therefore, U.S. schools must change their education and, as critically, their social policies so that students living in poverty have "access to an equitable, empowering education" that will enable them to "thrive in a technological, knowledge-based economy."[23] The "global gap" in educational achievement between students in affluent and poor communities is one that must be closed so that all students "will succeed as learners, workers, and citizens in today's global knowledge economy."[24] While Darling-Hammond's concern for students in poverty is commendable, what she ignores and what is ultimately detrimental to youngsters growing up poor, is that they and their families are becoming increasingly channeled in the U.S.-based portion of the global economy as workers doing low-wage work or as part of a surplus of competing applicants that further reduces the wages for low-wage work. How to explain why so many of the poor have no place in the U.S. economy except in these roles? The answer, of course, is that they are educational underachievers.

The "New" Global Economy

Certainly, we are living in a world with considerable technological newness. I wrote my first professional articles on a manual typewriter, but in the mid-1980s, I wrote my first book on a computer, although it required a floppy disk to boot up. As I revised one version of this chapter, I was on an Amtrak train connected to the Internet and listening to Beethoven, courtesy of a BBC streaming website. Certainly, for global capitalism this technology embodies monumental advances. Yet these vast transformations still leave open the question of how much they have *essentially* changed global capitalism, because in its essentials capitalism continues to embody the vertical distribution of power and wealth, profiting from labor through exploitation and abuse, control by powerful businesses of the resources of nations with little power, and military violence by major

nations in order to dominate, protect, and promote business interests abroad. All this is missing in discussions of education and the
"21stcenturyglobaleconomy."

Globalism 1.0 and Onward

Friedman's depiction of the advances of the global economy includes
the narrow, conventional tale of the long history of that economy:
for approximately five hundred years, the advances have largely been
about technological developments that spurred economic expansion, integration, and achievement. "Globalism 1.0," begun in 1492,
was generated by profound advances in navigation and related technologies that initiated the interconnections of the world. Globalism
2.0, extending from around 1800 to 2000, was propelled by multinational companies that were able to use advanced technologies,
especially those that reduced transportation costs and created forms
of telecommunication to go global for markets and labor. Businesses
in this second era, looking beyond national boundaries, were especially driven by the big question of "Where does my company fit into
the global economy?" As businesses created answers to this question,
Friedman explains, the world shrank from "size medium to size small,"
with Globalization 3.0 emerging at the end of the twentieth century.

Friedman's historic overview is remarkable in its extreme focus on
technology and its cleansing of most of the human content of these
eras. It is a familiar, comfortable history, narrowly economic, with
hierarchy and *despojo* having little place in it. Comfortably omitted
from Globalism 1.0, for example, is Columbus's assurance to Spain's
rulers that in his second voyage he would bring them as much gold
and as many slaves as they wanted. To meet the latter promise, in
1495 he led raids that captured hundreds of men, women, and children. Unfortunately for the Spanish economy, hundreds of slaves
died during transportation to Spain, thereby diminishing the size
of Columbus's cargo. As for the gold, the indigenous people on the
territory newly ruled by Spain were forced to collect the minerals
and were killed if they did not meet their quota. In two years, over

100,000 indigenous people on what is now Haiti were either killed by the Spanish or committed suicide. Chronicling the early Spanish conquests in Globalism 1.0, the Spanish priest Bartolomé de las Casas wrote that between 1494 and 1508, over three million people perished from war, slavery, and the mines."[25]

The young global economy continued with the slave trade and its massive human suffering for the profit of a relative few. This trade was not merely incidental to Globalism 1.0, it was central in the production of commodities, the accumulation of imperial wealth, and the commercial global connections that continued into roughly one-third of Capitalism 2.0. Yes, there were marvelous inventions: the Mercator projection, steam engine, chronometer, and many other such ingenious contributions advanced navigation and commerce, and helped beget a "smaller" world. At the same time there was another part of the global economy, namely, the approximately 11 million Africans who were forcibly transported for slavery, with at least 2 million dying during transport, to provide the labor power for products, such as cotton, coffee, tobacco, and sugar that advanced the global market and capitalist development. Additionally, the slave trade was itself a profitable global industry.[26]

Globalization 1.0 and 2.0, ever in quest of resources, markets, and profits, sought throughout the globe "great treasures of foods, minerals and other natural resources," which, as social critic Michael Parenti documents, have long been expropriated through imperialist domination that, in turn, has produced impoverishment in the dominated nations.[27] India, for example, at the beginning of Globalization 2.0 (1810) exported more textiles to England than England exported to it. However, through British military force, along with various competitive British economic steps, such as tariffs, India not only reversed its textile import-export relationship, it became a country that raised cotton for use in British textile factories. Additional British imperial economic and military practices, through the rest of the nineteenth century and into the twentieth, further impoverished India and contributed to the harsh construction of global capitalism.[28]

In the U.S. variation of Globalization 2.0, along with slavery and numerous forms of oppressed labor, and certainly along with technological advances, was military force, a central element employed for U.S. globalization's advance. Strikingly clear in a 1912 State Department Memorandum on the "Right to Protect Citizens in Foreign Countries by Landing Forces or the Use of the Navy,"[29] is the repeated use of U.S. military power on behalf of the global expansion of the nation's businesses. Enumerating the instances in which the United States "both alone and jointly with others, landed forces in times of Revolutions in foreign countries in order adequately to protect American interests," the State Department document includes China, 1854; Uruguay, 1855, 1858; Kisembo, Africa, 1860; Japan, 1864, 1868; Egypt, 1882; Haiti, 1888; Korea, 1888; Chile, 1891; Brazil, 1893; Hawaii, 1893; Nicaragua, 1899; China, 1900; Santo Domingo, 1903; Nicaragua, 1910; and Honduras, 1911.

For a century afterward, this 1912 memorandum has repeatedly been updated to justify further military interventions, right into today's 21stcenturyglobaleconomy. Consider the 2016 version, exemplified in the 2016 Congressional Research Service report, "Instances of Use of United States Armed Forces Abroad, 1798–2016, (spanning Globalization 2.0 and 3.0 so far).[30] Like its earlier iterations, the report provides a sequence of "hundreds of instances in which the United States has used military forces abroad in situations of military conflict or potential conflict to protect U.S. citizens or *promote U.S. interests*" (my emphasis).[31]

The complete list and description of military responses and interventions defending U.S. business interests around the globe covers nearly thirty-five single-spaced pages and illustrates that the advantage the United States has in advancing globalization has not simply been navigation and economic technology, but also military technology—from muskets and cannon to warships and bombers—and armed forces.

Yes, global capitalism certainly has, for a portion of humanity, achieved stunning advances in nutrition, health care, sanitation, transportation, housing, and an array of other developments in life's fundamentals and pleasures. But overall global capitalism has not been, and is not now, simply a sequence of advancing technological, communication, transportation, and trade practices. While over these centuries global capitalism has provided relatively good lives for many, for a huge portion of global humanity global capitalism, from so-called Globalization 1.0 through the current Globalization 3.0 has meant death, suffering, poverty, excessive work, illiteracy, slavery, punishing life conditions, and brief lives. Why? Because the world has been and remains cruelly vertical.

Educational policy runs away from this history, implicitly accepting the conceptualization of the global economy as one in which technological and more sophisticated educational advances have been and, more than ever, remain the central elements in the advancement of the market, work, and individual well-being. "Education to compete in the global economy" is stripped of the power, domination, suffering, and death that has been and remains global capitalism's composition. Through these deletions, this imperative not only rests on a false, immoral portrayal of the global economy, it also conveys expectations for students and their families that cannot possibly be fulfilled. STEM education will not, given the global economy's distribution of power, domination, profit-making, and actual occupational content, provide secure work for more than a small portion of humanity. Scrutinizing the actual substance of global capitalism helps explain why the ideological expectations fastened to STEM education must be challenged and rejected.

Riches and Poverty

The concept of the global economy and the new work skills it conjures are embodied in products like the Apple Smartwatch, which, at the time of its launching, received breathless reviews identifying its many potential contributions to "Life in Our 21st Century World." Typical were the *New York Times* travel[32] and digital age[33] columns describing test runs of the watch.

- "When I ordered an Egg McMuffin at a McDonald's, I never reached for my wallet. Rather, I paid instantly by double-click-ing the side button on Apple Watch (bringing up an image of my credit card), then holding it to a reader by the cash register."
- Also special was the Smartwatch's contribution to stress reduc-tion: "It mitigates a modern travel anxiety: fear of setting down your smartphone—in a cab, on a cafe table, in an airplane seat pocket—and kissing it goodbye. Your iPhone can remain in your bag or pocket while your Apple Watch hugs your wrist, subtly zap-ping it when a text message arrives, or flashing an alert when you pay for museum admission with your credit card."
- Finally, there was the seamless connection between one's brain and the digital world: "By notifying me of digital events as soon as they happened, and letting me act on them instantly, without having to fumble for my phone, the Watch became something like a natural extension of my body—a direct link, in a way that I've never felt before, from the digital world to my brain."

All this and more for a mere $349, although for the wealthy with a conspicuous consumption itch, there was the Watch Edition model that comes in either 18-karat yellow or rose gold, available at $17,000.

It's not that a smartwatch has no convenient uses, such as allowing the owner to very easily receive "text messages, answer phone calls, see emails and calendar alerts," or providing an on-body device that can monitor various health-related indexes. However, the market orchestration of these and similar products, especially in more afflu-ent capitalist countries, fosters a conception of these technological commodities as the representations of the global economy. Products like the Smartwatch misrepresent the countless people in the current global economy who have no guarantee of food or access to clean water each day, or the "2.4 billion still without sanitation facilities—including 946 million people who defecate in the open."[34] Absent too in Smartwatch portrayals of global capitalism are the vast number of underschooled and non-schooled workers, adults and children, who are central to production and profit.

This far-reaching, immiserated portion of humanity is not merely living in a transient moment alongside the high-tech economy, enduring privations until additional education opens their opportunities for better jobs and improved living standards for them. Rather, their meager or total lack of schooling is central to the profit-making and the ever-increasing verticality of wealth in the 21stcenturyglobaleconomy. From the former "dark satanic mills" of England to the contemporary clothing mills in Bangladesh, those at top levels of the economy have been able to wring hard work for minimum pay from the poorly educated.

In chapter 1, I discussed the manufacture of Nike shoes as emblematic of worldwide low-wage work in deplorable conditions. Apparel manufacturing is another example of horrific work in the global economy. In the garment plants of developing nations such as Cambodia, Bangladesh, Pakistan, and India, "malnourished workers working 14-hour days . . . earn little more than subsistence wage," and in many of these countries "the buying power of these wages is going down, not up."[35] Is this due to the meager number of well-educated workers who could do the work and get paid more? Of course not. Rather, global capitalism *needs* workers with little or no schooling, who have no choice but to accept this work because trying to earn a living in either the informal economy or through subsistence farming is even worse.

Bangladesh, the third-largest exporter of clothes in the world, after China and Italy, where thousands of workers have been killed in factory fires and building collapses, is a typically perfect place for labor exploitation of the barely schooled or unschooled: 42 percent of all adults have no schooling (for females the percentage is 47 percent); 21 percent of adults have a primary school education; 19 percent have completed high school; 3 percent have college degrees. From the heavily unschooled female population, global businesses are readily able to get workers to endure "grueling working conditions, violations of local laws and basic human rights, and abusive treatment" and "earn only a fraction of what constitutes a living wage."[36] Some 3.6 million women, with little education, work in the nation's $20 billion garment industry, earning a minimum monthly wage of 3,000 taka ($38.50) for labor that often extends over seven days. Their work may keep them above absolute poverty, but their incomes fail "to provide them and their families with adequate nutrition, decent housing, and other minimal necessities of a humane and dignified existence."[37] These conditions are typical in countries where apparel companies make products for the U.S. market. Moreover, in these countries the prevailing wage is commonly a small percentage of a living wage. For example, it is 29 percent of a living wage in Indonesia and 22 percent in Vietnam.

In the latter nation, where the garment and textile industry is the largest sector of private employment, suppliers to major U.S. apparel brands have required excessive work hours, employed child labor— "a significant problem in the Vietnamese garment industry"—and imprisoned workers who have attempted to organize against exhausting, poorly paid, unsafe working conditions.[38]

The Constant Global Search for Cheaper, Minimally Educated Labor

One might think that a society such as China, with an increasingly educated workforce, would be exactly what global capitalism wants. However, rather than looking forward to employing more educated workers and gladly paying them more for their skills, manufacturers in China, because wages there have been moderately increasing, have been heading to other countries such as Mexico, where less educated workers can do the work and will do it for lower wages. More precisely, in 2000, China's wages were somewhat lower than those in Mexico, but by 2015 they were slightly higher. Hence came a simple calculation and decision reported in the *New York Times*:

> With labor costs rising rapidly in China, American manufacturers of all sizes are looking south to Mexico with what economists describe as an eagerness not seen since the early years of the North American Free Trade Agreement in the 1990s. From border cities like Tijuana to the central plains

where new factories are filling farmland, Mexican workers are increasingly in demand.[39]

Or, as Christopher Wilson, an economics scholar at the Mexico Institute of the Woodrow Wilson International Center for Scholars in Washington, put it, "When you have the wages in China doubling every few years, it changes the whole calculus": unit labor costs in 2015 are approximately 30 percent lower in Mexico than in China. As for the calculation for U.S. workers, the wages on Mexican auto assembly lines are "often six or seven times lower," averaging about $3 an hour.[40] It is not because Mexican workers are better educated that many auto manufacturers have been moving south.[41]

Looking at sixteen countries that will replace China as low-wage manufacturing nations, political scientist George Friedman concluded that global capitalism "opens the door to low-wage countries with appropriate infrastructure and sufficient order to do business," even if that means the "brutality of early industrialism," because for the poor people in these countries industrial brutality is relatively less brutal than the lives they have endured. Attempting to forecast which nations will replace China, Friedman notes two important markers. One is "garment and footwear manufacturing, a highly competitive area that demands low wages but provides work opportunities," particularly for women. "A second marker is mobile phone assembly, which requires a workforce that can master relatively simple operations." Neither kind of work entails high-tech skills, but regarding the claim of the need of global capitalism for high-tech workers is the second marker: here is the cell phone, an extraordinarily technologically complex product, yet manufacturers seek a workforce with relatively minimal technical skills, not one possessing sophisticated STEM education.[42]

Student Workers and the 21stcenturyeconomy

While U.S. corporations criticize the public schools for producing deficiently educated students, it's obvious from real-life manufacturing that global businesses have no problem employing and exploiting students and youngsters who have less than the purported education workers need for high-tech production. For example, in tandem with Bill Gates's relentless expression of concern for the well-being of youth, Microsoft has had a work-study program for adolescents in one of its manufacturing factories in China. Most of the teenagers are sixteen- and seventeen-year-olds, with some reportedly even younger. "Work study" includes fifteen-hour shifts, six and seven days a week, with an hourly pay of about 65 cents an hour, which falls to a take-home wage of 52 cents an hour after the cost of factory food is deducted. In addition to the low pay and long hours, the work pace is grueling, with the study experience requiring twenty or thirty workers to complete a mandatory goal of assembling 2,000 Microsoft mice per shift.[43]

Other "work-study" has been created by Foxconn Technology, headquartered in Taiwan. Foxconn is a multinational technology company that produces an estimated 40 percent of the world's consumer electronics, such as Apple's iPhones and iPods, Amazon's Kindle, and many other electronic devices in factories in many countries but primarily in China. The factory's weekly work averages 56 hours at wages that most of the workers (64.3 percent to 72 percent of them) report are insufficient to cover their basic needs. Asked if they feel body pain after a full day's work, between 59 and 71 percent of workers in these factories replied "yes," with neck and back pain most frequently mentioned. How much education is needed in their factories? Various investigations have uncovered that Foxconn has often employed teenagers as young as fourteen, often under the guise of work-study programs. For these teenagers and the approximately 20 to 30 percent of workers who have only a middle school education, the answer would be: "not a lot."[44]

The work-study programs, with their harsh working conditions, are not unique to Foxconn. Other factories manufacturing for companies such as Hewlett-Packard, Apple, Intel, and Cisco do the same. For example, employed in these factories are tens of thousands of student "interns" hired during the summer months, with hundreds of thousands of teenage "interns" making up the regular workforce. These "internships" seldom have any kind of relationship to STEM education: "Vocational school students are from a wide range of majors: nursery, locksmith, security guards and so on. In other words, the work at [the factories] is totally irrelevant to their studies."[45]

Teenage "Labor Dispatch System" and the Global Economy

At HEG Technology, a company in China that supplies electronics for Samsung and Lenovo, an undercover investigation by China Labor Watch, a New York–based independent NGO, found fourteen- and fifteen-year-old workers in these factories, who explained they were hired through "a 'labor dispatch system' that often funnels child laborers to factories during the summer to help meet a surge in orders that comes just ahead of the fall and winter shopping seasons in the United States and Europe." The youngsters formally worked from "8:30 p.m. to 5:30 a.m., and then worked an additional three hours of overtime, six days a week."[46]

China Labor Watch also investigated Korean manufacturer Samsung's network of factories in China. Ranking as the second-largest tech company in the world in 2015, with $22 billion in profits,[47] Samsung had numerous

> illegal and inhumane violations . . . including but not limited to well over 100 hours of forced overtime work per month, unpaid work, standing for 11 to 12 hours while working, underage workers, severe age and gender discrimination, *abuse of student and labor dispatch workers,* a lack of worker safety, and verbal and physical abuse. Moreover, workers' lack of any effective internal grievance channel by which to rectify these transgressions [my emphasis].[48]

The investigators found that in one of the factories, about "60% of workers are students hired through schools." The students were required to work for up to a year and then return to their schools.

As vocational students, they had a modicum of skills far below the purported level needed for the claimed competition in the global economy.

The Education Required to Mine Minerals for High-Tech Products

The mantra of "education for the global economy" is further undercut when we look at the work involved in providing the minerals used in high-tech products. Tin, tungsten, gold, and dozens of other minerals are necessary for cell phones, laptops, DVD players, cameras, and various electronic devices. Gold, for example, is a valuable mineral for high-tech commodities because of its electrical conductivity, its corrosion resistance, and similar properties. Obtaining the minerals, not how they are obtained, is what counts most for global electronics corporations such as Microsoft, Apple, Dell, Nokia, Hewlett-Packard, IBM, Sony, Toshiba, Canon, Nintendo, Sharp, Philips, and Panasonic. Never mind that child and forced labor are used to mine these minerals in countries such as the Democratic Republic of the Congo.

Only because of broad grassroots campaigns publicizing the enforced labor behind these "conflict materials" have electronic companies begun to take steps toward reducing its use. Yet for all the activist pressure from community, church, and college groups, such as "Conflict-Free Campus Initiative," these corporations have largely continued to put profits ahead of human rights and have taken few and sometime no steps to trace, audit, or change their materials' supply sources.

A gauge of changes in corporate morality is available through the human rights organization Enough, which "has ranked the largest electronics companies on their efforts toward using and investing in conflict-free minerals in their products." In the organization's rankings, Intel, the most proactive corporation, received just a 60 percent rating for steps it took to combat the immoral labor conditions in obtaining conflict-minerals. Following Intel, the scores quickly drop. Hewlett-Packard landed just above the midway point with a 54 percent score, but Apple and Microsoft had a corporate morality score of

38 percent, IBM and Sony follow at 27 percent, Canon and Sharp at 8 percent, and Nintendo at 0 percent![49]

To help expose and address these deplorable working conditions, the 2010 Dodd-Frank financial-reform bill included a special section on conflict materials that called for publicly listed U.S. companies (those that offer stock shares and bonds for sale to the public through the stock exchange) to disclose whether any of their products included conflict minerals originating from the ten countries covered by the law: the Democratic Republic of the Congo, Tanzania, Zambia, Republic of Congo, Central African Republic, Angola, Uganda, Rwanda, South Sudan, and Burundi.

The bill was relatively restrained in its call for companies to disclose the use of conflict materials, but did not ban companies from using them. Nonetheless, simply disclosing the information was beyond the pale for the largest manufacturing trade groups in the United States—the Chamber of Commerce, the National Association of Manufacturers, and the Business Roundtable— which began a legal battle in federal court aimed at stopping the disclosure requirements from going into effect.[50] Coming to the aid of the business organizations was a federal three-judge panel of the District of Columbia Circuit court. It used the concept that corporations are persons (*Citizens United* decision) to strike down a portion of the SEC's conflict minerals rule, saying that requiring companies to disclose whether their products were free of conflict materials violated the manufacturers' First Amendment rights by "compelling speech."[51]

And so the immoral work continues. An estimated 320 tons of gold are used annually, without corporate regard to who is doing the work to mine it.[52] No worry that in Ghana, Niger, Peru, and Tanzania, boys and girls, some as young as eight, work twelve- to twenty-four-hour shifts to mine the mineral.[53] For the girls, life often is harder, because, in addition to their mining labor, they must fulfill their traditional female responsibilities at home.[54] Consequently, the girls have an overall fuller daily workload, less opportunity for daily rest and rehabilitation, and, in turn, even fewer educational opportunities.

Throughout the world these conditions are duplicated. In Bolivia, boys and girls mine tin, zinc, silver, and gold. In Columbia they mine emeralds, coal, and gold. In Tanzania, children work in gold mines, breathing in the deadly poisonous mercury that is used to extract gold.[55]

More Child Labor in the Global Economy

In Argentina children make bricks and garments. In India they make brassware, carpets, footware, and textiles. In Pakistan they help produce surgical instruments and glass goods. In the Philippines child labor is employed making fashion accessories and rubber products. Basic commodities valued in advanced capitalist countries, such as coffee, chocolate, cotton, beef, and sugarcane, depend on the use of child labor throughout the world.

Consider chocolate. Beth Hoffman, writing in *Forbes* magazine, describes the vast, $50 billion chocolate industry in the United States and Europe, whose products are made from cocoa pods, about two-thirds to three-quarters of which come from West Africa.[56] There, large numbers of children are employed to harvest cocoa for U.S. companies like Hershey, Mars, and Nestlé, each relying on cheap farming and labor for their profits. Though globalism has expanded and interwoven the connections between raw materials and finished products, even child labor is insufficient for providing a decent income for cocoa farmers, who have failed to profit. As adults and children work hard to produce cocoa, chocolate manufacturers have been paying less than half for cocoa than in 1980. Around that time, 50 percent of the cost of a chocolate bar went to pay for cocoa; today that cost is less than 6 percent.

Recommendations for ending child labor in cocoa production include having children spend more time in school than in harvesting cocoa, but this is usually is ignored. As Antonie Frountain, representing a European organization dedicated to addressing cocoa production, notes, "Your average cocoa farmer is earning about 10 percent of the absolute poverty line. In simple English, this means if you would increase a farmer's income tenfold, he would still be in the definition of the global society, absolutely poor." If most farmers were paid better for their cocoa, explains anthropologist Alfred Babo, they would not need their children to work on the farms and could send them to school.[57]

As economist Michael Yates underscores, from child prostitutes in Bombay to young boys and girls picking crops in Mexico, "work is hell."[58] For many millions of children throughout the world, the notion of "education for the global economy" is a bitter joke.

"No Longer Poor" in the Global Economy

For billions of extremely poor people who are not even part of the exploited workforce in the aforementioned manufacturing sector of the global economy—that is, the 1.22 billion who live on less than $1.25 a day, the poverty line established by the World Bank—life is continual suffering. However, for the World Bank, which looks at the bigger picture, these numbers represent good news: "poverty" has dropped from 1980, when the number of people living on less than $1.25 a day was close to 2 billion people.

For those lauding the World Bank's claims, the credit for this poverty reduction was encapsulated by the *Economist*, which attributed most of the reduction "to capitalism and free trade, for they enable economies to grow—and it is growth, principally, that has eased destitution."[59] the *Economist* does note the phenomenon chiefly responsible for the reduction is the growth of multinational production in China, though this is unlikely to be duplicated in poorer countries in the next twenty years. Or, were the phenomenon replicated, it would be at the cost of a diminution in the Chinese economy because capital would have moved to other countries to obtain workers who will work for less. Added to the link between poverty reduction and global sweatshop growth is the concomitant consequence of creating economic hardships for workers in advanced capitalist nations who have lost jobs to Chinese workers who work for less. In all, the race to the bottom that has been occurring throughout the world has also meant that poverty alleviated in one part of global capitalism has commonly increased poverty elsewhere.

Of course, any increase in income for human beings who have been living on $1.25 a day or less is to be welcomed, but exactly how self-satisfied the representatives of industries and banks who serve on the board of directors of the World Bank should feel is another question, one appraised by independent researchers. As would be quickly evident to anyone who actually has tried living on or slightly above the $1.25 level, researchers from Bristol University have determined that the $1.25 figure is "too low" and "artificial" for drawing conclusions about rises above a basic level of poverty. Studying the actual extent of global deprivation for shelter, sanitation, water, information, nutrition, health and education, the researchers found that while World Bank standards place approximately 5 percent of the world's children in poverty, 17 percent of children, when measured by actual food and basic needs standards, live in poverty, as do 23 percent and 30 percent of households.[60]

Similarly, United Nations researchers have estimated that poverty levels in Latin America are approximately twice the World Bank calculations. Latin American poverty as a whole is 28 percent and is projected to remain for future years, which, given demographic growth, would translate into an increase of 167 million people living in poverty. Among those in poverty, extreme poverty or indigence in Latin America was projected to increase to 71 million of the 167 million.[61]

Anthropologist Jason Hickel of the London School of Economics also argues that the World Bank's figures for a decline in poverty is "a comforting story, but unfortunately it is just not true." Hickel explains that the $1.25 figure is arbitrarily set with little data and a disregard for the actual cost of living in various countries. For example, "a 1990 survey in Sri Lanka found that 35 percent of the population fell under the national poverty line. But the World Bank, using [its International Poverty Line (IPL)], reported only 4 percent in the same year. In other words, the IPL [of $1.25] makes poverty seem much less serious than it actually is." Similarly, when actual calculations are made of survival threshold, the World Bank poverty line again fails to hold up. "In India, for example, children living just above the IPL still have a 60 percent chance of being malnourished."[62]

Further rejecting the $1.25 figure is the work of economist Peter Edwards of Newcastle University, who has estimated that to achieve normal life expectancy, people require a minimum of $2.50 a day, roughly twice the World Bank calculation. At $2.50 a day, global poverty increases to almost triple the World Bank's estimate. Even at a level of $10 a day—income surely a realistic step closer to any genuine standard of a "minimum poverty level"—nearly 70 percent of humanity falls into that category in the grand 21stcenturyglobaleconomy.[63]

Not to Worry

Despite these economic distributions and trajectories, the world's richest man, likely speaking both for himself and his 1 percent compatriots, ecstatically predicted in 2015 that "the lives of people in poor countries will improve faster in the next 15 years than at any other time in history. And their lives will improve more than anyone else's." Why is this? Because "the financial lives of the poor are very complicated" and the problem was not just a lack of income. Yes, Bill Gates recognized that the world's poor "don't have enough assets," but—and here was a key determinant out of poverty—they "also don't have access to a bank to help them use their assets effectively." Lack of bank accounts, that's the problem, Gates concluded, after he was astonished to learn that on this planet "2.5 billion adults are without a bank account." Nonetheless, the prospects of the poor were promising, he optimistically proposed, because of the new technology in the new global economy: "In the next 15 years, digital banking will give the poor more control over their assets and help them transform their lives."[64]

Still, the Beat Goes On

Despite the actual composition of the global economy, daily pronouncements like these continue:

- "Skill Up India" aims to bring global standards of education that will help meet the demands of a global economy through online and mobile courses.[65]
- Northern Ireland "must wake up to the opportunities of STEM education or face being left behind in a global economy."[66]
- "Nigeria: Vocation and Technical Education—A Key to Improving Nigeria's Development: The world has become globalized and the future prosperity depends on comparative advantage. This comparative advantage hinges on people and their technical or technological sophistication."[67]
- "Digital technologies are transforming every industry in our economy. Further, living in a hyper-competitive global economy, innovation is an imperative for almost every business. To not only survive, but to thrive, we [in Oregon] need to fill our companies with inspired talent that not only understands this reality, but is exhilarated by the challenge."[68]

These are variations of the education mantra. However, as this chapter delineates, the "global economy" is much more than technology, STEM skills, digital transformation, business competition, and properly skilled workers. It is also an economy in which physical commodities, services, and profit are created not solely in Infosys's flatscreen conference rooms, but in low-skilled production in China, Bangladesh, Vietnam, Mexico, and numerous other countries in which minimally skilled, low-wage workers are tethered to oppressive production.

Understanding and Feeling World Pain

For education, the prevailing conception of the global economy generates a misunderstanding of the term's actual construction and one's place in that economy, it also damages students' understanding of and sensitivity to global humanity and human rights. In Chaim Potok's novel *The Chosen*, Daniel is a brilliant son of a rabbi.[69] With his eidetic memory he shocks his new friend Reuven by reciting word-for-word long passages he has just read. When learning to read at age four, Daniel proudly recounted to his father the totality of a storybook he had just read. He did not merely "read the story," his father recalls, "he swallowed it, as one swallows food and water."

For Daniel, the employment and recognition of his superior abilities fill him with elation, but his father despairs because the story was about a poor, suffering man, about whom Daniel thought and cared nothing. His father worries that his brilliant son, who thinks only of his mental abilities, has no sense of or concern in his "cold mind" for those in the world who suffer, who "carry pain." The father decides to raise his son "in silence," that is, not talking to him at all. The son is confused and hurt, but the father holds fast because, though he is also wounded, he is certain that through "silence" his son will come to understand pain and suffering and extend those feelings to how he comes to know and respond to the pain in the world.

This method for teaching Daniel to become a person who can do more than employ and revel in his cognitive skills certainly is not one to recommend (and Daniel's father does express some misgivings over the suffering he caused both his son and himself). However, the story is pertinent when considering the kinds of persons educated to compete in the global economy. Fostered in the curriculum are cognitive STEM skills, languages for working across nations, knowledge for making various global market connections, resourcefulness for working cooperatively and innovatively with comparably skilled workers in other countries, and similar abilities for employment and participation in the global economy. Absent, however, is any education about the extent of harsh work, low income, poverty, illnesses, meager education, early mortality, and similar bitter conditions borne by a vast portion of humanity. It is a morally crippling education, one that narrowly educates the mind for the global economy, while largely excluding understanding of and social justice responses to the pain carried throughout the world.

3. The U.S. Economy, Schooling, and Knowledge

T he headline of a LaCrosse, Wisconsin, news article expressed the common framing of the purported national "skills-gap" issue: "Local Company Tackles Skills-Gap Issue; Experts in our area said there isn't an unemployment problem rather an unemployable problem."[1] Viewed at a national level, a 2015 appraisal by the Education Testing Service (ETS), the nation's major school testing company, reported that businesses across the country were being hurt because of an insufficiently skilled workforce, especially among the millennial generation (those born after 1980). This skills differential between the pace of technological advances and lagging educational development created underemployment, unemployment, wage inequality, and, of course, headaches for the nation's businesses because they were unable to get the skilled workers they need. "If we continue on this path," concluded ETS, "there could be serious consequences for America's economy and the future."[2] In community after community—Philadelphia,[3] Baltimore,[4] Indianapolis,[5] Chicago[6]—and state after state—Alabama,[7] California,[8] Indiana,[9] New York[10]—the problem is the same. Schools are failing to provide enough students with twenty-first-century skills, which then means that businesses cannot hire the skilled workers needed to build and sustain the twenty-first-century economy. Young people who lack these skills are especially hurting because they are locked out of the unfilled skilled jobs and, therefore, face a future of low-paying work and little chance to reach the middle class. Yes, claims about a current skills-gap and its consequences for U.S. businesses are loud and persistent, but there remain reasons to ask, "Is the story true?"

Are STEM Jobs New and Increasing at a Dazzling Rate?

All the focus on STEM jobs makes them seem they have suddenly burst into the economy and dramatically expanded their historical proportion of existing jobs. To appraise this perspective, let's look first at the current proportion of STEM jobs in the U.S. economy. The U.S. Bureau of Labor Statistics determined, "Depending on the definition, the size of the STEM workforce can range from 5 percent to 20 percent of all U.S. workers."[11] For the U.S. Department of Commerce, the size was at the low end, estimating that "in 2010, 7.6 million people or 1 in 18 workers held STEM jobs." This is about 6 percent, a figure that led the Department of Commerce to conclude that "STEM employment currently makes up only a small fraction of total U.S. employment." Projecting to the year 2018, the Department of Commerce estimated that STEM jobs would grow about 17 percent, which would put STEM jobs at approximately 7 percent of all jobs.[12]

These appraisals not only are far from what could be described as a STEM-work-dominated job market, their significance diminishes even more when put in historical perspective. Let's take the highest estimate of 20 percent as the current percentage of advanced technical work and look backwards. In 1850, around the start of the Industrial Revolution, these kinds of top-end jobs made up about 10 percent of all work. Consequently, we can conclude that the proportion of STEM jobs relative to the earlier and present economy has "doubled," but it has taken over 160 years to do so, and these jobs still represent only a significant *minority* of overall jobs—particularly if the 20 percent estimate is high. Nonetheless (or should I say "miraculously," considering the current focus on STEM jobs), for over 150 years the U.S. economy has managed to be built and sustained without a vast number of STEM jobs.

If we look back a shorter distance—to the 1950s—we again can ask: Why, suddenly, is there such a current stress on STEM education and work to advance the economy and provide Americans with a materially secure, relatively prosperous life? In postwar 1950s, after all, when the U.S. economy had become less militarized—albeit, in Eisenhower's words, still containing a large "military-industrial complex"—STEM jobs made up about 15 percent of all jobs, a proportion that continued into the 1960s.

Nonetheless, those years were a time when good-paying jobs expanded and the long-hailed U.S. "middle class"—defined as having a good wage, a house, vacation time, some savings, a retirement pension—was built. And profits accumulated as well. What, then, given these relative similar percentages of STEM jobs over decades, has affected the well-being of Americans? In other words, between the height of the American Dream years—the 1950s and 1960s—and now, the percentage difference in STEM jobs has been about 5 percent, and perhaps less. Is it really possible that with just 5 percent fewer STEM jobs, the age of the American Dream was built? Or, looking at the other side of the equation, how can we explain that the middle class was built with 85 percent non-STEM jobs, yet presently the middle class is collapsing with about 80 percent non-STEM jobs?

Shortage of STEM Workers?

In addition to the issue of the relative percentage of STEM jobs in the U.S. economy, there is the question of how many STEM jobs are being filled. Are many STEM jobs remaining vacant because there are not enough U.S. workers sufficiently educated to perform them? Do educational deficiencies explain why so many job seekers are unemployed or working poorly paid jobs? Did the additional 5 percent of skilled work create an educational goal that U.S. schools simply haven't been able to meet? Several studies have addressed these issues.

A 2004 Rand Corporation examination of STEM workers and the likelihood of a STEM worker shortage concluded: "Despite recurring concerns about potential shortages of STEM personnel in the U.S. workforce, particularly in engineering and information technology, *we did not find evidence that such shortages have existed at least since 1990*, nor that they are on the horizon" (my emphasis). The Rand study additionally concluded that in contrast to cries about a STEM worker shortage, in fact, except for engineering, "underemployment of STEM workers is relatively high compared with non-STEM workers."[13]

The Rand study did not find evidence that the United States would confront "an inadequate supply of STEM workers for the nation's current needs," nor were there "indications of shortages in the foreseeable future." The study also warned that with the continued cry about a STEM worker shortage, there was the risk that young people would complete years of training, and incur considerable debt doing so, "only to emerge into labor markets with surplus STEM workers."[14]

Robert Charette, an editor of the Institute of Electrical and Electronics Engineers (IEEE) magazine *Spectrum*, explained why claims about a "STEM crisis" in the United States, Japan, and several other countries were a myth. Supposedly, in the United States one million additional STEM graduates will be needed over the next decade, with similar shortages predicted in the United Kingdom, Germany, Japan, and similar industrial nations. However, Charette notes that various projections of increases in STEM jobs have not been substantiated by reality. For example, in contrast to one estimate that "2.4 million STEM job openings in the United States" would appear "between 2008 and 2018, with 1.1 million newly created jobs and the rest to replace workers who retire or move to non-STEM fields," in actuality, "more than 370,000 science and engineering jobs in the United States were lost" in 2011, according to the Bureau of Labor Statistics.[15]

Similarly, a study by the Economic Policy Institute (EPI) concluded that the "United States has more than a sufficient supply of workers available to work in STEM occupations," thanks to increased student enrollment following forecasts of employment opportunities in these jobs. For example, "the annual number of computer science graduates doubled between 1998 and 2004, and is currently over 50 percent higher than its 1998 level." Unfortunately, subsequent employment has not matched vocational expectations: "For every two students that U.S. colleges graduate with STEM degrees, only one is hired into a STEM job." In computer and information science and in engineering, "U.S. colleges graduate 50 percent more students than are hired into those fields each year." For computer science graduates, 32 percent say they could not enter the information technology (IT) workforce because an IT job was unavailable, and 53 percent say they found a better job outside the IT fields. The study concluded, "These responses suggest that the supply of graduates is substantially larger than the demand for them in industry."[16]

A study by Georgetown University's Center on Education and the Workforce drew comparable conclusions. Unemployment for Information Science graduates was 14.7 percent, higher than unemployment for all other majors (for example, 9.9 percent for sociology major and 9.8 percent for English majors; mathematics majors had a 5.9 percent unemployment rate; engineering majors had an unemployment rate between 7 percent and 8 percent, depending on specialized area).[17]

Adding to appraisals of the purported skills shortage was the work of economist Heidi Shierholz, who found that in 2012 the unemployment rate for workers in every sector of the economy was greater than in 2007, including the computer and mathematical sector, the architecture and engineering sector, health care practitioners and technicians, and life and physical sciences:

> If high-elevated unemployment were due to skills shortages or mismatches, we would expect to find some sectors where there are more unemployed workers than job openings, and some sectors where there are more job openings than unemployed workers. However, unemployed workers dramatically

outnumber job openings in all sectors. There are between 1.4 and 10.5 times as many unemployed workers as job openings in every industry. Even in the industry (Finance and Insurance) with the most favorable ratio of unemployed workers to job openings, there are still 40 percent more unemployed workers than job openings. In no industry does the number of job openings even come close to the number of people looking for work.[18]

Shierholz also looked at wage trends for evidence of a skills shortage, reasoning that if skills were in short supply, employers facing a shortage of skilled workers would offer higher wages to attract the workers they need. However, in no occupation, including computer work, engineering, and other skills jobs, is there evidence of wages bidding up that "would indicate tight labor markets or labor shortages." She concludes: "In sum, no matter how you cut the data, there is no evidence of skills shortages as a major cause of today's elevated unemployment."[19]

Discussing the purported insufficient number of skilled people in the U.S. labor pool who can do IT jobs, Michelle Davidson, editor of a technology website, responding to Bill Gates's claim that "anybody who's got good computer science training, they are not out there unemployed. We're just not seeing an available labor pool." "Oh really?" said Davidson,

> "Tell that to the thousands of unemployed IT workers out there. In fact, government figures showed 5.7 percent of IT employees were out of work last year compared with 5.5 percent of all workers. Many of those people will tell you that it's a matter of money—that employers don't want to pay U.S. workers the salaries they want. They say it isn't a shortage of skilled labor, but a shortage of cheap skilled labor."[20]

National Public Radio business correspondent Adam Davidson similarly argued, based on an investigation of college classrooms where high-skilled work is taught and of manufacturers who look to hire graduates of these classrooms, that the problem for industry is finding workers who will be docile and work for low pay. As one Milwaukee metal-fabricating manufacturer told him, he avoids hiring workers with a background in a "union-type job," and when he does hire skilled workers, their starting pay is $10 or $15 an hour. Davidson observes, "From what I understand, a new shift manager at a nearby McDonald's can earn around $14 an hour."[21]

With respect to a skills gap affecting manufacturing, the Boston Consulting Group (BCG), a "global management consulting firm and the world's leading advisor on business strategy," with clients in the world's 500 largest companies, found that "the U.S. is short some 80,000 to 100,000 highly skilled manufacturing workers. That shortage represents less than 1 percent of the nation's 11.5 million manufacturing workers and less than 8 percent of its 1.4 million highly skilled manufacturing workers." Focusing on the question of whether shortages were widespread, BCG found that "only five of the nation's 50 largest manufacturing centers (Baton Rouge, Charlotte, Miami, San Antonio, and Wichita) appear to have significant or severe skills gaps. . . . The findings underscore the idea that worries of a skills gap crisis are overblown." Evaluating the wages skilled workers receive, BCG echoed Michelle Davidson's response to Bill Gates: "Trying to hire high-skilled workers at rock-bottom rates is not a skills gap." BCG added, "Investment in training and skills development needs to be stepped up, but there's little reason to believe that the U.S. cannot remain on track for a manufacturing renaissance by 2020."[22]

Again, What Will Most Work Be in the United States?

Amplifying an important point made in previous chapters, contrary to the shrill claims that high-skilled work is speedily becoming pervasive in the U.S. economy, the reality, according to the National Employment Law Project, is that since the 2008 Great Recession the majority of jobs created have been low-paying and medium-paying.

Lower-wage jobs ($9.48 to $13.33/hr) comprise 44 percent of employment growth; medium-wage jobs ($13.73 to $20.00/hr) comprise 25 percent of employment growth; and high-wage jobs ($20.03 to $32.62/hr) account for 30 percent of employment growth.[23] Therefore, in terms of income, the majority of jobs created do not even pay the modest $15/hr currently being demanded as a start toward a genuine living wage, but which is considerably below a minimum living wage needed for a two-person family, which is around $20/hr.[24] Put another way, the income of the majority of jobs recently created are a long distance from the level needed to create a middle class.

The U.S. Bureau of Labor Statistics provided a similar perspective. In 2014, as in previous years, the occupations with the largest number of workers were not STEM jobs. The greatest number of workers were retail salespersons and cashiers, followed by food preparation and serving workers; general office clerks; customer service representatives; waiters and waitresses; laborers and freight, stock, and material movers; janitors and cleaners. Registered nurses were the only large occupation group that required advanced education.[25]

The work sectors that offer the greatest future growth was captured in the title of a *Foreign Policy* article, "More Unskilled Workers, Please." Michael Clemmons of the Center for Global Development argued that a 2013 immigration bill did not "do nearly enough to address America's real labor shortage," the need for "less-skilled essential workers—elder-care workers, farm workers, builders, cleaners, servers, and warehousers," and that "there aren't enough U.S. workers to do these essential jobs." Clemmons explained that the United States will need millions of additional workers over the next decade to fill the least-skilled jobs, ones that do not require a high school degree, to achieve projected economic growth. "These include jobs in home health, food preparation, freight, child care, cleaning, landscaping, and construction." He lamented that over the next decade millions of new low-skilled jobs will be created that U.S.-born workers will not fill. This call for foreign-born workers underscores the kinds of jobs that will continue to make up much of the U.S. economy.[26]

Twenty Years of Schooling

In his 1965 song, "Subterranean Homesick Blues," Bob Dylan sang that a worker's reward after achieving twenty years of schooling would be a promotion to the day shift. Ah, for those good old days. Now, twenty years of schooling and you're lucky even to get a job, and if you get one there's a good chance it will be one that someone with a high school diploma could have been hired to do a couple of decades ago. Furthermore, if you're working after twenty years of schooling, most likely your income is not enough for independent living or, if it is, it's probably not likely sufficient, as in years past, to be the sole income for adequately supporting a family.

These conclusions are corroborated by surveys the business consulting firm Accenture has done, which looked at the employment outcomes of recent college graduates. Fifty-one percent considered "themselves to be underemployed or working in jobs that don't require a college degree"; 39 percent were earning $25,000 or less, and low salary levels contributed to 42 percent of the graduates continuing to live at home. Moreover, less than half of the graduates (46 percent) had full-time jobs, down from full-time employment of 68 percent for graduates of just a year or two earlier. Nor were the low salary levels compensated for by good benefits, as indicated by the 52 percent of graduates who had to continue on their parents' health insurance. Overall, the trend for college graduates was toward more employment in work unrelated to college studies, less full-time employment, greater part-time employment, low pay, less personal independence, and long-term debt.[27] The Accenture findings were buttressed by a Federal Reserve Bank of New York study, which found that "underemployment among recent graduates—a condition defined here as working in jobs that typically do not require a bachelor's degree—has continued to increase. Many recent grads feel underemployed and disillusioned. The percentage of recent grads who feel underemployed—working at a job that actually does not require their degree—has risen 10 percentage points (41 percent to 51 percent) over the past three years," from 2013 to 2016.[28]

One significant cause of this underemployment is a process dubbed "upcredentialing." As the research organization Burning Glass Technologies (BGT) explains in a report, *Moving the Goalposts*, upcredentialing is a process in which employers seek to hire applicants who have "a bachelor's degree for jobs that formerly required less education, even when the actual skills required haven't changed or when this makes the position harder to fill." The following are examples of occupations for which the demand for a college degree is not commensurate with the tasks required:

- 65 percent of postings for Executive Secretaries and Executive Assistants called for a bachelor's degree, but only 19 percent of those who were currently employed in these roles had a B.A.
- 43 percent of sales jobs holders have a B.A., but the percentage of employment postings requiring a B.A. for sales jobs has increased to 56 percent.
- For office and administrative services, the percentage of job holders with a B.A. is 20 percent, although the percentage of postings requiring a B.A. for these jobs has jumped to 45 percent.

With respect to jobs overall, BGT reinforces a plethora of data that undercut the many claims about the need for job seekers to obtain twenty-first-century skills: jobs with skill requirements that had been filled by high school graduates constitute two-thirds of U.S. jobs and are not jobs that now require high-tech, STEM-like skills. Yes, in some cases the advanced technology employed in these jobs does require more skilled workers; however, for most middle-skilled work the job substance has not changed. The difference in degree requirements, BGT explains, lies primarily in employers simply raising the bar of required educational levels.[29] *New York Times* economics reporter Catherine Rampell framed it this way: "The college degree is becoming the new high school diploma: the new minimum requirement, albeit an expensive one, for getting even the lowest-level job." In the Atlanta area, for example, "in 2012, 39 percent of job postings for secretaries and administrative assistants requested a bachelor's degree, up from 28 percent in 2007." An example of credential inflation is a forty-five-person Atlanta law firm that hires "only people with a bachelor's degree, even for jobs that do not require college-level skills." The firm's documents courier has a bachelor's degree and earns $10 an hour.[30] The Center for College Affordability underscored the bleak reality of college payoffs in twenty-first-century work: currently more than one-third of college graduates hold jobs that require less than a college degree.[31] Similarly, the National Center for Education Statistics found that while nearly 19 million college students are to graduate with bachelor's degrees between 2010 and 2020, only 8.5 million job openings will require a B.A. during this period.[32]

Job Quality and Quality of Life

One measure of the job quality of employed college graduates is the proportion who "receive pension coverage from their own employer (either defined-benefit or defined contribution)." Based on U.S. Social Security Administration figures, the measure reveals both declining employment conditions and an insecure future for today's young, educated workers. For example, 41.5 percent of new college graduates (age 21–24) did have pension coverage in 2000, already a low percentage. However, in 2013, just over a decade later, the percentage had dropped to 35.2 percent. Furthermore, this declining and minor portion of pension coverage fails to consider the proportion of workers who have a pension that will pay a lifetime annuity based on years of work and final salary versus a pension in which future benefits are not guaranteed. The former "pensions are tied to employers who bear the responsibility for ensuring that employees receive pension benefits," and the latter are owned by employees who, therefore, bear the sole responsibility for their financial security. Over recent decades, most defined benefits plans have been replaced by employee-controlled benefits—if workers are lucky enough to have any kind of pension plan. And what will life be like for today's young, college-educated workers when they reach their retirement years? The Social Security Administration alarmingly concluded that, given the trend toward no pension coverage, "Social Security will increasingly become the only source of guaranteed lifetime benefits" on which these college-educated retirees will be able to rely.[33]

A College Degree in the Global Economy

Regardless of the reality of widespread reduction of wages and benefits for college graduates, getting a college degree will mean relatively better income than for jobs requiring less education. But what to do if obtaining that degree means accumulating substantial loan debt? One might think that the corporations and public officials bemoaning the nation's deficiently skilled workforce would be demanding the availability of free or low-cost college education. Yet, except for the 2016 Bernie Sanders's presidential campaign platform and his post-election call for free college, neither major U.S. political party has demanded this kind of reform.

The financial burden on young people hoping that a college education will help secure a good job is reflected in the following figures: from the college enrollment years of 1983–1984 to that of 2013-2014, the inflation-adjusted cost of a four-year education, including tuition, fees, and room and board increased 125.7 percent for private school and 129 percent for public school. Unfortunately, families of college students have been less able to help because higher education costs have increased far more rapidly than the 16.8 percent rise in median family income over the same period. Hence, students commonly have "little choice but to take out loans" and, worse yet, "upon graduating into a labor market with limited job opportunities, may not have the funds to repay the loans. What else is there for students to do but borrow money?"[34] Over 70 percent of college graduates have student loan debt averaging over $30,000, with more students than ever before taking on debt and projections of debt forecasting the total borrowing levels of future college classes continuing to rise; for students who attend graduate or professional school, the debt is likely to increase to six figures.[35]

Manufacturing Jobs That Built and No Longer Build a Middle Class

Given the actual limited number of STEM jobs currently available and projected for at least the next decade, is there another way to duplicate the conditions that generated the post–Second World War manufacturing jobs instrumental in creating the middle class? Although there are not as many manufacturing jobs now as then—currently, there are slightly more than 12 million such jobs in the United States, compared with about 15–16 million in the 1950s—today's 12 million or so manufacturing workers should, by themselves, demonstrate an area of employment through which, as before, the American Dream could be reached.[36] In other words, shouldn't the mantra be, If you get a STEM education *or* a manufacturing job, life can be good (or, at least somewhat economically secure)? The answer, unfortunately, is no, because, as a study by the National Employment Law Project (NELP) illustrates, today's manufacturers can pay workers deficient wages, so why should they pay them more?[37] In the 1950s, as economist Robert Reich calculates, manufacturing job wages were significantly higher than the average wage. "Fifty years ago, when General Motors was the largest employer in America, the typical GM worker got paid $35 an hour in today's dollars."[38] Wages for manufacturing jobs have continued to drop over the decades, however, with many manufacturing jobs now paying less than a living wage. Currently, the median wage in manufacturing is $15.66 an hour, with approximately one-quarter of manufacturing workers *earning less than $12/hour*, and many earning just $10–$11/hour. For example, General Electric workers in Louisville, Kentucky, earn $13/hour making electric water heaters. Remington, the gun company, pays workers $11/hour in its Alabama manufacturing facilities.[39]

Furthermore, the official median wage for manufacturing is inflated because it does not include "domestic outsourcing," that is, the manufacturing that industries formally transfer to staffing and temporary worker firms, where hourly pay is two-thirds or less than for workers employed by the primary manufacturing company. NELP research found that "workers looking for a manufacturing job, and especially ones in an auto plant today, increasingly find that the only open positions are placed by staffing agencies that pay lower wages and provide fewer benefits as compared with direct hires, and that offer limited opportunities to secure a permanent-employee position."[40] It's a clever scheme, with staffing agencies filling an increasing number of production jobs, even though the actual work difference for the employees at the manufacturing site, whether agency or direct-hire, is nonexistent because staffing agency workers usually work alongside and under the same supervision as direct-hire employees. Is something else going on besides greed? Are these manufacturing workers earning so little because the nation's schools have failed them? Is worker education the reason businesses are using crafty employment methods to lower wages? Or do current manufacturing wages have something to do with worker power? Is there now a lack of power to resist corporate avarice? Is it coincidence that in the past, wages were higher not because of anything inherent in manufacturing jobs, but because in the mid-1950s, the halcyon time of such "good-paying manufacturing jobs," 35 percent of that sector was unionized, whereas by 2016 union density had fallen to 10.7 percent, down 0.4 percentage points from 2015?[41] Is this a major reason why American corporations urge a focus on education, rather than on labor's bargaining power, to explain why most U.S. jobs do not pay more than they do?

The Skills Shortage, H-1B, and Other Replacement Workers

Another reason for the clamor about a U.S. skills shortage and the failure of the nation's schools to provide an educated workforce is business's desire to replace U.S. workers with those from other countries who will work for less—or, more precisely, who will have to work for less if they want a job in the United States. One method for accomplishing this employee switch is the H-1B visa program, which allows U.S. businesses to temporarily employ foreign workers in specialty work, such as in information technology (IT). As explained by public policy analyst Ron Hira in testimony before the U.S. Senate Judiciary

Committee, the accruement of profit is what drives the H-1B program, not overcoming a national skills shortage. Businesses can use the program simply by claiming that they cannot find a sufficiently skilled U.S. worker to do a job and then, using legal loopholes, hire foreign workers.[42] In practice, Hira explained, the program serves as a vehicle for businesses to hire H-1B workers who essentially can be paid wages lower than the market wage for an American worker.[43]

Not So Funny

In the 1936 animated comedy, *Mickey's Rival,* Mickey Mouse asked his sweetheart, Minnie Mouse, about another mouse looking to replace him. "So you still think that guy's funny?" Computer workers at Walt Disney World in Florida were readily able to answer the question when they were told in 2014 that they would be fired and replaced by computer workers brought in from a firm in India.[44] Was inadequate education of the currently employed workers the reason for Disney's decision? No. Was Disney facing a year of low or no profits? No. In 2014 Disney had its most profitable year ever, with profits of $7.5 billion, up 22 percent from the previous year, and 2015 promising even greater profits, providing enough cash for the $46 million take-home pay of Disney's CEO.[45] No, the issue was simple: why employ one worker, when a replacement would do the same job for roughly $40,000 less?[46] Disney management, like some Disney cartoon characters, did exude a degree of warm fuzzies when the company offered the fired employees the opportunity to keep their jobs a bit longer if they agreed to train their replacements.[47] (To be fair to Disney, it has not been the only company to require employed workers to train their replacements.)[48]

Using the Flat World of Global Tech Workers

The H1-B program is an additional profit-maker for U.S. companies, because they use outsourcing firms as official employers of H-1B workers. Northeast Utilities, for example, using India's Infosys, replaced 200 IT workers.[49] Agribusiness Cargill replaced 900 IT workers with substitutes hired by Tata Consulting Services in India.[50] Tata and Infosys have also provided hundreds of replacement workers for Southern California Edison.[51] Motorcycle manufacturer Harley-Davidson used Infosys to replace U.S. workers and set up a new tech facility where Infosys is located.[52] Through these global outsourcing machinations, U.S. companies can save between 25 and 50 percent in wage and benefits costs.

The extent to which this kind of policy gift to corporations creates a dog-eat-dog global economy is well illustrated in the mendacity of the criticism of U.S. schools. In 2011, at a time when U.S. colleges were graduating "50 percent more computer science majors than were able to find a job in IT," guest workers filled one-third to one-half of new job openings, while U.S. IT workers under the age of thirty filled the rest. As explained in an Economic Policy Institute study on "guest worker" legislation, these young guest workers not only provided "competition to new U.S. graduates, but also provided a large supply of younger, lower-paid workers who [could replace] older workers."[53] In other words, U.S. college graduates in IT were competing with a pool of guest workers who would work for less pay and fewer, if any, benefits, and who would accept being disposable. This occurred while Congress was proposing to substantially increase the number of H-1B workers available to IT and other industries.

Crowdsourcing/Crowdwork: Skilled Labor at Unskilled Labor Wages

While the education for the global economy mantra suggests that someone with STEM skills has a strong possibility of having a job in the conventional sense of one employer and some form of a steady workweek and wages, even this expectation has diminished as businesses find ever-new ways to reduce labor costs and use workers "as needed." One new employment method, for example, which advances the tenuous conditions of outsourcing, is crowdwork or crowdsourcing, a method of temporary employment for particular tasks, with potential workers commonly bidding against one another to be hired.

Like day laborers who wait on street corners, making themselves available for work and negotiating a wage for doing a job, these high-skilled workers wait and negotiate at their computers to be tapped for narrow projects and periods of work.

Crowdwork is processed through professional online market-place businesses, such as Upwork (formerly oDesk), Freelancer, and Amazon's Mechanical Turk (named after an eighteenth-century chess-playing robot that was operated by a human). Upwork has about 9 million registered freelancers, with about 3 million job postings a year. Freelancer reports having about 15 million freelancers. Mechanical Turk workers, known as Turkers, number approximately 500,000, 40 percent of whom come from the United States, about 33 percent from India, and the remainder from about a hundred other countries.[54] Although crowdworkers tend to be well educated, their income levels seldom reflect their education because with crowd labor an employer can use someone at a competitive, rock-bottom price.[55] Writing in *Forbes* magazine, Haydn Shaughnessy warns that crowd-sourcing is "a troubling development" in its "drift to highly educated, low-paid labor" and its "capacity to drive income through the floor."[56] IBM, for example, in 2013 enhanced its profits by firing thousands of employees, using crowdsourcing as a new employment tool to "rehire the workers at contracts for specific projects as and when necessary," that is, as crowdwork freelancers, without benefits—they became "independent contractors."[57]

Yet, as bad as crowdwork can be for potential workers in the twenty-first century, if no other work is available, crowdwork has, for many workers, become a grueling means to at least some income. Labor and civil rights attorney Moshe Marvit describes one woman, an unemployed nurse (that is, a skilled worker), whose story is all too common. One month she did crowdwork approximately sixty hours a week and earned about $150 a week—a good crowdwork income. However, the following month, because the pay rates were lower, she earned only about $50 per week. Often, she stayed up all night with the crowdwork screen open, because when work requests are posted, they tend to go quickly.[58] Writing on this low-wage work, employment law professor Miriam Cherry (who herself tried and failed to earn a minimum wage as a crowdsource worker) underscored the exploitative nature of this equal-opportunity low wage employment for potential workers across a spectrum of skill levels.[59] Following Cherry's article, several crowdsource workers posted comments expressing the common plight endured by many unemployed workers who face little choice but to be exploited by earning low crowdsource wages rather than none. One respondent wrote:

> I am a Mechanical Turk worker. I am American, and our family has found ourselves in a hard place financially. I work at Turk for about 12 hours a day, and my average pay is $1.40 an hour. (How odd that it is exactly the median pay!) I keep track because I was told that I could make more, and I keep hoping to find a way. I keep working because we need money to be OK right now. I can't wait until some unknown future date when I might find a better job. Matter of fact, we are at risk for having our electricity shut off, and I need $179 fast and am hoping to have that total deposited in my account soon. I have been working for Mechanical Turk for just under a month. At first, I was excited to be able to earn money easily from home. I would be sad [if I could not work for Mechanical Turk] because that would lower my income. Then I would feel more hopeless. At the same time, I do feel like a sweatshop employee. I do not make minimum wage. I work really hard. I also feel somewhat trapped. I have to keep working at Turk to get the 16 or 17 dollars deposited into my bank account each day. This leaves me no time to find other money-earning opportunities. I do not know if . . . crowdsourcing is ethical or not. I clearly see the dichotomy of not enough pay and yet not wanting this small amount of income to lessen or disappear. Just thinking about it is a source of anxiety.[60]

This is a heartrending story, at least from the perspective of a worker, but for an employer the facts can provide a different, uplifting tale. As the business organization Everett Group explains, in an essay titled, "Every Crowd Has a Silver Lining": "Crowd labor is phenomenally cheaper on account of low wages, no benefits, and no facilities or support costs. Due to the anonymous relationship with the crowd, the employer also does not need to bear any recruitment, training, supervision, or turnover costs."[61] This "silver lining" is possible because, Moishe Marvit underscores, crowdworkers are "categorized as independent contractors, they are not legally entitled to minimum wage, overtime pay, workers' compensation, unemployment insurance or the various other statutory protections that cover employees."[62] When crowdworkers sign a participation agreement, they consent that they are not employees of the Requestor or the Crowdsource company.

While the dominant national mantra is "obtain a good education, preferably a technical-science-based education," the reality, as illustrated by crowdsourcing or other forms of outsourcing, is that even after obtaining this level of education, a decent life within capitalism is far from guaranteed and many wholly qualified educated workers find themselves crowdsource workers one way or another. Research on future "independent" workers has projected that they will become the majority of workers by 2020, between 65 to 70 million, comprising more than half of all workers, a large proportion of whom will have advanced skills and education. For these independent contractors, their work future in the stellar twenty-first-century economy will consist of "scraping for new jobs and dealing without health care and other safety net provisions."[63]

Taylorism of White- and Blue-Collar Work

Under the banner of "Everything Old Is (Or, Can Be) New Again," the overlords of the twenty-first-century economy have been retrofitting a central mechanism of the "old economy"—Taylorism—to extract maximum profitability from workers' labor, regardless of, as in days of old, the toll on the workers. Taylorism was yesteryear's scientific management of manufacturing, in which the production process was broken down into specialized routine, repetitive tasks to be done within allotted times. Currently, whether the work is in wholesale, retail, financial services, education, or health care, the trend in all areas of work is to employ new and very powerful "scientific management" work control methods, known as Computer Business Systems, which apply yesterday's Taylorism to new forms of contemporary work.

Simon Head, who has researched various kinds of employment and production processes, concluded that workers' knowledge, experience, and autonomy are increasingly "under siege from ever more intrusive forms of monitoring and control." Whether a shop-floor employee at a Walmart store or an Amazon fulfillment center. or a worker making electronic products, processing a bank loan, or providing health care—whatever the worker's skills—increasing control systems govern the organization, speed, and time of work routines, all with the aim of increasing productivity to maximize profit. Furthermore, while the idealized conception of today's "highly skilled workforce" is one of workers "going about [their] business within autonomous, self-directed teams," current monitoring and control is much greater in the white-collar than in the blue-collar economy.[64]

Employers use a management "cost breakdown structure" to make work more organized and overseen by digital management in which human work is represented by various monitoring metrics on computer screens. Management programs display how well the critical elements of a process are being performed, how well the process is performed in real time and against a target time, and contain an "alert view" that identifies when and how an employee's performance is missing established targets. In turn, management superiors monitor management performance. Apart from the use of information technology, Head concludes, "there is not much to distinguish [these new work control] methods from those of the primitive American and European capitalism of the late nineteenth and early twentieth centuries."[65] The "21stcenturyglobaleconomy" just can't seem to abandon that old-time profit-making religion!

Not Working for the Company You Work For

Increasingly fundamental for business profits is an ever-expanding domestic outsourcing of jobs, such as the manufacturing jobs noted above. Workers at an Amazon fulfillment center in Pennsylvania unload boxes, for example, fill and ship orders in brutal working conditions. Workers in receiving must "stand fairly stationary throughout an "8–10 hour shift, while they also have to lift, bend, stoop and squat repetitively." These workers are paid $10.50 an hour for day shifts, and $11 an hour for nights; however, the responsibility for any injuries incurred from this labor is not entirely Amazon's because it does not employ many of the workers. Rather, they are employed by a temporary employment company, that is, a domestic outsourcing company, Integrity Staffing Solutions. ISS is the biggest temporary-employment company in the area and one of the fastest-growing temporary employment companies in the United States, supplying workers for Amazon in Arizona, Delaware, Indiana, Kentucky, Nevada, Tennessee, and Virginia. Amazon also keeps labor costs low and profits high by employing workers for less than the 12-month period legally required for workers to receive compensation because of sickness or injury.[66] In turn, employment companies that hire Amazon workers for a limited work period also relieve Amazon of the unemployment insurance responsibility it would have had if it were firing the workers. As an *International Business Times* headline put it, describing "Amazon Warehouse Blues": "Amazon.com's Workers Are Low-Paid, Overworked and Unhappy; Is This the New Employee Model for the Internet Age?"[67]

Amazon is a graphic example of what David Weil, the U.S. Wage and Hour Administrator in the Department of Labor, calls the "fissured workplace," in which work is distributed through subcontracting, franchising, third-party management, and outsourcing to multiple organizations in order to reduce costs for a primary organization. Fissuring occurs not only in work requiring fewer skills, such as janitorial services, security work, hotel cleaning, retailing, and restaurant labor, but in higher-skilled work, such as information technology, paralegal and legal jobs, and accounting. Driving this fissuring is a desire for greater profits and greater returns for investors, as well as the elimination of unionization of a sector of workers. While the National Labor Relations Act prohibits closing down a workplace because there is a union presence or a threat of a union, "shedding employment can provide more subtle ways to shift away from a highly unionized workforce or can move work to forms of employment that are both legally and strategically difficult for unions to organize."[68]

Fissured work includes Uber drivers, FedEx drivers, graphic designers, information technology workers, gutter installers, and physicians. While traditional employment included "Social Security, a 40-hour workweek with time-and-a-half for overtime, worker health and safety, worker's compensation if injured on the job, family and medical leave, minimum wage, pension protection, unemployment insurance, protection against racial or gender discrimination, and the right to bargain collectively," fissured work puts employment outside of all such benefits and labor laws.[69]

These employment changes will continue and expand, according to a study titled *Workforce 2020,* conducted by the business research organization Oxford Economics. Exploring twenty-first-century business practices, the researchers found that "a hefty 83 % of executives say they are increasingly using consultants, intermittent employees, or contingent workers." Of course, being a contingent, intermittent worker means in turn that the "independent contractor" had better look out for number one, rather than the contracting company, so it is not surprising that company executives also list "lack of employee longevity/loyalty" as a chief business problem. The research does not make clear if this finding surprised the executives.[70]

Public Sector Job Losses in the U.S. Economy and Communities

The attention to high-tech jobs and the need to acquire the education to compete for them in the twenty-first-century economy also diverts focus away from public sector jobs at the local, state, and federal levels—the "twentieth-century jobs" that have continued to be critical to community and individual well-being. These jobs include teaching school, policing, fighting fires, driving buses, inspecting buildings for safety, planning and supervising environmental services, food safety inspection, controlling air traffic, and doing an array of infrastructure maintenance and repair work. Many of these jobs, requiring moderate or considerable levels of STEM skills education, such as municipal engineers, have been eliminated, not because they are no longer needed, but because of an ideology that smaller government for the public's benefit is better government and the best government services are those that are privatized, profit-directed, corporate-run, and without public sector unions.[71]

Since the 2008 Recession, while the U.S. rich have gotten richer, accumulating more wealth than the rest of society, and the corporate tax rate is at a near half-century low, over 550,000 public sector jobs have officially been lost. Furthermore, Economic Policy Institute economists noted that this large figure fails to measure this loss relative to population growth. Formulated this way "the economy is short 1.8 million public sector jobs."[72] A similar calculation, one pertinent with respect to labor force recovery since the 2008 Recession, determined that if public sector spending had been proportional to such spending after previous recessions, the nation would have added more than a million jobs.[73] The Brookings Institution concurred, finding that the recent "record decline" in public sector jobs "has been among the largest contributors to unemployment in the United States since the end of the Great Recession."[74]

And, of course, vast numbers of teaching jobs have been lost. I will say more about this in chapter 6, but for now here are a few examples. In California, thousands of teachers have lost jobs—contributing to overcrowded classes and a downsized curriculum.[75] In Wisconsin "73 percent of school districts have cut teachers' jobs."[76] A *Detroit Free Press* headline read, "Even Well-Off Michigan School Districts Can't Avoid Layoffs"—as they "struggle to keep revenue in line with expenses."[77] The Anchorage School District fired teachers and other staff because of insufficient funds.[78] New Jersey governor Chris Christie is typical of politicians who, on the one hand, speak of the need to "deliver a strong and relevant education" for "our young people . . . entering the 21st-century global workforce and economy,"[79] while, on the other hand, cutting education spending by at least $1 billion and handing out $2 billion in corporate tax breaks.[80]

Look This Way, Not That Way

We are targets of an extraordinary ideological sleight of hand, in which corporate overseers and their minions encourage our misperception in one direction while their deceptive acts occur elsewhere. Americans are urged to focus on a mythical new economy in which skilled jobs predominate, for which skill education and worker competition are regarded as fundamental prerequisites. In turn, despite the reality of the economy, educators are blamed for failing to provide students the skills that will provide them income and a modicum of well-being in the 21stcenturyglobaleconomy. Additional blame for not getting a decent job in this economy is cast on those students who, their critics accuse, do not have the single-minded focus on achieving STEM skills that other students possess.

Blaming schooling and students turns the nation's focus away from the reality of the array of jobs and from U.S. capitalism's numerous ways for extracting ever-greater profits, such as paying the lowest wages here and abroad, substituting foreign workers for U.S. workers, reducing or eliminating an array of job benefits, outsourcing work, and creating an ever-growing temporary workforce. While all the blame is foisted on teachers, students, and Americans generally, the "failure of education" ideology is meant to keep the eyes of all workers and future workers on one message: YOU are responsible for yourself; getting a decent job and having a decent income depends solely on YOU; and if YOU don't have a good job and income it's because YOU haven't had the right kind of education, for which educators are to blame. Your problem is not a consequence of corporate policy, corporate greed, and corporate attacks on the public good, not a problem of how wealth is acquired and used. YOU and your teachers are the problem, and most of all, YOU are a problem for American business and America because YOU have failed to become part of the skilled workforce these businesses and the nation need.

4. Corporate "Support" of Schooling and Protecting Corporations

Along with corporate America's relentless insistence that U.S. businesses are suffering because of a deficiency of skilled workers, and schools are to blame for this suffering, many STEM corporations, rather than merely complaining and criticizing, seem to have stepped up by funding STEM education in schools across the nation. In this chapter I review these corporate efforts and suggest various classroom STEM-related projects that illustrate issues of concern regarding the education and miseducation in STEM-course content. I begin with a model of corporate participation in today's schools—IBM's partnership in Chicago's Sarah E. Goode STEM Academy.

The "School That Will Get You a Job"

The Sarah E. Goode STEM Academy, named after the Chicago inventor who was the first African-American woman to receive a U.S. patent, opened in 2012. The school offers a six-year program (high school plus two additional years) to "connect high school, college and the world of work to prepare students, mostly African-American, for technology jobs of the future." IBM, a "corporate partner" and "key developer of the curriculum," promises graduates "a $40,000-plus opportunity" with IBM. Reflecting this promise, a *Time* magazine article announced that the Academy, in the forefront of realigning "American education for the jobs of the future," is a "School That Will Get You a Job."[1]

The *Time* article underscored the view that the purpose of schooling should be largely about a future job and that the major creators of these jobs should be involved in crafting the curriculum. As a principal at a similar academy in New York City exuded, "It's incredible how much further children can reach when industry is closer to them to help set the context for learning." Nearly giddy over corporate involvement in constructing education, *Time* lauded the Goode Academy leadership of an "enlightened blue chip" company, like IBM, although the magazine cautioned that enlightened corporate involvement was not necessarily accompanied by corporate cash. As the article put it, corporate leadership

> doesn't mean pouring in corporate money—Chicago's programs are paid for entirely with existing public funds. When IBM and the other private-sector sponsors sign on, they are essentially promising to help mentor kids and develop a curriculum that will churn out the kind of workers to whom they can guarantee decently paid jobs.[2]

Hence, IBM is a helpful corporate "partner" in the Goode Academy, but not a cash-pouring one.

Nevertheless, IBM's job promise seems terrific, until the key word "opportunity," as in promising that Academy graduates will have an "opportunity" to attain "a $40,000-plus" job, is closely examined. Stanley S. Litow, the president of IBM's International Foundation, explained that the IBM employment futures for graduates from Goode Academy or other STEM schools associated with IBM were not guaranteed; rather, IBM would give these students "preference for openings."[3] In other words, the title of the *Time* magazine article and its implied high likelihood of a job entry—a "School That Will Get You a Job"—is more than a bit misleading.

Nonetheless, whether or not a future job with IBM is a sure thing for Goode Academy graduates, the value of the curriculum supposedly lies in the purported great need for STEM-educated workers and the now-familiar story: corporations are searching for these workers, schools are failing to supply them, and this failure is having a damaging effect on the nation's economy. Using IBM's employment needs as an example, Litow complained that "currently almost 1,800 jobs at IBM alone are going unfilled" due to a lack of appropriate candidates.[4] However, Litow's complaint was a strange one, to say the least, given that IBM had cut and was continuing to cut thousands of jobs at the time the article appeared.

IBM Job Cuts

IBM might have begun looking for these 1,800 suitably skilled workers in Vermont, New York, Iowa, Arizona, Missouri, North Carolina, and several other states where the company was busy firing technically skilled employees. How many? IBM wouldn't say, claiming "privacy" and the right to refuse to release documents containing information needed to calculate the number of employees fired. Why IBM's need for privacy? One IBM worker observed, "This is just another attempt by IBM to hide the number of job cuts taking place and the continued destruction of the IBM employee population in the U.S. Federal and state governments should look into this and demand transparency or tell IBM no more tax breaks."[5]

Nonetheless, despite IBM's refusal to release the numbers of fired U.S. workers or what divisions were most affected, pieces of information revealed that the numbers had been extensive. For example, as of June 2013, Alliance@IBM, an IBM employees union, put the total number of firings in North America at 2,792.[6] More significantly, in 2014 IBM officially reported reducing its global workforce by "51,620 people (from 431,212 to 379,592 employees)."[7] In January 2015, IBM was reported to be on the cusp of firing approximately 100,000 more workers from its global workforce.[8] In 2016, IBM fired an estimated 14,000 workers.[9]

Whatever the exact numbers, IBM's complaint that it had 1,800 unfilled jobs, supposedly evidence of a STEM worker shortage, provides material for the kind of valuable STEM lesson that can help students more fully understand and evaluate STEM activity not only as productive processes, but as part of the corporate "global economy" context that affects the lives of individuals, communities, and nations. This is the kind of thinking and evaluation nearly wholly absent in today's classrooms, as illustrated by curriculum questions I provide in this chapter, questions which are seldom raised when studying corporate STEM production.

STEM math question:

To assess an example of the claimed national STEM-worker shortage, do the following math calculations:

(a) At the time of IBM's complaint that it had difficulty finding skilled applicants for 1,800 unfilled STEM jobs, the company's worldwide employees numbered approximately 400,000. (434,246 IBM workers were employed globally at the end of 2012).[10] Calculate what percentage 1,800 is of this rounded-off number? (Answer: .0045 or .45 percent.)

(b) IBM does not divulge its number of employees by country, but if we take the estimate of the International Business Times and put the number of IBM's U.S. workers at about 80,000,[11] 1,800 needed workers comes to what percent? (Answer: .0225 or 2.25 percent).

•   STEM critical thinking question (a): Discuss why IBM would think the .0045 global job vacancy rate or a .0225 U.S. job vacancy, especially in terms of skilled workers IBM fired, would indicate a serious STEM job vacancy problem.

- STEM critical thinking question (b): Discuss whether you
  think U.S. 2.25 percent is a number crying "skilled-worker
  shortage" for IBM and is evidence that U.S. public schools
  are doing a poor job providing STEM skills education.

While IBM had cut jobs in states across the nation, in states where
jobs have been retained, the retention was largely due to state and
local governments making tax deals with the company. Unfortunately,
knowing whether these deals really saved jobs is difficult because, as
the *Washington Post* reported: "Counties and school districts often
permit IBM to pay lower property taxes in exchange for creating or
retaining local jobs . . . but governments have no way of knowing
whether the company has made good on its promises and whether
the tax cuts actually work."[12] For example, in New York State, where
IBM has been associated with schools similar to the Goode Academy,
a New York State Republican assemblyman complained about IBM's
lack of accountability and the hundreds of millions of dollars in "corporate welfare" that it has received from New York State taxpayers:
"It's impossible to tell what we're getting back in return if we don't
know how many IBM jobs there are in a particular region or state.
It's complicated, because every level of government to some extent is
subsidizing IBM." [13]

- Social Studies and Economics research project: Write
  IBM, asking for the figures for the tax breaks the company received in various states and the number of jobs
  IBM created and retained in those states. As best you can,
  determine the number of jobs created and maintained,
  the actual funding sources for these jobs, and the profits IBM made at the facilities in these states. Using your
  math calculations, write an essay on who benefits most
  from these arrangements and outcomes, and whether
  you agree with the Republican senator that the arrangements are "corporate welfare"—and discuss what is or
  isn't wrong with that.

Given IBM's employment history, what are the prospects that graduates of the Sarah E. Goode STEM Academy and other IBM-related STEM schools will get a job with IBM? Considering that employment history, the students would do well to temper their expectations. More certain, in light of IBM's school partnership, the curriculum surely will omit any critical examination of the "STEM worker shortage," IBM's treatment of its workforce in the United States and elsewhere, and the general issue of public tax contributions to the profits of STEM-based corporations.

Project Lead the Way

A nationwide program self-described as embodying the corporate desire to promote STEM education is Project Lead the Way (PLTW), which provides curricula in "over 6,500 elementary, middle, and high schools in all 50 states and the District of Columbia," including rural, urban, suburban public, private, and charter schools, across all income levels. PLTW, with its membership of "nearly 100 leading corporations," aims to help "students develop the skills needed to succeed in the global economy," thereby solving "America's STEM challenge" by "transforming STEM education in the United States." [14]

PLTW focuses on basic STEM instruction and advanced STEM subjects such as aerodynamics, digital electronics, microbiology, and computers. This might appear to be valuable subject material but, as I will discuss, the curricula are considerably deficient because the focus of this instruction is wholly detached from the impact of PLTW corporations' employment of STEM on communities, society, and the environment. More generally, this instruction is separated from deeper and essential educational goals in social studies, citizenship, and critical thinking (even though the latter is often identified as an important STEM-education goal). Especially pertinent in this regard is the absence in PLTW STEM curricula of any in-depth study of the STEM corporations that support PLTW, such as their products, production methods, social purposes, and ethics. [15] Because of these omissions, the following will suggest what could be learned through some study of the PLTW corporate members themselves.

Chevron

One of the chief PLTW corporations is the Chevron oil company, dedicated, in a clever fossil-fuel simile, to supporting PLTW's work to "build talent pipelines." In 2013 Chevron, in partnership with PLTW, began a $6-million, three-year initiative to bring "PLTW's world-class STEM education programs to thousands more students across the United States." Announcing the funding, a Chevron executive intoned on the necessity of a "STEM-skilled workforce that is prepared to meet business and social needs and compete in a global marketplace." One important educational goal was to "arm students today with the critical skills they need to succeed in the jobs of tomorrow." [16]

Nicely put, but among the "critical skills" students surely will not be encouraged to use extensively are those for appraising the effect of fossil fuel production on the environment, especially the production in which Chevron is involved. Chevron-supported STEM curriculum is not likely, for example, to include the reasons for the criminal charges brought against the company for oil spills in Brazil[17] or for its hydraulic fracturing explosion, 50 miles from Pittsburgh, which caused a fire lasting four days. [18] Perhaps Chevron was trying to provide material for the following STEM-based learning activity:

- STEM education lesson: Following the hydraulic fracturing explosion near Pittsburgh, Chevron offered each nearby resident a coupon for a free large pizza and a two-liter drink. Employ critical thinking to explain the humor in social media responses to Chevron's offer, such as: "The Chevron Guarantee: Our well won't explode . . . or your pizza is free." [19]

Read various accounts of the explosion and answer the following questions:

- Prior to the explosion, what were the complaints of local residents regarding the effects of Chevron's hydraulic fracturing? (Answer: polluted drinking water; foul odors; ailing pets and livestock; headaches and nausea; and skin rashes.)
- How many days did the fire burn before it was finally extinguished? (Answer: 4)
- Despite don't-worry reassurances from Chevron, in the fiery aftermath what did residents in the area continue to worry about? (Answer: toxins)

- Chevron could only compensate residents with a pizza and soda because in 2013 its profits were just (a) $100,000, (b) $21 million, (c) $100 million? (Answer: $21.42 billion [sorry, trick question]).

- STEM Research Project: Research hydraulic fracturing, a.k.a. fracking. Study the STEM-based processes supporting the extraction of natural gas. Compare the arguments for and against the process, such as those concerning the amount of water used and polluted, and the effect of hydraulic fracturing on the climate, and human and animal health. Study and appraise New York State's decision to ban hydraulic fracturing.

Dow Chemical: PLTW Partner

In 2015, Dow Chemical Company, the largest chemical maker in the United States, announced "a significant partnership to increase K-12 students' access to high-quality STEM education programs." Through a $400,000 grant, Dow funded PLTW programs in seventeen schools, with a combined enrollment of more than 14,000 students—about half of whom were students of color—in Indiana, Louisiana, Michigan, and Pennsylvania. The curriculum was described as one in which "students become engaged in STEM fields while developing *critical thinking, problem solving,* and collaboration, those skills identified as crucial by today's employers" (my emphasis). Announcing the program, DOW portrayed itself as a company whose dedication is to "passionately innovate what is essential to human progress" and "to help address many of the world's most challenging problems such as the need for clean water, clean energy generation and conservation, and increasing agricultural productivity." [20]

To grasp DOW's exemplary goals, a number of curriculum projects should be considered:

- STEM Chemistry Project: Study the chemistry of dioxin associated with Dow's hometown chemical plant in Midland, Michigan, and analyze the effects of dioxin pollution in the waters of nearby Saginaw Bay and two major rivers. [21] Include in this examination an explanation of the association between Dow's STEM-based dioxin production and the higher rates of breast cancer in women who live near the Midland plant.

- STEM Math question: The Michigan Department of Environmental Quality reported that the levels of dioxin were a "thousand times higher than the residential standard" in some places around Dow's Midland plant. What is the "residential standard" versus the amount a "thousand times higher"?

- STEM Critical Thinking question: Discuss the adequacy and justice of the $2.5 million civil penalty Dow agreed to pay to settle the lawsuit brought against it for violating environmental laws around Midland. [22]

Lockheed Martin: Another PLTW Partner

In 2014, the District of Columbia schools received a multimillion-dollar, multi-year grant from "global security and aerospace company" Lockheed-Martin, in partnership with PLTW, as part of a plan to support the expansion of STEM education "in select U.S. urban schools." PLTW's Chief Development Officer declared the grant a "model for how public and private partnerships can help solve the education and workforce development challenges facing our nation." [23]

Of course, one person's "challenges" can be another person's obfuscations. Aside from the overriding false issue that the nation is facing "education and workforce development challenges," as Lockheed-Martin's vice-president acclaimed "the excitement of STEM" work, the curriculum is not likely to include any exciting study of the STEM work of Lockheed-Martin, the nation's largest weapons manufacturer. Neither will exciting study explore whether Lockheed-Martin is a stellar example of the military-industrial complex that President Dwight Eisenhower warned about over fifty years ago.

Additionally, the Lockheed-Martin–supported curriculum is not likely to have students "challenged" with fact-based math and critical thinking questions like these:

- Math question: Considered a top federal contractor, the Project on Government Oversight, a Washington-based watchdog group, ranks Lockeed-Martin the top federal contractor in its list of contractor instances of misconduct FY2015. Calculate the total amount of penalties the company paid for seventy-five instances of misconduct since 1995 that include overbilling, fraud, and water pollution. (Answer: The penalties totaled $745 million.) [24]

- Critical Thinking question: Besides making STEM-based weaponry, Lockheed-Martin has contracts for other military work, such as military "interrogation" [25] that includes the use of enhanced interrogation techniques (a.k.a.

torture) for prisoners in Iraq and at Guantánamo Bay, Cuba.[26] Investigate whether Lockheed-Martin used any STEM-based techniques in its "interrogation."

"Analytical and Critical Reasoning Skills" the PLTW Way

In 2014, Billings, Montana, schools received a $25,000 check from ExxonMobil to fund PLTW STEM education.[27] Like Chevron and other PLTW corporations big on "critical thinking," an ExxonMobil Refinery manager noted that the STEM curriculum "really takes us down the path of critical thinking, analysis and logic. So when children approach texts or approach logics, they understand how to solve them."[28] She stressed that "businesses like ExxonMobil . . . *support efforts to encourage more analytical and critical reasoning skills* to the texts students are reading and the math problems they are solving" (my emphasis). Not included in this educational exuberance was an explanation of whether these "capabilities," as she called them, would include looking closely at the corporate benefactor that provided the opportunity for applying this critical thinking STEM skill:

- Math question: Calculate how much ExxonMobil has paid in penalties for contractor misconduct. (Answer: $2,886,069,576 as of 2015, with 18 pending instances of misconduct.)

Three years before Billings received the check from ExxonMobil for funding the PLTW STEM curriculum, the company created a STEM-based local catastrophe by spilling an estimated 63,000 gallons of crude oil into the nearby Yellowstone River.[29] The pipeline broke when ExxonMobil chose not to shut it down at a time the river was prone to seasonal flooding and erosion. Although at least one other company decided to close its pipeline in the same area, a federal investigation concluded that ExxonMobil's "failure over an extended period of time to recognize those threats ... was a major cause" of the pipeline break.

- STEM Research question: Study the federal investigation of ExxonMobil's pipeline break and determine whether its explanation for the oil spill was correct; that is, should ExxonMobil have kept the pipeline open, considering that another company recognized the threat to the river and closed its pipelne?

ExxonMobil's desire to "encourage more analytical and critical reasoning skills" could also be fulfilled by applying these thinking skills to another portion of ExxonMobil's history:

- STEM Research Project: An *Exxon Valdez* supertanker ran aground in Alaska in 1989, spilling 11 million gallons of crude oil. [30] Research the event and determine whether this spill was (a) average for this kind of oil spill, (b) a moderate spill of this kind, (c) the worst oil spill up to that point in American history?
- Math question 1: Research and quantify the various damages to people, the fishing industry, subsistence hunting, birds, and marine animals along the 1,300 miles of shoreline affected by the spill.
- Math question 2: In 2014, twenty-five years after the tanker ran aground, the spill continued to pollute Alaskan waters. A U.S. government study done in 2007 found that "more than 26,600 gallons of oil" remain in the water, "declining at a rate of only 4% a year and even slower in the Gulf of Alaska." [31] Given these calculations, approximately how many years will be required before the respective bodies of water are free of oil from the disaster?
- Social Studies questions: Was justice fully served when the $5 billion that ExxonMobil was initially ordered by a federal court to pay for the spill's damage in 1994 got reduced upon appeal to $2.5 billion in 2006, and further reduced by the U.S. Supreme Court in 2008 to just over $500 million? Was the amount the company had to pay in damages to people,

the local economy, and wildlife sufficient for covering ExxonMobil's responsibility for causing these problems? [32]

Global Warming and PLTW Partners

Another major PLTW partner is the Kern Foundation, whose grants raise questions about how PLTW pedagogy will explore global warming, the STEM-related issue most crucial for humanity and the planet. Kern's funding record isn't reassuring, considering, for example, that the foundation has given over a million dollars[33] to the American Enterprise Institute that the Union of Concerned Scientists describes as routinely trying "to undermine the credibility of climate science."[34] This funding is in keeping with the Kern Foundation's overall "interest in conservative-oriented causes and programs" and reflects the individual political contributions of Robert and Patricia Kern, the foundation's founders.[35] For example, Governor Scott Walker of Wisconsin, whose politics have included attacks on public schools and teachers, support of school choice and voucher programs, denial of climate change, and promotion of fossil fuel development,[36] has benefited from the Kerns' campaign contributions.[37] As such, Robert and Patricia Kern stand shoulder-to-shoulder with billionaire Walker supporters Charles and David Koch, who have made a fortune in fossil fuels.

Nor are the Kerns alone among PLTW partners who rebuff concerns about global warming. Returning to ExxonMobil, considering that its economic blood is made of fossil fuel, it is no surprise that, following a 2007 investigation, the Union of Concerned Scientists (UCS) found that "ExxonMobil funneled nearly $16 million between 1998 and 2005 to a network of 43 advocacy organizations that seek to confuse the public on global warming science." Moreover, in a 2015 investigation, UCS documented that despite the 2007 UCS report, ExxonMobil, as well as PLTW partner Chevron, has continued to fund fossil fuel misinformation organizations that have opposed all legislative efforts to reduce carbon pollution. This misinformation campaign aimed "to deceive the American public by distorting the realities and risks of climate change, sometimes acting directly and sometimes acting indirectly through trade associations and front groups."[38]

The UCS's report also discussed how the American Petroleum Institute, of which ExxonMobil and Chevron are members, has targeted teachers and students with materials aimed at emphasizing "uncertainties in climate science." One of its curricula for elementary schools asserts that "renewable energy sources such as oil, natural gas, and coal" are "more reliable, affordable, and convenient to use than most renewable energy resources."[39]

- Math question: Dividing ExxonMobil's $16,000,000 funding to 43 global warming skeptic organizations, on average how much did each of these organizations receive?
- Critical Reading Project: Read the UCS's 2015 report, "The Climate Deception Dossiers: Internal Fossil Fuel Industry Memos Reveal Decades of Corporate Disinformation" and the American Petroleum Institute's (API) policy statement, "An Overview of the Climate Change Issue from the U.S. Oil and Natural Gas Industry." Then evaluate and discuss whether ExxonMobil and other fossil fuel companies have deliberately been spreading disinformation about the consequences of carbon emissions for global warming, life, and the planet. The UCS report concludes, "Recognizing that the tide might turn against fossil fuels, the API pushed out materials for teachers and their students that directly countered scientific evidence." Discuss whether the UCS report provides evidence for this conclusion and, if it does, whether you think ExxonMobil and other fossil fuel companies should be involved in influencing STEM instruction in schools.

Not all PLTW partners are engaged in socially and environmentally damaging business practices, funding of one-sided corporate-crafted research, or creating murderous weaponry. However, the leading and largest partners funding the PLTW STEM curriculum can be described as such in one or more ways, characteristics we will again see in Change the Equation, which follows.

Change the Equation

Change the Equation (CTEq) is self-described as an organization promoting "high-quality STEM learning programs to every K-12 community in the United States, whose corporate members include CEOs of Fortune 500 companies." When the organization was launched in 2010, President Obama applauded the CEOs "for lending their resources, expertise, and their enthusiasm to the task of strengthening America's leadership in the 21st century by improving education in science, technology, engineering and math."[40]

CTEq does indeed promote STEM education across the country, providing classroom curriculum resources, teacher professional development, after-school STEM programs, STEM summer camp programs, classroom involvement of STEM employees, special STEM programs for girls, online STEM courses, STEM curricula for "diverse student populations," and summer STEM business-education partnerships for teachers—called Teachers in Industry, a "partnership" that places teachers in paid STEM jobs during the summer.

Like PLTW, CTEq might at first glance seem like a noble corporate effort and curriculum contribution, but consider that of the forty-six members, thirty-nine (85 percent) are businesses that have been found guilty of one or more criminal charges (or settled lawsuits in order to avoid being convicted of criminal charges), and/or are entrenched in the military-industrial complex, a phrase that was insightfully expanded by Senator William Fulbright in a 1968 speech at Stanford University to the "military-industrial-academic complex."[41] Astonishingly, only seven CTEq members have committed no corporate crimes or are not part of the military complexes (Caroline Biological, EMC2, PASCO, Sally

Ride Science, the Niels Company, Time Warner, and Valen Analytics). As for the rest, I will begin with the polluters in my review of the CTEq corporate members that schools across the country are counting on to help solve the STEM crisis.

The Polluters

Having already discussed the polluting crimes of PLTW members Chevron, Dow, and ExxonMobil, which are members of CTEq, here is a brief review of other major polluters who are CTEq members (listed alphabetically).

AT&T

For many years, AT&T had failed to dispose properly of toxic substances in "more than 230 AT&T warehouses and facilities across California," substances that cause serious health problems, such as cancer, hormonal disorders, brain disorders, liver damage, and immune deficiencies. Finally caught and convicted in 2014 for "illegally dumping hazardous waste" over a nine-year period, AT&T had to pay a $23.8 million settlement payment and about $28 million for cleanup.[42] While these settlement amounts are considerable, for a California consumer watchdog group they were insufficient because the settlements did not require AT&T to do the full cleanup necessary to ensure public health and deter similar dumping by other companies.[43] In other words, based on this decision, a company might calculate that, if caught polluting, their cost of a settlement would be less than the cost of preventing the pollution.

- STEM Research Project: Using AT&T's polluting STEM-based products and the company's court settlement as a gauge, calculate the business costs for properly and improperly disposing of one or more of these hazardous products, such as electronic equipment, batteries, aerosol cans, gels, liquids etc. Assess the financial and ethical considerations involved in a business decision on the cost of using and disposing of hazardous STEM products' waste vs. the costs of fines and settlements if a company like AT&T is caught.

DuPont

In 2004, DuPont paid $300 million in a settlement with residents in Ohio and West Virginia whose drinking water had been contaminated by a chemical used in making the STEM-based product Teflon.[44] DuPont knew for decades about the contaminant but hid it from communities, the water utility, and state regulators.[45] At its plant in Tonawanda, New York, DuPont violated the Clean Air Act by allowing hazardous air pollutants to be released; for example, 193,836 pounds of methyl methacrylate and 27,183 pounds of vinyl fluoride, which accounted for 24 percent of all "Toxic Release Inventory" releases in the county. In 2014, DuPont paid a $440,000 fine for these violations.[46] At its chemical manufacturing plant in New Jersey, the Environmental Protection Agency fined DuPont $531,000 for other Clean Air Act violations.[47] In this case, DuPont had allowed chlorofluorocarbons (CFCs) to leak into the environment, thereby contributing to the damage of the Earth's ozone layer and, in turn, contributing to global warming.

- STEM Research Project: Research and explain how chlorofluorocarbons damage Earth's ozone layer and, in turn, contribute to global warming. Estimate the amount of chlorofluorocarbons DuPont has released.

Freeport-McMoRan Copper & Gold Inc.

Were I ranking the CTEq polluters by the extent of their environmental crimes, rather than alphabetically, Freeport-McMoRan Copper & Gold Inc. would be a strong competitor to head the list. Its $276,000 fine in 2009 for discharging an estimated one million gallons of a

highly acidic fluid that contaminated local waterways and ground-
water in New Mexico[48] makes it a moderate contender to head the
polluter crime list, but its $6.8 million fine for discharging pollution
from an Arizona mine in 2012[49] makes the company even more competitive. However, beyond these achievements, the company would
get my top vote because of the environmental damage caused by its
gold mining operations in Indonesia, where it has dumped a "billion
tons of mine waste directly into the mountains surrounding the mine
or down a system of rivers in what had been one of the world's last
untouched landscapes."[50] Nonetheless, apparently with a straight face,
the company states in its description of its mining in Indonesia that it
supports "programs . . . in environment."[51]

- STEM Research Projects: (a) Research and discuss the use
  of gold as an excellent conductor in electronic products,
  such as computers, cell phones, global positioning systems,
  etc., as well as in other products, such as medical devices
  and aerospace vehicles. (b) Explain some of the environmental and health effects caused by a billion tons of gold
  mine waste in Indonesia. (c) Given the environmental
  damage in mining gold in Indonesia and elsewhere, discuss the benefits and problems of, and alternatives to, the
  uses and constant replacement of STEM products, such as
  smartphones, that use gold.

Intel

Intel describes itself as a technology company that works with "communities, and schools worldwide to bring the resources and solutions
needed for advancing education." Oregon's largest private employer,
Intel has been sponsoring school STEM expos in and making various
donations to Oregon schools, but the company has also been polluting the state with fluoride releases, going back to 1978. Although
Intel's releases have been substantial, the state's responses to the company's pollution violations have been mild.

Why did the state's largest employer fail to include fluoride in its air-quality permit? The omission, concluded the state, was no more than a slight oversight. Unfortunately for Intel, however, while Oregon was inclined to minimize the company's crime, the federal government was less forgiving, finding Intel guilty of failing to report accurate emissions for *thirty years*, including failing to obtain necessary air emissions permits when constructing a $3 billion facility expansion. Quite a crime, but nevertheless a corporation as large as Intel often can obtain a sympathetic response when appealing for legal mercy, and doing so, the federal government was not much more punitive than Oregon in punishing Intel's three decades of harmful fluoride releases. Yes, the federal penalty of $143,000[52] would be a large amount for most people and many small companies, but for Intel, whose 2014 full revenue was $52.7 billion and net income $9.6 billion, the penalty was far less than a profits-buster.[53]

While Intel was polluting Oregon, in New Mexico environmental activists, neighborhood organizers, and scientists were accusing the company of poisoning the air through the release of "hazardous metals and toxic chemicals."[54] Additionally, because the manufacture of Intel products requires vast amounts of pure water, which Intel obtains with a reverse osmosis system (which rejects two-thirds of the water it pumps), in the midst of drought conditions in New Mexico the company was drawing about 3 billion gallons of water a year from the aquifer, contributing greatly to the state's water crisis.[55]

- Advanced STEM Research Project: Barbara Rockwell of New Mexico describes herself as someone who became a "reluctant community activist when Intel began to fill local homes with toxic fumes that sickened us." In her May 21, 2015, blog entry, she quotes retired Los Alamos National Laboratories chemist Fred Marsh on the difficulty of identifying the toxicity of Intel's emissions:

    When toxicity information is available, it is always for a single chemical, whereas Intel's toxic emissions are always mixtures. It is well known that a mixture of two (or more) chemicals can be much more toxic than the sum of their individual toxicities. Because Intel can release nearly 100 toxic chemicals, the resulting mixtures can be exceedingly complex. There is no way to study all possible combinations; all we can do is recognize that the synergistic toxicities of mixtures can be much higher. . . . In a very real sense, residents who are forced to breathe Intel fumes serve as guinea pigs for exposure to untested and unknown health threats.[56]

- STEM Project 1: Choose two or more chemicals Intel has released in the area around its New Mexico plant. Study the contributions of these chemicals in Intel's STEM-based production and the possible toxic effects on people when the chemicals are released in fumes.
- STEM Project 2: Research Fred Marsh's statement to determine if there is evidence for its validity.

The Ethically Challenged

Many CTEq partners that have not polluted can be aggregated under the heading of "ethically challenged." While manufacturing and selling various STEM products, they have committed crimes for which they were penalized or decided to pay a "settlement" to avoid legal conviction and paying even larger penalties. The CTEq corporate partners in this category include the biotechnology company Amgen, steel company ArcelorMittal, food company Archer Daniels Midland, telephone company AT&T, military contractor BAE Systems, software company CA Technologies, medical products and services company Cardinal Health, pharmaceutical company Celgene, outsourcing company Cognizant, financial advisory company Deloitte, global technology company Eaton, pharmaceutical company GlaxoSmithKline, electronics company Hewlett-Packard, and aerospace company Northrop Grumman.

The array of charges brought against CTEq corporate partners have included illegally marketing drugs, price-fixing, allowing the trafficking and forced labor of children, illegally adding charges to customers' bills, defrauding the U.S. government, overcharging states and the District of Columbia for products and services, selling medication to chain and Internet pharmacies without any oversight or controls, illegally preventing the manufacturing of a generic version of a cancer drug that would have been more affordable to patients, short-changing employees' wages and benefits, failing to exercise proper oversight to prevent money laundering through banks, violating anti-trust laws, promoting drugs that had never been proven beneficial for various medical problems, manipulating illiterate parents to participate in a vaccine experiment in which fourteen babies died, bribing officials in other countries to win technology contracts, and submitting fraudulent proposals for military contracts.

- Critical Thinking Research Project: Select a company from the "ethically challenged" list and research the lawsuits brought against it. Explain the criminal charges brought against the company and discuss whether the charges were fair and the fines and settlements suitable penalties. Bring these research findings to a class discussion of why these corporations acted as they did and why the drive for business profit can supersede a business's goal of adhering to normal ethical standards, particularly with respect to the well-being of communities and the environment.

STEM Businesses and Teaching about the Environment

Given the extent of environmental damage caused by CTEq and PLTW-member corporations, and the members' concomitant funding of organizations that deny and obfuscate the reality and effects of global warming, it is not likely that STEM curricula will delve extensively, if at all, into the most dire issue facing the planet and humanity. For example, put the term "global warming" into CTEq website's search engine and nothing appears. Entering "climate change" is more encouraging in that it produces a link to a June 2015 article, "Could Climate Change Spoil the Winter Olympics?" This promising article answers the question affirmatively, explaining that temperatures have risen over the past century. This appraisal would seem to be a good start for studying climate change, until CTEq explains the problem with respect to the winter Olympics.

What's the problem created by climate change? According to CTEq, it's finding a city cold enough to host the winter Olympics. What's the cause of climate change: fossil fuel use? Not a word about that. What's the climate change solution? Why, it's employing STEM knowledge, of course, used the CTEq corporate way, to make a snow product:

> Without Mother Nature as a reliable snow producer, resorts spend millions creating winter playgrounds. Snow whisperers, snow managers, snow technicians and snow groomers are hot commodities—as is the STEM know-how that is creating innovative, high-tech snowmaking systems.

Yes, that's the answer: STEM-based businesses. Yes, they contribute heavily to global warming, but rely on them to provide the remedies.

Such is the argument of Carly Fiorina, former CEO of CTEq partner Hewlett-Packard, and an early Republican presidential candidate in the 2016 elections. Certainly global warming is a reality, Fiorina acknowledges,[57] but she opposes any government regulations or international treaties to reduce it. Government regulations would "destroy lives and livelihoods," and international treaties "won't make a bit of difference in climate change" because the nations that would sign them would not abide by them.[58]   Moreover, Fiorina stresses, there are more terrifying concerns facing the United States, which she highlighted when running for the California Senate against Senator Barbara Boxer. Mocking Boxer's concern about climate change, a Fiorina ad stated, "Terrorism kills, and Barbara Boxer is worried about the weather!"[59]

Similarly, while the CEO of Hewlett-Packard, Meg Whitman, acknowledges the reality of human-caused global warming, the company's website insists that the answer is "technical innovation,"[60] not government regulation. When running as the Republican gubernatorial candidate in California in 2010, Whitman said that, if elected, her first act would be to suspend the state's climate change law, AB 32,[61] in order to "fix it" so that it would not damage businesses and jobs.[62] Signed into law in 2006 by Republican governor Arnold Schwarzenegger, AB 32 "sets increasingly stringent caps on greenhouse gas emissions, leading to a 25% reduction by 2020."[63] Whitman, however, described the law as an abomination that would lead to higher energy costs and damage job creation. Her concern for job loss seems not to have extended to Hewlett-Packard, where under her leadership, the company eliminated over 50,000 jobs.[64] However, no doubt concerned about her own possible job loss, Whitman's contract entitled her to $51 million if she found herself on the unemployment line.[65]

- STEM Research Project: Compare and evaluate the evidence and arguments from PLTW and CTEq member-supported organizations that deny or are skeptical about climate change against the evidence and proposed solutions from organizations such as the Union of Concerned Scientists and 350.org, and books, such as James Hansen's *Storms of My Grandchildren: The Truth About the Coming Climate Catastrophe and Our Last Chance to Save Humanity* and Naomi Klein's *This Changes Everything: Capitalism vs. the Climate.*

CTEq's Military-Industrial Complex Members

A number of the CTEq members are primarily military manufacturers, part of the military-industrial complex.[66] One wonders how President Eisenhower would feel learning that weapons manufacturers that are part of the current military-industrial complex are members of organizations shaping school curricula. In the present construction of this complex, what, for example, is the ethical and moral impact of the killer robots manufactured by CTEq member Northrop Grumman? Announcing its support of STEM education, the corporation underscored that such support was "critical for our business and for U.S. competitiveness," but ignored in this narrow focus on "competitiveness" was the condemnation of killer robots[67] by organizations such as Human Rights Watch,[68] and the joint call[69] by Harvard Law School's International Human Rights Clinic and Human Rights Watch for an international treaty that would prohibit the manufacture of these weapons. Titled *Losing Humanity: The Case Against Killer Robots,* the joint call profoundly echoed Eisenhower's concern for the military-industrial complex's damage of society's "spiritual" development.[70] Besides criticism from organizations such as these, killer robots have been opposed by major international scientists, such as physicist Stephen Hawking, Nobel Laureate; MIT physics professor Frank Wilczek; and artificial intelligence expert, Harvard University professor Barbara J. Grosz.[71] Yet none of these expressed concerns or policy demands over these STEM products enter the CTEq STEM curricula.

Another CTEq member, the Rand Corporation, further illustrates the reasons for Eisenhower's warning. Political scientist and former CIA consultant Chalmers Johnson described the company this way:

> RAND became a key institutional building block of the Cold War American empire. As the premier think tank for the U.S.'s role as hegemon of the Western world, RAND was instrumental in giving that empire the militaristic cast it retains to this day and in hugely enlarging official demands for atomic bombs, nuclear submarines, intercontinental ballistic missiles, and long-range bombers. Without RAND, our military-industrial complex, as well as our democracy, would look quite different..... [It] remains one of the most potent and complex purveyors of American imperialism.[72]

Other CTEq members—such as Booz Allen Hamilton, Lockheed-Martin, Rolls-Royce, United Launce Alliance, Verizon, the Aerospace Corporation, and Space System-Loral—demonstrate how the contemporary military-industrial complex has advanced to a stage that even Eisenhower might not have imagined. Companies are directly involved in military activities, so that war, like schooling and numerous other functions that had been part of government, has become increasingly privatized.[73]

- STEM Research Project: Read President Dwight Eisenhower's remarks on the "Military-Industrial Complex." Select a CTEq corporate member that is part of this complex and discuss whether you agree that, as President Eisenhower observed, the influence of STEM-based military production of this kind of corporation has "economic, political, even spiritual effects" throughout the nation.

Add the Financial Institutions

Comedian, singer, and actor Jimmy Durante had a signature catchphrase, "Everybody wants to get into the act!" And so it seems with America's dominant financial institutions, which, like the corporate members of PTLW and CTEq, want to step up to promote STEM education. For example, Standard & Poor's (S&P) has, as part of its self-proclaimed "corporate responsibility,"[74] helped open a combined high school and community college in New York City that will enable students to earn "a high school diploma and an associate degree in business systems or engineering technology." The students will learn "how to help the world run better, using technology to solve everyday world problems . . . [and will get] a competitive edge in tomorrow's employment marketplace."[75]

When students study how to "solve everyday problems," they will not likely study how S&P's executives dealt with people's everyday mortgage problems by manipulating and inflating mortgage ratings to obtain more fees from mortgage issuers. Disregarding warnings from its own analysts, S&P continued defrauding investors by inflating credit ratings, which increased mortgage-related profits that, in turn, contributed to the 2008 global financial crisis and the massive loss of homes of everyday people. As Attorney General Eric Holder stated, "S&P executives made false representations to investors and financial institutions, and took other steps to manipulate ratings criteria and credit models to increase revenue and market share. Put simply, this alleged conduct is egregious—and it goes to the very heart of the recent financial crisis."[76] Having been caught in 2015, S&P agreed to pay $1.4 billion to settle charges related to its role in causing the 2008 financial crisis.[77]

Surely the S&P-supported STEM curriculum, aimed at teaching students "how to help the world run better," will not have much to teach about these manipulations nor will any math lessons include calculations of how much money S&P saved by "settling." As securities lawyer Andrew Stoltmann noted in his own math calculation, the accepted $1.4 billion settlement—a long financial distance from the $5 billion in penalties the Justice Department had demanded—was "a classic example of a regulatory slap on the wrist" in which S&P avoided the expense of further litigation and larger penalties, and did not have to admit wrongdoing.[78]

Investment bank Goldman Sachs also stands on the stage of STEM education boosters. In Utah, for example, the bank supported various events to "raise funds for a state initiative to support STEM education training for students and teachers." A soccer tournament it supported raised $20,000 for this purpose (not exactly a stunning sum, but every dollar helps). At Bucknell University in Pennsylvania, the investment bank hosted a STEM symposium.[79] At the University of Michigan, Goldman Sachs presented an "event to learn more about engineering at GS and how to utilize your STEM degree."[80]

When Goldman Sachs discusses the bank's self-proclaimed "citizenship" activities,[81] surely nothing will be said about how the bank severely damaged people's lives through its illegal mortgage manipulations, for which the federal government required it to pay $1.1 billion to settle claims for the bad mortgage-backed securities it sold.[82] Nor will there be anything but silence about the bank's "scam" that contributed to the 2007–2008 economic crash.[83]

Then there is Bank of America. In 2014 in Charlotte, North Carolina, it opened the Bank of America STEM Center for Career Development. The Center, said the bank, arose from Bank of America's "commitment to corporate social responsibility" that guides how it operates "in a socially, economically, financially and environmentally responsible way around the world."[84] Any discussion of these "responsible" ways is not likely to include how the bank defrauded taxpayers in the sale of thousands of defective home loans and why it paid $1.3 billion for "a program that caused heavy losses to federally-backed mortgage" organizations.[85] Nor will the Center have anything to say about the criminal fines the bank had to pay: $30 million for violating the rights of accounts owned by U.S. military service members[86] and $2 million for race discrimination. But, certainly, Bank of America will have much to say about STEM careers.[87]

- STEM Math Project: 1) Calculate the amount of settlements or fines paid by Goldman Sachs, Standard & Poor's, and Bank of America for criminal acts related to the 2008 financial crash, various mortgage violations, and other criminal acts; 2) Which of the three paid the most in settlements and fines?; 3) Identify and explain the kind of advanced math knowledge these financial institutions used to amass illegal mortgage profits.

Were Teachers STEM Corporations?

The very corporate forces that have been so vocal in claiming there is a STEM crisis supposedly created by the schools and threatening the U.S. economy and workforce, especially the future workforce, have been implanting themselves as corporate saviors in schools across the country. Schools encourage and welcome them because of their financial support, their self-proclaimed embodiment of the twenty-first-century global economy, and their curriculum contributions to students' occupational futures.

Yet imagine this occurring at a school faculty and not corporate level, in which a school system is seeking science teachers for several elementary and high schools. A group of certified teachers apply, and a background check reveals that they have committed an array of crimes, not simply against individuals but whole communities; and not only against whole communities but even against the biosphere. In their present occupations they have been responsible for vast pollution, home evictions, job losses, community health problems, and even deaths. At least one of the applicants had done work associated with torture. For many of these crimes they have either been convicted or have arranged settlements to avoid a likely court conviction and a larger financial fine. Moreover, although they had science teacher certifications, evidence revealed they had deliberately miseducated students about scientific issues. And if this history alone were not sufficiently immoral and clear justification for not hiring them, considerable evidence also revealed that the applicants had continued to engage in the criminal activities after their convictions.

Were teachers with these immoral, antisocial, and criminal histories—histories that also included the falsification of scientific evidence—to apply for teaching jobs, what school system would hire them? What school system would hire them and say not a word about their criminal activities and their purposeful distortions of knowledge? What school system would feel that not revealing anything to parents and caretakers about the applicants' background is ethical? What school system would conclude that the applicants "know their subject matter" (even if they misrepresent their subject matter) and that's all that mattered for hiring them? Of course, not one school would. Yet when appraising corporations that have even greater power to influence students, schools overlook all corporate immorality and criminality as they welcome these corporations' curriculum contributions.

Possibly, if STEM education promoted by these corporations could really serve as an occupational answer for today's young people, then parents and other citizens might, in desperation, accept the immorality inherent in this corporate-intrusion. However, as discussed in previous chapters, STEM jobs at best will make up only a small portion of future work. By not challenging and rejecting these corporate intrusions, which distort full understandings of the impacts of profit-making STEM production, schools and teacher organizations help construct education that does not provide study of the full impacts of this corporate work, and thereby fail to serve the young people it is their mission to care for and educate.

5. Constricting the Curriculum

"Education for the global economy" requires the creation of a correspondence between what students think and the thinking necessary for the dominant political-economic order. At the start of the First World War journalist and social critic Randolph Bourne described the orchestration of minds and feelings necessary for soldiering in support of a nation's war: the national ideal must be undisputed, while "other values such as artistic creation, knowledge, reason, beauty, the enhancement of life" must be sacrificed to it. Educating people to use "their intelligence to realize reason and beauty in the nation's communal living," is an "alien" goal.[1] A century later, Bourne's observations apply equally well to the current curriculum, supposedly devised to create competitive workers for the global economy. In the process of achieving that goal, any education not aimed directly at that target is considered by corporate forces and their political representatives to be irrelevant and even harmful. If qualities such as artistic creation and critical reasoning are included in the curriculum, they must be useful for commodity creation and production processes that serve employers.

This schooling orchestration of thinking and feeling to serve the dominant economic and political order was described by economists

Samuel Bowles and Herbert Gintis in their 1976 book, *Schooling in Capitalist America*. Education is guided by a "correspondence principle," they argued, in which the organization, content, and values taught in schools reflect and reinforce the social order.[2] Or, as education philosopher David J. Blacker put it, "Nazism yields Nazi schools, Communism communist schools, apartheid apartheid schools, capitalism capitalist schools, etc."[3]

Nonetheless, recognizing the preponderant success of this correspondence does not mean that the content, values, organization, roles, and practices of schooling have been achieved in a stable fashion, any more than the achievement of correspondence between citizens and a dominant economic and social order is attained without conflict between rulers and the ruled. For example, around the time Bourne was describing the orchestration of mind and feeling supportive of the First World War, Eugene Debs, Helen Keller, and Jane Addams were among numerous social activists who opposed the war, and many were jailed to serve as examples of the punishment accompanying opposition to the dominant political-economic dictates. Those who would not "correspond" included the nearly million Americans who voted for Debs in the 1920 presidential election, while he was in a federal prison, suggesting that even within the severe repression of antiwar, anti-capitalist views, the maintenance of the dominant order can require considerable repression of alternative perspectives.

So too for schooling. Efforts over the last half-century by teachers, parents, and activists to create educational alternatives demonstrate that the correspondence has been in constant contention and only considerable resistance, attacks, and enforcement by dominant political and economic forces have kept these challenges to "correspondence" from blossoming into established educational alternatives. The current efforts to constrict the curriculum around "education to compete in the global economy" derives from a long history, particularly the fifty-or-so-year history extending back to efforts in the 1960s to challenge the prevailing school curricula and classroom practices. Looking back from the present, the history makes apparent that though the fight against the "correspondence principle" has been a series of losses, many educators have sought to keep alive, against considerable political-economic muscle, a vision of education that helps students engage thoughtfully, rather than submissively accept dominant assumptions about the world and how they should live their lives.

"Free the Children"

In the 1960s, as part of the array of political challenges to the nation's militarism, racism, and sexism, alternative modes of schooling, that is, objections to the correspondence principle, emerged. These included free schools, open classrooms, and various alternative curricula within public schools that challenged the top-down, established curricula that reinforced the societal ills political activists identified and rejected. The alternatives included more student-generated topics, more critical views of the social order, more cooperative learning, more examination of students' communities, and more integration of curricula areas, such as between the arts and social studies.

The radical political content of these alternatives varied. For example, many free schools served merely to provide enriched curriculum for youngsters from affluent families seeking the "best" education that would enhance their children's possibilities of future "success." However, for the most part, these alternatives included exploration of war, power, community, gender, culture, equality, poverty, and peace that, to one degree or another, went beyond the ideological boundaries of standardized education. Educators were influenced by the works of Paulo Freire, Jonathan Kozol, Maxine Greene, and Ivan Illich, who proposed sharply different alternatives to conventional schooling. *Pedagogy of the Oppressed, Compulsory Mis-Education, The Open Classroom, Deschooling Society,* and *Free Schools* are book titles reflecting the thinking of the time.

Appraising these educational alternatives, Allen Graubard, educator and organizer of a free school in Santa Barbara, California, wrote, in *Free the Children,* a book about the free school movement, that while the politics of organizers and teachers of these schools varied, as did the explicit political and social justice content and aims of the curriculum, it would have been "difficult if not impossible to find a free school person—student, teacher, or parent—who support[ed] the American role in Vietnam or [thought] that Richard Nixon [was] a fine president and Ronald Reagan an admirable governor. . . . It follows from this that free school people would want a society rather different from the dominant social order that exists today." Moreover, despite the cultural, spiritual and political diversity of "free school people," Graubard underscored that "the great majority would be included in the vague and diverse constituency that wishes to transform the political culture of America." It is within the context of the "growth of political insurgencies throughout most areas of institutionalized social life in America" that free schools should be seen. An aim of the "free school idea was to free education from the political indoctrination expressed in the form, content, and organization of public schools."[4]

The same could be said for open classrooms, which, although like free schools were predicated on questionable assumptions about "natural learning," also offered teachers and students the opportunity to examine critically dominant and alternative views of social class organization, distribution and allocation of wealth, political power, militarism, U.S. and world history, social and personal values, and all other aspects of that economic, political, and social system whose name could not be spoken in conventional public schools.

By the 1970s, with social movements and alternative schools loosening "correspondence," leaders holding dominant economic and social power faced a threat that had to be confronted and overcome. A major expression of that fear was the 1975 report *The Crisis of Democracy*, published by the Trilateral Commission, an organization of global business and political leaders. The report expressed worry about and cautioned against the continuation of the "excess of democracy" contained in the antiwar, anti-racism, expanded unionism, and similar activism that was part of the "democratic surge of the 1960s and produced a variety of challenges to existing systems of authority." For example, the 1970s began with a minority of Americans thinking that the government was "run for the benefit of all people," while a dissatisfied majority thought it was "run by a few big interests looking out for themselves." The report also underscored that more young voters under thirty identified themselves as Independent than as Republicans and Democrats combined. Especially worrisome was the "rise in political participation" that accompanied these changes in public opinion. Though such participation might be considered evidence of a flourishing democracy and educational system, the report described this democratic vigor as an "excess of democracy" that "contributed to a democratic distemper."

Certainly, alternative modes of schooling could not be held solely responsible for these changes, but in the eyes of the interests represented by the Commission, schooling was a critical institution that required a reassertion of top-down governance. As when "armies in which the commands of officers have been subject to veto by the collective wisdom of their subordinates have almost invariably come to disaster on the battlefield," so too authority from above must be reestablished and democratic "overindulgence" eschewed.[5]

Educators echoing these concerns about an "excess of democracy," employed a no-nonsense empirical tactic of criticizing "free" and "open" learning for its poor academic achievement outcomes compared with those of more conventional classroom instruction. The criticism supposedly had nothing to do with political and ideological requirements. No, it was simply based on academic goals and the hard evidence of academic failure, there for everyone to see! Open classroom critics, for example, claimed that research showed "students in open classrooms had significantly lower academic achievement than students in traditional classrooms," a finding that helped generate pubic hostility toward various alternatives to conventional instruction. Evidence did not support the criticism, but the judgment simply needed loud volume, not evidence, to succeed in contracting the curriculum, students' thinking, and teachers' power.

Following the elimination of open classrooms, later retrospective studies determined that the so-called evidence against the pedagogy produced "no clear conclusion about the superiority of one form of instruction over the other."[6] Nonetheless, the baseless criticism was persuasive and "top-down governance" of classroom practice and curricula was strengthened.

Yet even with the demise of free schools, open classrooms, and similar educational alternatives, the opposition to "correspondence" education continued, reformulated largely through a reading approach called "whole language." Although based heavily on linguistic and cognitive theory applied to literacy acquisition—a theory that conceptualized learning to read as a process using predictable, meaningful texts and, as needed, instruction in sound-symbol association—whole language teaching also encouraged student involvement in deciding what to read, rather than reading education prescribed by pre-packaged reading programs (commonly known as "basal readers") that often were filled with vapid stories.

From the perspective of those concerned about the development of a new form of alternative education and a "democratic surge" in students' thinking, there was good reason to worry about whole language as a Trojan Horse opening the gates of thinking. On the one hand, the pedagogy was based predominantly on linguistic theory and evidence pertaining to oral and written language acquisition, but on the other whole language could incorporate the educational goals that had, indeed, emerged in the 1960s. As such, whole language provided an opportunity that helped attract many educators desirous of putting a "democratic surge" back into classrooms. For example, reading educator Carole Edelsky insisted that whole language should be explicit about creating pedagogy that "opposes social stratification and promotes an egalitarian social order." To create "a curriculum aiming for justice and equity" there must be "a deliberate, active search for materials that try to promote [these aims], for projects that could reveal the less dominant sides of issues, for resources that feature voices not usually heard."[7] Although not all teachers identifying as whole language teachers employed this social justice perspective and classroom practice, the viewpoint Edelsky articulated was a sufficiently prominent part of whole language writings and teaching to be of concern to dominant political-economic power.

Accepting Top-Down Management Starts with Learning to Read

The counterattack on whole language extended from purported research-based dismissals in academic publications to restrictive federal policy, in the form of No Child Left Behind, which established so-called scientifically based reading instruction—a top-down, intellectually restrictive pedagogy—as the law of the land. Prominent in the counterattack was the work of Harvard reading professor Jeanne Chall, whose 1967 book, *Learning to Read: The Great Debate*, assailed reading instruction that stressed engaging children in meaningful language activities ("meaning emphasis").[8] This approach, commonly called "look-say," which had been used from the nineteenth century through the first half of the twentieth century, had students learn individual words separately, in sentences and in stories, and eventually master—either intuitively or explicitly—specific skills for identifying parts of words. Reading textbooks ("basal readers") created for each grade were the instructional materials for the look-say method, with the "Dick and Jane" and "See Spot run" family stories most commonly associated with the method. Chall argued that reading instruction had to be grounded in a tightly controlled "code-emphasis method," that is, mastery of the alphabetic code.

Chall introduced her educational model by asking, "How in essence do readers change as they advance from the *Cat in the Hat* to the financial pages of the *New York Times*?" Her answer was pre-programmed instruction, orchestrated by a middle-manager teacher, that took students through a hierarchical progression of reading stages, each purportedly linked with a particular cognitive organization, beyond which students' thinking was not allowed to stray.

In Stage 1 (corresponding to grades one and two), thinking about meaning was eschewed because it could interfere with the central aim of reading instruction in these grades, which is to help children gain control of the correspondence between symbols and sounds. At Stage 2 (around grades two and three), meaning occupied a relatively larger place in the curriculum, but because of children's cognitive limitations, meaning activities are confined primarily to content with which the child is already familiar. Chall stresses that in these first two stages, "*very little new information about the world is learned from reading*" (my emphasis).

At last, in Stage 3 (beginning around fourth grade and continuing into high school), students arrive at the first stage of "reading to learn the new—new knowledge, information, thoughts and experiences." However, "new" was confined to "conventional knowledge of the world essentially from one point of view."

Not until Stage 4 (the high school years) do multiple viewpoints become part of the curriculum. Yet even here thinking is proscribed. Students can think about a variety of perspectives, though not yet their own. Finally, at Stage 5 (usually in college or at age eighteen or above), students begin to develop their own views, that is, read what others think, "construct knowledge" for themselves, and create their own "truth." Of course, having spent a decade with no opportunity or encouragement to think for themselves, the likelihood that students would "construct knowledge" was captured by physicist Leo Szilard's observation: "Americans are free to think what they want to think; the problem is, they don't think what they're free to think."

Top-Down Management Is Justified by "Verified Practices"

In addition to the curriculum history I have outlined, the road to crafting students' thinking for the global economy included a series of national reports, supposedly justified by scientific research, such as *Becoming a Nation of Readers*, written in 1985 during the Reagan administration by the Commission on Reading of the National Academy of Education.[9] Echoing Jeanne Chall, the report claimed that tightly controlled beginning reading had to be based on "verified practices," of which the proven centerpiece was composed of phonics instruction, primers (basal readers), and workbooks, all orchestrated through top-down management. Reining-in thinking had nothing to do with reinforcing and protecting the dominant ideology and power; it was solely about scientifically verified research findings. Absent in the report was any discussion of reading that had been raised in alternative educational approaches. The following year (1986), Reagan's Secretary of Education, William J. Bennett, repeated the recommendations in his *A Report on Elementary Education in America*.[10] As educator Ira Shor documented a few years afterward, the drummed-up literacy crisis that these reports purportedly addressed used concepts such as excellence, standards, accountability, and research—apolitical terms that cloaked a conservative attack on the experiences, content, and purposes of schooling—all aimed at implanting dominant ideas in students' minds.[11]

To ensure that thoughtful education would not flourish, pedagogical attacks on its use were buttressed with national legislation. A Republican policy paper, "Illiteracy: An Incurable Disease or Educational Malpractice," appeared in 1989[12] and acquired political power the following year through a provision in the Adult Literacy Act, in which phonics instruction—the leading edge of correspondence education—was added to the list of instructional methods eligible for federal funds, while other methods purportedly lacking scientific support were excluded. Hailing the inclusion as a big victory, the chair of the Republican Policy Committee stated, "Research shows phonics is the most effective way to teach people to read." In fact, the paper did not support this claim, but the smoke-and-mirrors policy achievement served as another step to control and constrict the ideas allowable in classrooms.

The Reading Excellence Act

Despite reports, claims, and funding supporting lockstep, do-as-you-are-told instruction, whole language continued to appeal to teachers as an effective alternative, which, in turn, produced a rising political, educational, and media backlash. *Time* magazine, *U.S. News and World Reports*, and *The Atlantic Monthly* were part of a media drumbeat that helped garner support for a major federal bill, the 1998 Reading Excellence Act, which served to eviscerate further teachers' power and students' thinking.

The Act emphasized lockstep instruction, supposedly supported by "replicable, reliable research," a term that, as I explain below, had no more factual basis at the end of the twentieth century than it had in previous decades. Nonetheless, according to the legislation, this purported research was the foundation for controlling the curriculum and ideas in the classroom. The Act's primary author was House Education Committee staff member Bob Sweet, who had no professional training or experience either in reading or education. However, Sweet's politically conservative credentials were impeccable. In New Hampshire he had led the Moral Majority, a right-wing political organization that pushed schools to teach creationism, make school prayer mandatory, and ban "immoral" books. The organization also opposed abortion, the Equal Rights Amendment, and the reduction of the U.S. nuclear arsenal.[13]

Further bipartisan support for legislation that contracted classroom teaching, learning, and thinking occurred with the passage in 2001 of George W. Bush's No Child Left Behind, whose literacy mandates supposedly were based on a gold-standard of scientific research contained in the *Report of the National Reading Panel* (2000). The multitude of deficiencies and distortions in the Panel's research review makes the report fool's gold, offering no evidence to justify the support of the sure-to-fail-children "Reading First" top-down, constricted instruction.[14] Sadly for students, this deficient literacy instruction became the law of the land in the No Child Left Behind Act, and it took nearly a decade before test scores revealed what was evident to anyone who had been paying attention to the evidence. Students taught with this "scientifically based reading instruction" scored no better on reading comprehension tests than did students not taught with it.[15] Yet even this outcome did not convince supporters that it was fundamentally flawed. No, the problem was improper implementation. Hence, it rolled on with a new face in the Common Core Standards promoted by the Obama administration—the same grade-by-grade skills-heavy, thinking-lite, publisher-crafted curriculum.[16]

Commenting on the link between the attack on whole language reading education and the contraction of thinking in the classroom, Kenneth Goodman observed:

everything that we as educators have learned about literacy through our research and the theory we have built from that work is less valued than conceptions of literacy that serve the political and economic purposes of those who have the power to control the decision-making.[17]

With the introduction of the ideology that education must be designed to provide students with the occupational means to compete in the global economy, efforts to confine classroom teaching and learning within "correspondence" boundaries now had a purpose grounded in the material well-being of the American people. Thinking had to be directed toward enabling young people to obtain work, have an income, and be constantly equipped to retool themselves for those fast-changing productive innovations that generated a continual advance of skills. At the same time, the contraction of thinking was justified by evoking the concern expressed in *A Nation at Risk*, that the nation's schools were failing to create a competitive workforce, thereby putting the entire national economy at risk.

Social Studies

The contraction of student thinking is vividly evident in the reduced time devoted to social studies. For example, a 2007 study of the time school districts devoted to various subjects and activities found that 44 percent of districts reported cutting time from one or more other subjects or activities—social studies, science, art and music, physical education, lunch, and/or recess—at the elementary level, with 36 percent of school districts reporting a decrease in social studies in elementary schools.[18]

When Arne Duncan, secretary of education in the Obama administration, maintained that social studies needed to be emphasized in schools for a "well-rounded education" and for "creating contributing and responsible citizens," the president of the National Council for the Social Studies replied that while the Council welcomed and supported Duncan's words, the reality was that in schools that do not do well on national Adequate Yearly Progress tests, students are pulled from subjects deemed "unnecessary," such as social studies, "to prep for the high stakes tests of accountability." Rather than contribute to a "well-rounded education," social studies—which seeks to promote "knowledge, skills and attitudes" that will contribute to "lifelong . . . informed and thoughtful . . . participation as citizens"—has been marginalized. Despite lofty pronouncements about citizenship, "our students are not as well versed in the knowledge of our political system and its operations as we would like."[19]

Several of the Council for Social Studies instructional goals are worth enumerating to see how far they are from the dominant imperative of preparing students to compete in the global economy. Stressing that the elementary social studies curriculum should not be a "mere collection of enjoyable experiences focusing on food, fun, families, festivals, flags, and films," the Council projected a curriculum that would:

- "enable students to understand, participate in, and make informed decisions about their world"
- promote "responsible citizen participation locally, nationally, and globally"
- promote "independent and *cooperative* problem solving to address complex social, economic, *ethical*, and personal concerns" (my emphasis)
- ground "children in democratic principles" and immerse "them in age-appropriate democratic strategies"
- promote "civic engagement"
- "provide opportunities to practice critical thinking skills while examining multiple perspectives"
- teach students "to question, evaluate, and challenge informational sources"[20]

These have been the curriculum goals that educational activists from the free schools to whole language have sought; and they are precisely the goals that promoters of "correspondence" abhor and crush.

The Demise and Distortions of Social Studies

Social studies and history instructional time not only has diminished, it has often been filled with corporate-funded curricula dedicated to reinforcing a corporate-controlled world. One such curriculum comes from the Bill of Rights Institute (BRI), a project created primarily by the billionaire Koch brothers, owners of a fossil fuel empire and funders of right-wing politicians and causes. In a BRI essay contest on "Being An American," the top winning themes expressed a Koch brothers definition of Americanism. Of twenty-two top essays, "individual liberty," "private property," and "limited government" were prominent themes, while "all men are created equal" was the theme of a single winning essay.[21]

Lauding its influence in schools, the Institute claims it has "provided a better understanding of the Constitution and Bill of Rights to more than 4.3 million students and over 50,000 teachers. Additionally, the Institute has directly trained over 22,000 teachers through its constitutional seminars."[22]

The BRI's political views and purposes are evident in its lessons, such as those concerning the Occupy Movement, a worldwide action in 2011–12 that protested economic and social inequality, particularly as represented by the richest "1%." The focus on the "Occupy Movement and the Bill of Rights" was not on whether the 1% has abused human rights, but on how the Occupy Movement violated the rights of others. One issue concerned an article about a crackdown on Occupy in New York City. Was the crackdown justified? Yes, it was, concluded BRI, because while the Bill of Rights is meant to help protect American citizens from government abuse, the demonstrators in this instance had violated their First Amendment rights by damaging both the park that was the center of demonstrations and the neighborhood adjoining the park. Consequently, the government had a right to inflict pain (with pepper spray, for example) on the Bill of Rights abusers.[23] Similar abusers, according to BRI, could be found in the Occupy Movement in Tulsa, Oklahoma. As a BRI lesson article explains, quoting experts from the First Amendment Center, Tulsa

Occupy could not offer any First Amendment defense arguments that would hold up in court.[24]

Wholly omitted from the Occupy lessons is any reference to the Occupy movement specifically targeting the Koch brothers for the damage they have done to First Amendment rights. For example, Occupy Atlanta marched on the headquarters of a Koch business, criticizing the brothers for spending vast amounts of

> money to ensure that legislation in Washington benefits their private and corporate interests, rather than the American people. This means less protections for you and your family, and less taxation and regulation for them. We need to get the power in Washington into the hands of the people, the 99%, and out of the hands of the 1%.

Explained one demonstrator, the Koch brothers are the "poster children for corporate corruption of the political process."[25]

Beyond BRI's various seminars, teaching, conferences, and contests that constrict thinking about democracy, the Institute has also developed curricula at the state level. In North Carolina, the state's Department of Public Instruction encouraged teachers to use a history curriculum written by BRI to fulfill an instructional requirement established in the state legislature's 2011 Founding Principles Act, requiring high school students to pass a course on "Founding Philosophy and the Founding Principles of government for a free people."[26] The BRI curriculum was the perfect choice because the bill was based on model legislation provided by ALEC, a conservative group also funded by the Koch brothers and other right-wing individuals, corporations, and foundations, such as the Richard Scaife Foundation, John Olin Foundation, and ExxonMobil.[27] Flowing from the BRI ideology, the curriculum emphasizes individual rights and limited government action. In a lesson on "rule of law," for example, students are asked to analyze how the Constitution serves to "ensure liberty" by requiring a limited government that does not infringe on individual rights. One comprehension question asks: "What is the fundamental reason why, according to Locke, government's main purpose must be to protect the rights of individuals?"[28]

BRI underscores that it "envisions a society in which all individuals enjoy life, liberty, and the pursuit of happiness," but the Institute fails to note that this key phrase comes from the Declaration of Independence, which focuses on *collective* rights and action. The Declaration is filled with phrases such as "one people," "entitle and impel *them*," "the public good," "our people," "us" and the "good people of these colonies." While this declaration excluded women and slaves, and was therefore less than expressive of collective society, the declaration is not primarily about "individuals." Nonetheless, the entire BRI curriculum, with its emphasis on individuals and omission of the social collective, fits perfectly into schooling increasingly shaped by "education for individuals to compete in the global economy."

Khan Academy

With the Internet has come a vast amount of digital learning in and out of the classroom. As the U.S. Department of Education stated, this form of communication "supports learning 24 hours a day, 7 days a week" and "builds 21st-century skills." It ushers in "a new model of connected teaching" and opportunities to improve "instruction and personalize learning."[29] Not described in this laudatory overview is the content in the delivery system. Does new twenty-first-century global technology convey new understandings and thinking, or does it fit the cliché of "old wine, new bottles"? For example, with the clamor for schooling that will meet the needs of the new global economy, what kind of understanding of globalization is conveyed in the new digital curriculum?

The 24/7 digital curriculum of the Khan Academy helps answer the question. Using educational videos that can be freely accessed through the Internet, the Kahn Academy describes its aim as providing "a free, world-class education for anyone, anywhere." By 2012 Kahn Academy videos had been viewed more than 200 million times by "6 million unique students each month (about 45 million total over the last 12 months)" and was "(formally or informally) part of the curriculum in 20,000 classrooms around the world."[30] By 2013, more than 30,000 classrooms had begun incorporating the Khan videos into their curriculums,[31] and a year later the number of unique users had risen to 10 million per month, about 65 percent of whom were in the United States.[32] By 2017, the Khan Academy had nearly 57 million unique users, with 70% of users from the United States.[33]

Is the Khan Academy the future of education?, asked the CBS program *60 Minutes*? in 2012. Begun by Salman Khan, a former hedge fund analyst who has degrees in mathematics, computer science, and electrical engineering from MIT, and in business administration from Harvard, the initial videos first garnered $2 million support from billionaire funders Ann and John Doerr, whose foundations also contributed to charter schools and for-profit education businesses, thereby making clear the values of schooling they promoted. Bill Gates then joined as a "founding partner." Donations falling in the $1,000,000–$1,999,999 group came from Mexico billionaire Carlos Slim, the Broad Foundation, the Helmsley Charitable Trust, the Walt Disney company, and the Craig and Susan McCaw Foundation (the McCaws were major fund raisers for George W. Bush). Donors contributing lesser amounts include those with similar right-wing politics, such as the Bradley Foundation. Given the political perspective of these donors, it is reasonable to question how that perspective has been reflected in the curriculum, particularly with respect to the instruction about the global economy.[34]

Globalization, According to the Khan Academy

Khan Academy lessons on "Globalization II: Good or Bad" begin with an approving summary of certain U.S. "collectivist" programs, such as Social Security, enacted in previous decades. However, before students get too comfortable with the "collectivist" concept, the instructor quickly underscores that "since the 1960s, the ascendant idea of personal freedom, minimally limited by government intervention has become very powerful." This thereby injects a definition of democracy consonant with the views of the Koch brothers' Bill of Rights Institute, without any reference to how this idea ascended and for whom and why it has become "powerful." A 2015 Gallup Poll, for example, found that 63 percent of Americans felt the distribution of wealth was unfair and should be more evenly distributed among a larger percentage of people. Moreover, about half of Americans (75 percent Democrats, 50 percent Independents, and even 29 percent of Republicans) support "heavy taxes on the rich"—surely not a view of "limited government intervention." And 47 percent of Americans hinted that collectivism maybe isn't so bad when they said they would consider voting for a socialist candidate. None of this kind of public opinion appears in the Kahn curriculum.[35]

The Kahn teacher in the "Globalism II" video quickly runs through a variety of disturbing contemporary concerns, such as climate change, overuse of resources, and "ethnic and nationalistic violence," but just as quickly refocuses on globalization from a very positive perspective, explaining that there is an "ideological shift in the age of globalization that does seem pretty new, and that's the turn to democracy." For example, the teacher continues, "the governments of most Latin American countries during most of the 20th century" were "ruled by military strongmen, with a couple of exceptions." What are these exceptions? In *sotto voce* and a slightly comedic tone he says, "Fidel, Hugo . . ." and at the same time, popping up behind the narrator are the faces of the two remaining leaders he considers to be antidemocratic strongmen, Cuba's Fidel Castro and Hugo Chávez, the former elected president of Venezuela. The teacher in the video then feigns fear that the images of the two might be real and, therefore, are menacing threats he does not want to anger. He then looks at the video viewer and springs the grand finale joke, asking, "Are they behind me right now? Because if they're behind me, I am in favor of collectivizing oil revenue and distributing it to the poor. If they're nowhere around me, that's a terrible idea."

Of course, since they really are not behind him, then yes, students can be told the truth: nationalizing resources and using the revenue for the poor *is* a "terrible idea." Why it's a terrible idea is never explained and the Khan curriculum's horror of collectivizing oil says nothing about Chávez using oil revenues to expand public education, particularly for children of the poor; instituting land reform to help small farmers and the landless; expanding worker cooperatives; starting special banks to assist small enterprises; and initiating similar reforms opposed by Venezuela's wealthy.[36]

Nor does the narrator note that the "military strongman" Chávez was in fact the democratically elected president of Venezuela in 1998, 2000, 2006, and 2012, precisely because his nationalization of key industries helped address the multitude of needs of the poor.[37] Nor does the Khan course say a word about the 2002 U.S.-supported coup d'état to overthrow him,[38] despite Chávez becoming president through a fair election.

The Khan lesson explains that the history of governments of most Latin American countries have been ruled by military strongmen, but is silent on how these governments maintained their rule through U.S. support and, moreover, were often created after the United States toppled or helped topple democratic governments, such as Jacobo Arbenz in Guatemala in 1954, Joao Goulart in Brazil in 1964, Salvador Allende in Chile in 1973, Jean Bertrand Aristide of Haiti in 2004, and Jose Manuel Zelaya of Honduras in 2009. And, of course, the lesson includes nothing about the U.S. attempts to overthrow Fidel Castro since the Cuban Revolution toppled U.S.-backed dictator Fulgencio Batista in 1959 and instituted agrarian reform that included the expropriation of land, particularly foreign-owned property, such as the hundreds of thousands of acres owned by the notorious United Fruit Company.[39]

The Khan lesson continues by noting three stellar examples of the contemporary global economy—Brazil, India, and South Africa—where, says the teacher, democracy is "flourishing" and "the combination of democracy and *economic liberalism* has unleashed impressive growth that has lifted millions out of poverty" (my emphasis). Unfortunately for the students, but surely to the satisfaction of the approval of the billionaire funders of the Khan courses, this summary omits any details of the "flourishing." The following brief review of South Africa illustrates the actual history that Khan Academy's viewpoint excludes when naming the "flourishing" nations in the global economy.

South Africa

At the end of apartheid in 1994, a more egalitarian society was expected, but in the following years, the promise did not materialize. For example, overall unemployment was approximately 32 percent when apartheid ended, but in 2013 it had risen to 36 percent, with youth unemployment in black townships at 57 percent.[40] In 2014, an economic appraisal using the appallingly low national poverty line of $43 per month, found that 47 percent of South Africans remained poor, a percentage not lower than the 45.6 percent in poverty in 1994.[41] Using the Gini coefficient, which measures inequality, South Africa was categorized as one of the most unequal countries in the world.

Although there have been gains in housing, schools, roads, infrastructure, pensions, health care, and similar social needs, alongside these gains remain "gross inadequacies and inequities in the education and health sectors; a ferocious rise in unemployment; endemic police brutality and torture . . . an alarming tendency to secrecy and authoritarianism in government; the meddling with the judiciary; and threats to the media and freedom of expression."[42] Workers' rights have been brutally suppressed, as illustrated by the police killing of thirty-four striking miners in 2012 at a mine owned by the London-based Lonmin Company.[43]

What are the roots of these injustices? They can be traced to the African National Congress (ANC) eliminating legal apartheid but not touching the economic apartheid that serves big business through an array of neoliberal economic policies, especially opening wide the privatizing of public enterprises and eviscerating social welfare funding.[44] Nelson Mandela made clear to journalist John Pilger just how far the ANC would go in pursuing change: "The policy of the ANC is privatization," Mandela said, in which the World Bank and the

International Monetary Fund provide key policy guidance. As Pilger explained: Enveloped in the hot air of corporate-speak, the Mandela and (second post-apartheid president) Mbeki governments took their cues from the World Bank and the International Monetary Fund. While the gap between the majority living beneath tin roofs without running water and the newly wealthy black elite in their gated estates became a chasm, finance minister Trevor Manuel was lauded in Washington for his "macro-economic achievements." South Africa, noted (billionaire investor) George Soros in 2001, had been delivered into "the hands of international capital."[45]

Using access to water as one measure of the effect of the post-apartheid economics on children, 93.7 percent of young white children and 97 percent of Indian/Asian children had piped water inside their homes, whereas only 27.1 percent of black African children had such access. Sanitation is another measure: all Indian/Asian children and 97.1 percent of white children lived in households that used flush toilets; however, only 40.2 percent of young black African children had similar facilities.[46]

Comparable disparities were found for electric, gas, and other energy sources for cooking, heating, and lighting. Medical care for black children was overwhelmingly provided by public hospitals and clinics, while the majority from white and Indian/Asian groups received medical care from private doctors. Hunger occurred along comparable groupings, with approximately 30 percent of black children living in households where, through the year, there was no or too-little food whereas only about 2.3 percent of white and Indian/Asian children faced this problem.

These are the realities ignored in the Khan Academy's rendition of the glories of global "economic liberalism" and the impressive economic growth this configuration of the global economy promoted in South Africa. Similar conditions exist in the other two examples, India and Brazil, about which the Kahn curriculum raves. With respect to India, in chapter 1 I noted Arundhati Roy's characterization of the vast "gush up," not "trickle down," of wealth in India, a country with the largest, and growing, number of poor in the world, whereas its number of billionaires has increased. As for the Khan curriculum's third example of impressive growth through contemporary global "economic liberalism," Brazil too has one of the world's largest disparities between rich and poor, as graphically depicted in the Gini index, which ranks Brazil number 16 in inequality in a list of 141 countries.[47]

The Big History Project

Another Internet-delivered curriculum is Big History, extending "from the Big Bang to modernity." Devised by Australian historian David Christian, Big History is heavily funded by Bill Gates, who, while viewing it during treadmill workouts thought, "Everybody should watch this thing!"[48] Since the debut of the free curriculum in five high schools in 2011, the course has been used by "more than 15,000 students in some 1,200 schools, from the Brooklyn School for Collaborative Studies in New York to Greenhills School in Ann Arbor, Mich., to Gates's alma mater, Lakeside Upper School in Seattle." A version of it is in the Khan Academy curriculum.

Like the Khan Academy history lessons, Big History's rendition of the last few hundred years is a model in obfuscation of the "global economy," with the term "modernity" used as the chief operating descriptor of that economy. The overall tale of the creation of modernity is comforting and uplifting, despite acknowledgment of some unsavory episodes, such as slavery and the deaths of black Africans as they were being transported to become slaves or the "vast amounts of silver that the Spanish acquired from the Americas" (with the narrator using air quotes for the word "acquired").

Yes, Big History teaches, there have been some grim occurrences, but these should not detract from grasping the deeper, largely positive essence of "modernity" that is very much about global linkage—"link[ing] up globally through shipping, through trains, through telegraph, through the Internet, until now we seem to form a single global brain of almost seven billion individuals." And best of all, we are on the cusp of an advanced stage of modernity that will provide a "growing benefit" for "all humans, rather than just a privileged few." Collective learning has expanded, many inventions have been created, many products manufactured, and the future is promising because soon billions of "potential innovators" will be able to advance "new ideas" and "products." The mostly good, some bad, often breathtaking modernity tale is summed up this way: Along with all this horrific stuff, the unification of the world zones was a good thing for collective learning, which would eventually prove our salvation in many ways. This global system continues to increase in complexity and connectivity today, which is why people can now look at this (video) on their smartphone.

In this glowing panorama of the "global system" of "modernity," the "horrific stuff" is strikingly minimal. To take just one example, slavery and slave deaths, as I described above, are briefly noted in Big History; however, there is no lesson about how many native peoples were killed in the construction of modernity. A valuable history-math lesson could explore whether it was approximately 100 million people who were destroyed, as historian David Stannard calculated, in the Euro-American genocidal wars that began with the Spanish attack on the Arawak people of Hispaniola in the 1490s and continuing through the U.S. slaughter of the indigenous peoples of North and South America.[49] Or was it fewer, depending on one's definition of genocide. For example, political scientist Rudolph Rummel, according to his strict definition of "genocide," puts the number at 2 million to 15 million, much smaller than Stannard's calculation, but not exactly a negligible number of deaths. As Rummel writes, "Even if these figures are remotely true, this still makes this subjugation of the Americas one of the bloodier, centuries-long [genocides] in world history."[50]

Also absent in Big History's rendition of "the unification of the world zones" is the blood spilled elsewhere by U.S.-backed dictators—approximately 70,000 Salvadorans; in Guatemala an estimated 100,000 were killed and an additional 60,000 "disappeared"; in Indonesia the U.S.-backed military government killed between 500,000 to one million in 1965,[51] which the *New York Times* called "one of the most savage mass slaughters of modern political history."[52]

The end of the Big History course contains a few brief additional commentaries, including one by Bill Gates, that acknowledge all is not entirely well in the connected globe. David Christian observes, "We're burning fossil fuels at such a rate that we seem to be undermining what made it possible for human civilizations to flourish over the last 10,000 years." Henry Louis Gates Jr. mentions "huge class differentials" and a "third world of poverty and a first world of economic prosperity and economic development." A few other commentators also note extensive global poverty. How do we solve these problems? Either the commentators provide no answer or the answer is embraced in the vague Big History model of "our power of collective learning" in a "connective global system" and in the avoidance of any understanding of corporate economics and power shaping global capitalism and social class. M. Sanjayan, a researcher at the Nature Conservatory, states that "technology can really help to move us forward to solving some of the big intractable problems." Sanjayan's observations lead directly to Bill Gates's commentary in which he ponders where the world is right now and will be in fifty years. He concludes, in somewhat jumbled prose, "We've come to value the work that's been done, but in other countries, making great products and really think together about humanity's common future. The pace of innovation will need to surprise us in some ways. What form will this great energy source be that will avoid us destroying the environment? That's an invention that's very, very important."[53] Presumably, Gates, like Sanjayan, is counting on the capitalism that has brought massive global poverty and environmental destruction to be the same global economic system that will sufficiently address poverty and end environmental destruction with a new technology or a new invention.

Overall, this Big History view of contemporary problems is quite different from that expressed by many global economy organizations and activists from countries around the world. The answer for them is not new technology or invention, or "collective learning." Rather, as the 2015 "Statement of the World's Peoples' Conference on Climate Change and the Defense of Life" says:

The world is being battered by a multiple global crisis that manifests itself in a climate, financial, food, energy, institutional, cultural, ethical and spiritual crisis and a state of permanent war. This tells us that we are living an integral crisis of capitalism and a society model. To survive, humanity must break free of capitalism that is leading humanity towards a horizon of destruction that is a sentence of death to nature and life itself. ... We rise up against capitalism that is the structural cause of climate change and intends to submit the life cycles of Mother Earth to the market rules under the domination of capitalist technology.[54]

This kind of viewpoint is wholly absent from Big History, thereby preventing students from engaging in the full connectivity of knowledge the creators and funders of the course claim to laud.

Shrinking Arts Education

With the purported educational goal of equipping students to compete and obtain work in the global economy, arts education is another part of the curriculum that has been losing time and importance. For example, expressing the job market reality of the contribution of the arts to one's employment, President Obama observed, "I promise you, folks can make a lot more, potentially, with skilled manufacturing or the trades than they might with an art history degree."[55] Following extensive criticism of the remark, he apologized, but the apology changed nothing about his appraisal that the job market must be the chief shaper of the curriculum.[56]

With this assumption shaping the curriculum across the nation, art education courses, not surprisingly, have diminished. A 2012 U.S. Department of Education survey of visual arts, dance, and drama classes found that fewer public elementary schools offered these courses than in the previous decade. Theater and drama programs over that time period went from 20 percent to 4 percent of schools, while visual arts classes dropped from 87 to 83 percent of schools.[57]

Though the overall size of the latter reduction seems modest with respect to the amount and quality of arts education provided, the percentages fail to provide a full depiction of the diminution. In New Jersey, for example, reflective of a nationwide change that formally, but not substantively, fulfilled the meaning of "arts education," some 97 percent of the state's students had arts classes at school, but the actual amount of class time devoted to the arts had been cut.[58] Among states, the instructional policies for arts education vary greatly, particularly with respect to how often and by whom arts instruction should be taught. Twenty-seven states, slightly more than 50 percent define the "arts" as core subjects, with about the same number (twenty-six states) having an arts requirement for high school graduation. In practice, however, the latter requirement usually means one or two semesters of an arts course.[59] The severe cuts in art education across the country are illustrated by budget decisions in Los Angeles, where one-third of the arts teachers were fired between 2008 and 2012 and arts programs for elementary students dwindled to practically zero.[60]

For schools serving low-income students, the cuts in the arts have been even more severe. For example, whereas 100 percent of high schools with low-income students had a music class in the 1999–2000 school year, a decade later the percentage had dropped to 81 percent. Moreover, simply offering these courses does not take into account the increased class size and reduced art class instructional time, especially in elementary school, where arts are often taught as part of other subjects. Among low-income students, poor urban students have been especially affected. Philadelphia schools, facing a budget shortfall of over $300 million, completely eliminated funds for art and music programs. Cuts in the Chicago schools similarly crippled arts education, with the majority of schools unable to provide even two hours of arts instruction per week.[61]

STEAM

With job preparation described as the chief task of schools, arguments by those who strongly support the inclusion of the arts in the curriculum have frequently stressed how the arts create academic benefits that, in turn, can contribute to job preparation. For example, students with high levels of art engagement from kindergarten through elementary school have higher test scores in science than do students with low levels of arts engagement over the same school years.[62] Supporters of arts education also underscore its particular attributes for low-socioeconomic status students (SES). Several studies have found that those low-SES students who had a history of in-depth arts involvement had better academic outcomes—earned better grades and had higher rates of college enrollment and attainment—than had low-SES youth with less arts involvement.[63]

This arts-job performance linkage has been an argument the National Performing Arts (NPA) organization has employed in explaining how the arts promote creativity, communication, and risk taking, all of which enhance the performance of the new workforce. To help gain support from influential policymaking groups, the NPA has provided arts education advocates a list of "useful quotes," starting with those from political and business leaders. Leading the recommended quotes is one from billionaire Apple creator, the late Steve Jobs: "It is in Apple's DNA that technology alone is not enough—it's technology married with liberal arts, married with the humanities, that yields us the results that make our hearts sing."[64] The quote, typical of current arguments for justifying the value of the arts, has led to an amplification from STEM to the concept of STEAM in which Arts are integrated into technical-vocational education and occupations. STEAM provides an occupationally functional view of the arts far from more soaring visions, such as Picasso's conviction that "the purpose of art is washing the dust of daily life off our souls." For STEAM, the purpose of art is clear: to help create a new-something, Windows-something, virtual-something, cloud-something, or smart-something. Not another *Guernica*.

Why the Reduction in Arts Education?

A curriculum devoted to preparing students for future occupational

competition in the global economy nicely minimizes or wholly elimi-
nates the kind of thinking that philosopher of education Maxine
Greene observed can be fostered through arts education:

> We know that the arts cannot change the world, but, as [Herbert]
> Marcuse reminded us, those who can engage reflectively and
> authentically with the arts may be awakened in startling ways
> to the scars and flaws in our society . . .[and] may be imagina-
> tively awakened and uniquely moved to choose themselves as
> actors committed to alter some corner of our suffering world.[65]

For Greene the aesthetic, imaginative experience embraces
"awareness, wide-awakeness, and the passion for the possible." Its
opposite, she notes, quoting John Dewey, is the "anesthetic" experience, which embodies passivity and apathy and "the very notion
of what it signifies to be human." A great potential of the arts, she
argued, is their capacity to allow us to look at things as if they could
be otherwise, to build alternative realities, perhaps *alternative visions
of the world—visions of what might be, of what ought to be*. Encounters
with the various arts enable us to break with the habitual, the wholly
conventional (and, we must remember, not always for the good), to
think about our own thinking, to reflect on our own stories, our own
experiences.[66]

Art education also nurtures empathy—that is, understanding and
vicariously experiencing the feelings, thoughts, and lives of others.
Empathy is vital, art education professor Carol S. Jeffers observes,
because "it offers the promise of intersubjective understanding so
essential to the survival of the human community." Discussing evidence of empathetic connections in art education classes, Jeffers
concludes that the arts have "community building potential" and can
"enable young people to grasp the meaning, the power of connection,"
especially "if we are to share so fragile a planet."[67] Similarly, Candice
Jesse Stout, in an essay titled "The Art of Empathy: Teaching Students
to Care," describes a curriculum she developed for stimulating imagination, developing empathetic awareness, and instilling a capacity to

care, a curriculum "intended to evoke empathetic response to fellow human beings as well as to other creatures with whom we share this earth."[68]

These goals are precisely the opposite of current assumptions about preparing students to work and compete in the twenty-first-century economic and social order. For this new order, the arts can contribute only if they help produce persons who will devote their imaginations to what are regarded as core human behaviors, that is, job performance, and product and service creation.

What's the Point of Liberal Arts?

The vocational refashioning of schooling has extended to higher education, where the number of liberal arts colleges and programs has declined and been replaced by a job-oriented, "practical" curriculum attuned to the twenty-first-century economic "reality."[69] As Victor E. Ferrall, former president of Beloit University and author of *Liberal Arts at the Brink*, wrote in 2015, three years after the publication of that book:

> I reported that student demand for liberal arts courses and majors—the humanities, social sciences, and physical sciences—was rapidly declining and being replaced by demand for vocational, directly career-related courses and majors. *Liberal Arts at the Brink* focused on liberal arts colleges, but the student-demand shift was also occurring at universities with both liberal arts and professional programs. As the book's title suggested, I thought the future of liberal arts education was bleak, but not hopeless. Now, I believe I was too optimistic. There no longer is reason to believe the decline of liberal arts education will be stayed or reversed.[70]

Focus on vocational preparation has intensified because students now anticipate high college debt (a prospect boosted by cuts in state funding of higher education) and the need to pursue coursework that may lead to enough job income to repay the debt. With the question "What courses are worth it?" Ferrall explains, liberal arts courses decreasingly are the answer, while "practical" programs increasingly are proclaimed as the road to economic well-being.[71]

Pay For It Yourself, If You Think It's Worth It

In addition to reductions in liberal arts courses in colleges, liberal arts education has been directly attacked as extraneous to the economy's needs. For example, North Carolina governor Pat McCrory, questioning whether state-funded universities should even be teaching liberal arts, groused, "I think some of the educational elite have taken over our education where we are offering courses that have no chance of getting people jobs." State funding of universities and community colleges should be based not "on how many butts in seats but how many of those butts can get jobs." Using gender studies courses at UNC-Chapel Hill as an example, McCrory complained that indulgence courses such as these should not receive public funds. "If you want to take gender studies that's fine, go to a private school and take it. But I don't want to subsidize that if that's not going to get someone a job."[72]

Florida governor Rick Scott, noting that liberal arts and social science programs do little to contribute to the state's economy, advocated a similar utilitarian educational policy in which university programs are tailored to the job market. "If I'm going to take money from a citizen to put into education then I'm going to take that money to create jobs," he insisted. "So I want that money to go to degrees where people can get jobs in this state." Scott's intention, in keeping with the prevailing ideology of what counts most for students' futures, was to shift more funding to the STEM disciplines. Supporting Scott, the state senate's president added that Florida was a "second-tier" state in attracting companies because the universities were not producing graduates with the right skills. Therefore, the budget issue for Florida lawmakers was whether to increase funding for STEM programs or to reduce funds for liberal arts programs, such as psychology, and shift them to STEM areas.[73]

On a national scale, Republicans have fought to reduce federal funding of university social science and related research, including the study of climate change. In a bill titled the "Frontiers in Innovation, Research, Science, and Technology Act of 2014," National Science Foundation research funds for the social, behavioral, and economic sciences were to be cut by more than 40 percent, with $160 million shifted from social, behavior, economic, and climate sciences to areas that would contribute to the global economy: the physical and biological sciences, engineering, and computer and information science.[74] In the words of Representative Lamar Smith, a Texas Republican who chaired the House Science Committee, "Funding for social science should not come at the expense of areas of science—math, engineering, computer science, physics, chemistry and biology—that are most likely to produce breakthroughs that will save lives, create jobs, and promote economic growth."[75]

But Liberal Arts Can Serve Capitalism!

North Carolina governor McCrory's remarks about education aimed only at "butts that can get jobs" were widely criticized, but much of the response was framed in terms of the benefits a liberal arts education can have for working and surviving within global capitalism. One history professor criticized the governor for not understanding how a liberal arts education can prepare students for employment in the twenty-first-century labor market. Given the likelihood that today's eighteen-year-olds will *switch jobs every four to six years, accumulating five to seven jobs over their lifetimes*, a liberal arts education, with its honing of critical thinking, writing, and speaking skills, would be ideal preparation for this ever-changing work demand. A liberal arts education, in other words, provides a utilitarian benefit for the challenging and ever-stressful demands put on future workers throughout their lifetimes, and "critical thinking" is conceptualized as an intellectual process contained within and serving the givens of global capitalism. Vivek Ranadivé, CEO of a billion-dollar software company, also recommended a liberal arts education for its utilitarian value. In "expensive labor markets like the United States," those people who "succeed" will be those "who can think creatively and generate the IDEAS that will propel economic growth." These profit-making goals "are best fostered" by the intellectual capabilities developed "in a traditional liberal arts environment."[76]

Nor should the benefits of a humanities education for the military be overlooked. At the U.S. Military Academy at West Point, "future officers are required to take humanities and social-sciences courses such as history, composition, psychology, literature, and languages." Why? As one cadet explained, in philosophy you learn that "there's no right answer, and that's very useful in the Army, so you're not so rigid." A brigadier general added, "It's important to develop in young people the ability to think broadly, to operate in the context of other societies and become agile and adaptive thinkers." The liberal arts teach future members of the military "to deal with complexity, diversity, and change . . . to think very intuitively to solve problems on the ground."[77] No one commented on where esteemed antiwar literature, such as the poems of Wilfred Owen or Dalton Trumbo's novel *Johnny Got His Gun,* fit in the curriculum.

Commission on the Humanities and Social Sciences

In 2010, the American Academy of Arts and Sciences formed the Commission on the Humanities and Social Sciences, in response to a somewhat bipartisan group of members of Congress (three Republicans and one Democrat) concerned about the "top actions that Congress, state governments, universities, foundations, educators, individual benefactors, and others should take now to maintain national excellence in humanities and social scientific scholarship."[78]

The appointment of Richard H Brodhead, president of Duke University, a scholar in nineteenth-century American literature, to serve as co-chair of the Commission, was a credible one. However, the same could not be said of co-chair John W. Rowe, former CEO of Exelon Corporation, owner of the largest number of nuclear plants in the United States. Under Rowe's leadership, Exelon had a history of leaking large amounts of radioactive water and not reporting it to regulatory agencies or the public,[79] as well as being found guilty of radioactive leaks in some of its power plants.[80] Along with heading Exelon, Rowe's occupational background included running other power companies and serving as general counsel for a rail corporation. Extending from his corporate work, Rowe had endowed a university chair[81] in the Sustainable Energy Institute at the Illinois Institute of Technology (the Institute's research includes nuclear energy and "clean coal" technology).[82] Financial contributions to parochial and secular charter schools headed Rowe's work in education. What humanities background did Rowe have that would qualify him to co-chair the panel? He has endowed chairs in Byzantine History and Greek History at the University of Wisconsin.

The panel did have members from various cultural and scholarly activities, including cellist Yo-Yo Ma and singer Emmylou Harris, but heavily represented was corporate power and its defenders, such as former CEOs of Lockheed-Martin and Boeing, members or former members of banks and investment companies, a right-wing *New York Times* columnist, and various academics whose work did not extend beyond the assumptions of capitalist economics and culture. The result was *The Heart of the Matter*, a report that praised various benefits of liberal arts, such as the contribution of the humanities and social sciences to a "more civil public discourse, a more adaptable and creative workforce, and a more secure nation."[83]

The panel also put forth the proposition that a "grounding in history, civics, and social studies" would be useful because it "allows citizens to participate meaningfully in the democratic process—as voters, informed consumers, and productive workers." The report does not explain how a national humanities organization thinks that "productive workers" or "informed shoppers" relate to participating meaningfully in a democracy. Nor does the report note that since productivity has outpaced wages for decades, perhaps more focus should be aimed as well at the degree of citizenship of business owners who have inordinately taken advantage of and profited from the productive work of their employees. Voting is, of course, part of what citizens should do, but narrowly defining "citizenship" to choosing between a candidate from one of the two dominant political parties surely is an attenuated definition of political participation.

As for workers who will be scrambling perpetually for jobs in the new global economy, a humanities education would also serve them because it would provide another tool for survival:

> Students should be prepared not just for their first job but for their fourth and fifth jobs, as there is little reason to doubt that people entering the workforce today will be called upon to play many different roles over the course of their careers. The ones who will do best in this new insecure employment environment will be those whose educations have prepared them to be flexible. Those with the ability to draw upon every available tool and insight—gleaned from science, arts and technology.[84]

Finally, not neglecting a mainstay in today's world, the Commission explained that warfare, too, will benefit from liberal arts education. The "U.S. military requires the kinds of expertise that students can acquire only through advanced study and immersion in other cultures." The nation needs "experts in national security, equipped with the cultural understanding, knowledge of social dynamics, and language proficiency to lead our foreign service and military through complex global conflicts."[85]

BEGINNING WITH RESPONSES TO eliminate the 1960s free school movement, efforts to strengthen the "correspondence" between schooling and the social order have been relentless. Curricula have been packaged in new technologies, but the long-enforced ideological curricular constraints on students' thinking remain unaltered. Further advancing these constraints have been intrusions into the schools by the very corporations and billionaires that have dominated and profited most from global capitalism and offer less and less for people in the United States and around the world. As the well-being of workers has deteriorated and economic injustice has accelerated, the more the overriding mission of schooling has been not only to avoid exploration of these issues but, instead, to focus singularly on a mission to make students combat-ready for the global economy.

6. U.S. Capitalism's Pretense of Supporting Education for the Global Economy

If only U.S. schools, teachers, and students were treated like iPhones. Take the first-generation iPhone. To enable users to swipe, pinch, and scroll with their fingers, "making for a more immersive experience," Apple, in the early 2000s, spent approximately $150 million in development costs.[1] Consumers who could feel, embrace, and afford the experience bought more than 250 million iPhones. Given this profitable result, Apple's iPhone research and development money has increased at least 32 percent annually since 2009,[2] to make every part of an iPhone as cutting-edge as possible. To equip newer ones with a scratch-resistant crystal, Apple invested a *billion dollars* for a steady, high-quality supply of sapphire.[3] Nobody at Apple yelled, "Stop throwing money at it! That won't make the product better!" No, "not resting on its laurels, even with record sales of its iPhone and Mac, the company again spent heavily," putting nearly $2 billion into research and development in 2015, an increase of more than 40 percent over the previous year's amount.[4]

From the perspective of what the overall economy needs, or, to put it more bluntly, what corporate heads and their political allies decide it needs, similar investments in schools and students are not regarded as comparable, because, as educational psychologist Milton Schwebel concluded in his analysis of the "three-tier" U.S. educational system, the U.S. economy "has no need for a well-educated populace. The hard fact is that the economy operates perfectly well" with the top school tier providing well-skilled workers, the middle-tier providing workers for the middle tier of jobs (in offices, retail stores, hospitals and wherever dependability and accuracy are required for routine tasks), and the third tier fills the ranks of unskilled service work and the unemployed.[5] Hence, funding and resources are proportionately distributed across these tiers. Were there really a crisis of public schools not meeting business needs for skilled workers, surely corporations would look at "what works" among schools, families, students, and communities that do produce the needed skilled workers and would strive to duplicate throughout the nation those quality elements for success. As discussed in this chapter, research does not point to charter schools as the answer. Therefore, if public schools were not meeting corporations' personnel needs, what kind of high-quality educational system across the nation would these corporations want to promote and fund?

Ensuring Educational Achievement

To create the well-educated workforce U.S. businesses claim they need, a solid starting point would have to be children's basic well-being. Yet, in 2015, students living in low-income families, defined as children eligible for federal free and reduced-price lunches, made up the "majority of the schoolchildren attending the nation's public schools" from preschool through 12th grade.[6] Yes, "low income" now describes the conditions in which most U.S. children live. Moreover, the term describes not just certain states or cities but, as a report by the Southern Education Foundation reveals, familial and child impoverishment runs throughout the nation. While low-income child poverty is extremely high in the southern states—for example, 65 percent for students in Louisiana and 71 percent for Mississippi children— the extent of child poverty is deplorable even in states with the least percentage of low-income students, such as 27 percent in New Hampshire and 30 percent in North Dakota. Below these "top-ranked" states are those with almost one-third of their students living in poverty.

Within the vast numbers of "low-income" children are those for whom life is even more desperate, that is, those children living at poverty's bottom, defined in 2015 as $24,600 for a family of four with two children.[7] This subgroup composes 21 percent of U.S. children, up from 17 percent in 1990. What does the future hold for many U.S. children? Judging from the 23 percent of U.S. children under six who now live in "poverty," more students will be living in economic conditions substantially worse than what is now categorized as "low income."[8]

What is more, international comparisons reveal both more extensive child poverty and deeper policy callousness toward the young in the United States than in other nations. A UNICEF report, comparing children's well-being in the world's "rich" (or developed) economies, found that in key areas, such as housing, health, and education, the United States ranks appallingly near the bottom in the "overall well-being" of its children. As UNICEF put it: "The bottom four places in the table are occupied by three of the poorest countries in the survey, Latvia, Lithuania and Romania, and by one of the richest, the United States." With respect to educational support, based on preschool funding and enrollment, health services, nutritional aid, and years attending school, the United States ranks even lower. far behind countries such as Estonia, Slovakia, and Greece.[9]

Educational Impact of Poverty

The impact of poverty on academic achievement has been amply documented by many researchers and summarized by organizations such as the American Psychological Association (APA) and the Economic Policy Institute (EPI). Certainly, some poor children do well in school and even attain advanced college degrees and fame, such as writer Alice Walker, who grew up in a sharecropper family, or scientist Jonas Salk, creator of the polio vaccine, who grew up poor in New York City. Nevertheless, a substantial portion of poor children tend to develop academic skills more slowly compared to children from more affluent homes; live in families with more chronic stress which, in turn, negatively affects pre-academic skills; and live in homes with fewer books and other fundamental educational resources that can have an adverse impact on initial reading competence.

Conditions of poverty that undermine educational growth are housing instability, hunger, poor nutrition, and an array of health issues, such as vision impairment, hearing problems, lead exposure, and iron deficiency anemia.[10] Although various famous achievers such as Walker and Salk demonstrate that poverty is not an inexorable cause of educational underachievement, as educational researcher Richard Rothstein[11] and educational historian Diane Ravitch document,[12] a vast body of evidence identifies poverty as the single most reliable predictor of school success or failure. Nevertheless, despite this evidence, corporate America, while carping about the nation's educational underachievement, is happy to hoard mountains of cash, a portion of which could be used to address the plight of impoverished children, working families, and an array of school conditions, all of which would boost academic achievement of economically poor students.

Education Should Start with Good School Infrastructure

The conditions for successful schooling should begin with the physical condition of the nation's schools. Business leaders should be asking, Are the facilities, such as buildings, classrooms, electrical and gas power, and other infrastructure conducive for learning? For education leaders who are in a good position to appraise the matter, such as the board of directors of the Council of the Great City Schools, a coalition of sixty-seven of the nation's largest urban public school systems, the answer is a decisive "No," summing up the issue this way:

Many educators maintain that the debate over how to improve education in the United States has ignored one critical element: the physical condition of schools. Students and teachers are held accountable for their performance, but it is extremely difficult to raise levels of academic achievement when teaching and learning take place in crumbling, antiquated facilities.[13]

As the Council underscores, the physical conditions of schools are not inconsequential to learning. Students in substandard schools "perform at lower levels than students in newer, functional buildings," even when controlling for income level. Especially affected by school facilities are poor and African-American students, whose schools are in greater need of repair, in large part because their schools tend to receive about "half of the funding for their school buildings as their more affluent peers."

Infrastructure conditions have, year after year, worsened considerably in school districts coping with reduced budgets, because repairs have been delayed or semi-repairs have been made to "save money" to meet more immediately pressing educational needs. However, as the Council has found, the choice will have devastating consequences for subsequent budget options because half-measures and delays accelerate the deterioration of school buildings and component systems.[14] Ultimately, more money is required for repairs or replacements, thus forcing communities to "borrow large sums of capital funds (with their accompanying debt service costs) to upgrade and/or replace facilities."[15]

An indication of the neglect of the nation's schools can be seen by comparing the amount school districts have spent on school construction and what they should have spent. Between fiscal years 2009 to 2011, the nation's school districts allocated approximately $51 billion per year for school construction and about $49 billion per year for operations and maintenance, a combined annual spending of about $100 billion. While these billions are quite a sum, it was much below the estimated $271 billion to $542 billion that should have been spent for America's crumbling schools. Corroborating the

Council's assessment is a study done by the American Society of Civil Engineers, which notes the severe decline in spending on school construction and facilities and gives the infrastructure condition of the U.S. schools a "D+."[16]

For many schools beyond just needing repair, their infrastructure grade does not even reach the D level. The Detroit public schools, for example, have broken and buckled floors, crumbling walls, leaking classroom ceilings, leaking toilets, rodents, and mushrooms growing on walls.[17] The Philadelphia schools are rife with "fire hazards, electrical hazards, safety and tripping hazards, water damage, damaged and deteriorating masonry, and other damaged building elements."[18] Hundreds of Chicago school principals described their schools as "filthy," with "dead vermin and garbage sitting in classrooms overnight."[19] In High Point, North Carolina, school officials complain of deteriorating schools with damaged roofs, green mold scales on walls, mortar no longer keeping bricks together, and falling ceiling plaster.[20] Richmond, Virginia, parents and teachers have, for years, been criticizing schools that have broken ceiling tiles and cracked floors, and are in the process of crumbling. But what are parents and students to do? A typical answer is that of the Richmond school board and mayor. Facing a budget of only "$5 million of the $18 million requested to fix aging school buildings and address safety and health concerns," and no expectations for future budget increases, they have proposed closing six schools.[21] With these additional closings, the problems for parents and students would pile on: more overcrowded classes, more difficult teaching conditions, massive transportation problems for many students, and additional strains on parents having to navigate new and often complex travel arrangements. Meanwhile, alongside these budget shortfalls, seven Fortune 500 companies in Virginia have avoided paying $9 billion in state and federal taxes by stashing massive profits overseas.[22]

Goodbye, Teachers

While the wealthy have grown wealthier and corporations have avoided paying taxes that could support public education, school funding shortages have led to the firing of hundreds of thousands of school personnel (teachers, teacher assistants, aides for disabled students, etc.), with many more teaching jobs in danger of being lost, including the purported must-have-for-STEM math and science teacher jobs.[23] In California, 82,000 teaching jobs were eliminated from 2008 to 2012.[24] Arizona's teacher shortage was described as at "crisis levels,"[25] with a loss of a record number of teachers,[26] despite, as the state's Department of Education put it, the need (in education-for-the-global-economy-speak) to "create the workforce of tomorrow."[27] In Wisconsin, in 2012, 73 percent of school districts cut a combined 1,500 teaching jobs.[28] Similar teacher shortages abound across the nation—in Kansas,[29] Indiana, New Mexico,[30] Oklahoma,[31] Kentucky, Rhode Island, Nevada, North Carolina, and Texas.[32] Among the consequences of reduced teaching staff, according to the Center for Public Education, class size has increased, while much else has been eliminated, such as high school courses not required for graduation, summer school, extracurricular activities, and field trips, hardly the qualities of a nation's great school system.[33] In 2016, the Learning Policy Institute, an education think tank, described the teacher shortage problems as substantial, worsening, and without evidence of adequate implementation of solutions to reverse the problem.[34]

Who Wouldn't Want an Overpaid Teaching Job?

Despite nationwide finger pointing at the "overpaid" teaching profession—part of what economist Robert Reich labeled "the shameful attack on public employees"[35]—a report from the Center for American Progress found the opposite to be true: teachers commonly are poorly paid. For example:

> In Colorado, teachers with a graduate degree and 10 years of experience make less than a trucker in the state. In Oklahoma, teachers with 15 years of experience and a master's degree

make less than sheet metal workers. Teachers in Georgia with 10 years of experience and a graduate degree make less than a flight attendant in the state. The average annual salary for a teacher in South Dakota with a bachelor's degree and 10 years of experience is $33,100 per year, well below the state's median household income of $49,091, and approximately the wages of a printing press operator in the state. Even at mid-career a South Dakota teacher supporting a family of four can potentially be eligible for seven government assistance programs.[36]

California's teacher shortage has increased in recent years and the state now has the highest teacher-student ratio in the nation. In the state of Washington, 45 percent of the state's principals reported they could not "fill all of the teacher positions in their schools with fully certified teachers who met job qualifications" and that the "burden of this shortage falls heavily on schools serving highly diverse, poverty-impacted students—schools where students already are more likely to be taught by less-experienced teachers."[37]

Were teachers not blamed for an array of failures, from the educational underachievement of poor children to the purported deficient workforce ruining the U.S. economy, perhaps by accepting the low pay that historically has been part of the "noble profession," the teaching shortage would be less. However, the castigation of teachers combined with a corporate-driven, government-mandated, vacuous curriculum harnessed with incessant testing has made teaching unsatisfying, stressful work. A 2013 MetLife teacher survey found that from 2008 to 2012 the percentage of teachers who felt "very satisfied" with their work plunged 23 percentage points, from 62 percent to 38 percent, the lowest level in twenty-five years. A "majority of teachers" reported feeling "under great stress at least several days a week, a significant increase from 1985, when this was last measured."[38]

Charter School Teacher Shortage

Nor can we look to charter schools to provide the educational conditions that will attract and retain teachers. At the premier charter school chain, the KIPP (Knowledge Is Power Program) schools, teachers stay an average of four years. Although charter schools have disputed teacher attrition figures, even their calculations are high.[39] New York City charters, for example, calculate an attrition rate of 26 to 33 percent, "or one in three teachers, compared with traditional public school attrition rates of 13 to 16 percent."[40] Using the figures of the city's premier charter school, Success Academy (SA), roughly "one in three SA teachers (32.8 percent) either switched to a different (non-SA) school, in New York City or elsewhere, or exited the teaching profession entirely."[41]

In other parts of the country, attrition is similarly high. In Texas, "the average teacher turnover rate for charter school districts was 46 percent, compared with 13 percent for traditional school districts."[42] At the Houston YES Prep network of thirteen charter schools, the average classroom teacher stays about 2½ years.[43] In Colorado, the Charter School Institute, which has thirty-four charter schools throughout the state, had a 36 percent turnover rate in 2014–15, albeit an improvement from 48 percent in 2013–14.[44] A 2015 Florida study found that the state's charter schools had a within-school-year attrition rate of roughly 10 percent, "more than twice" the approximately 4 percent at traditional public schools.[45] Combining charter schools' within- and end-of academic-year teacher departures, the national turnover rate was at least 20 to 25 percent a year.[46]

Brian Harris, the president of the Alliance of Charter Teachers and Staff, a Chicago-based union affiliated with the American Federation of Teachers, argues that given the nature of teachers' work (or, overwork) at charters, high turnover rates are, in fact, expected because they use an industrial employment model favored by factory owners in the past: use up workers, pay them little, and replace them. [47] In today's charters, the work hours are long—"as high as 60 to 80 hours per week"—and intense, and the salaries are low.[48] Not surprisingly, a study of teacher satisfaction in charter schools in Georgia found that the teachers "are less satisfied with their jobs than teachers in traditional public schools," with teachers in for-profit managed charter schools being the least satisfied.[49] In contrast, a high satisfaction rate was found for teachers in a charter chain on the U.S. East Coast, but at the same time 57 percent of these teachers "said they could not envision themselves having long-term careers" at charter schools. The charter chain's co-CEO acknowledged that a "high workload, teaching that was emotionally and physically draining," a longer workday, and an extended school year deterred teachers from long-term employment in the charters.[50]

Charter school teacher-turnover rates have also been affected by charter school reliance on the Teach for America (TFA) program, in which college graduates receive five weeks of summer training and then teach in schools with poor, high-needs students. Better named "Teachers for Awhile," participants tend not to remain beyond their two-year commitment, most assuming that the job is a transient occupation in a move onto something else, perhaps graduate school or a better job. The title of one article, "Most Teach For America Instructors Plan to Flee Teaching," nicely sums up the reality of the extent to which TFA will answer the need for quality teaching in charters or public schools.[51]

Is There Really a Teacher Shortage?

Those who criticize the claims that there is a nationwide teacher shortage insist that, contrary to alarmist misreadings of the data, there are sufficient numbers of teachers in the nation's schools, overall class size is fine, and claims of overcrowded classes are "exaggerated,"[52] particularly because some states have no overcrowded classes at all.[53] When we calculate teacher-student ratios—that is, count the number of educators and students in a school system or at the state or national level—it strongly undercuts teacher shortage claims and concomitant demands to increase school spending. According to the U.S. Department of Education, teacher-student ratios have been about the same—1:16 or 17—for the last three decades. Yes, in 2015, the ratio was 1:16, which was higher than the record low of 1:15.3 in 2008, but nonetheless it was better than 1:17.9 in 1985, and much, much better than the 1:26.9 ratio in 1955, one of the years in which the American Dream was occurring.[54]

The problem with such statistics is that, although the 2015 teacher-student ratio seems pretty good in relation to previous years, it is misleading because it has nothing to do with class size. Rather than basing class-size figures on the number of students taught by individual teachers in a classroom or a course, teacher-student ratio includes the number of "full-time equivalent" (FTE) instructional staff employed by a school or school district. The FTE formula could include special education teachers, librarians, speech therapists, art teachers, second language teachers, part-time teachers (two half-time teachers equals one FTE), along with, of course, classroom grade teachers. Consequently, a student-teacher ratio of 10:1 represents ten students for an aggregate FTE, a very misleading representation of class size. That is, when the FTE calculation is compared with appraisals based on a single teacher in a classroom of students, "the difference between student-teacher ratio and average class size is 9 or 10 students."[55] In other words, using the FTE formula, a teacher-student ratio of 15 in a grade would typically translate to an actual average class size of 25 or 26 students in that grade. Moreover, "average" does not depict the variation of class size across a school district, city, or state, or by the wealth or poverty of a community.

Swelling Class Size

Summing up the national phenomenon of increased class size, the *New York Times* reported:

> Millions of public school students across the nation are seeing their class sizes swell because of budget cuts and teacher layoffs, undermining a decades-long push by parents, administrators and policy makers to shrink class sizes. Over the past two years, California, Georgia, Nevada, Ohio, Utah and Wisconsin have loosened legal restrictions on class size. And Idaho and Texas are debating whether to fit more students in classrooms.[56]

When we look more closely at some of the class size reductions many states and communities are trying to achieve, we see the formidable barriers faced in educating countless young Americans. In the Los Angeles school district, where classrooms can exceed forty students, the goal of reducing overcrowded high school classes has been to reach a ratio of thirty-five students-to-one-teacher.[57] In New York City the teacher's union reported class-size progress in 2015 when overcrowded classrooms in city schools dropped by 15 percent, an achievement that went from 6,447 overcrowded classrooms in 2014 to 5,485 classes in 2015, the lowest overcrowded size in recent years! This reduction still left 3,400 high school classes exceeding the thirty-four students permitted in the teacher's contract, while more than 2,000 elementary and middle schools exceeded the twenty-five to thirty-three students range.[58]

Class Size Research

If there were one educational reform, backed by a substantial body of research, in which corporate America could put its money for advancing educational outcomes, it would be small class size. The evidence that this single reform significantly improves academic achievement, especially for students injured by poverty and racism, comes from a considerable body of research, begun in the mid-1970s with a series of studies named Project STAR (Student/Teacher Achievement Ratio). This research compared students in three kinds of classes: small classes (thirteen to seventeen students) with a single teacher; regular-sized classes (twenty-one to twenty-five students) with a single teacher; and regular-sized classes with a teacher and a teacher's aide.[59] (It should be noted that by the standards of many of today's schools, twenty-one and twenty-five students in a classroom would be regarded as "small"!)

At the end of first grade, youngsters who had been in small classes had reading achievement scores two months ahead of the students in regular classes without an aide, and one month ahead of students in regular-sized classes with an aide. Thus, even when a regular classroom was augmented with a teacher's aide, small classes proved superior in promoting literacy achievement. Through third grade, students in small classes continued to score significantly higher in reading and math than did students in the other two class sizes, whether compared by community (rural, urban, inner-city, suburban) or by race.

White students scored on average higher than minority students in reading and math, but minority children in small groups had scores within or near the range of scores for white children, and minority students in small classes always outscored the minority students in regular and regular/aide classes. Overall, minority children in small classes had a pass rate of 64 percent on a reading test, compared with minority children's average pass rate of 45.4 percent in regular and regular/aide classes. In suburban schools, 74.7 percent of minority children in small classes passed the reading test, compared with 53.1 percent in other class sizes. Clearly, the researchers concluded, "few well-defined interventions have shown as consistent an impact as this one on the performance of minority students in inner-city settings, not to mention both their minority and non-minority peers in other settings."[60] Would small classes be the answer to the underachievement of minority students? Although the answer is "No," the achievement differences in this research demonstrate that small class size would have a substantial educational impact.

When Project Star pupils returned to regular-sized classes in fourth grade, a follow-up study, named "Lasting Benefits," tracked their progress and found that in every grade through the eighth, students from Project STAR small classes "showed clear, consistent and statistically significant advantages over Project STAR students from the other two" class-size arrangements. Superior academic achievement held not only in reading and math, the two areas tested throughout STAR, but in spelling, science, and social studies, all areas tested from grade four onward.

A third phase of this extended research was Project Challenge, an application of Project STAR in Tennessee's poorest counties, in which the average rankings of the Challenge school systems were compared within the rankings of the state's 138 school system. Among the latter, "a ranking of 90 would be below average" (not so good), and "a ranking of 69 would be average," that is, in the exact middle of the 138 school systems, and a ranking of 50 would be closer to the top and therefore "above average" (good). During the four years of Project Challenge, the small-class second-grade pupils in these poorest counties continued to move upward in the rankings. In reading they went from a ranking of 98.9 to 78.5 over the four years and in math the respective rankings were 85.2 to 56.6. In addition to the academic benefits in the face of poverty's undermining effects, later research found that the benefits of early grades' small classes extending through high school course selection, high school graduation/dropout rates, and college entrance, particularly for low-income students and for reducing the black/white gap.

Why Do Smaller Classes Make a Difference?

Reduced class size makes possible instruction that might not be unique but is not easily done in larger classes. For instance, a study of Project STAR's "effective teachers"—teachers whose students ranked in the top 15 percent of largest achievement gains in reading and mathematics—revealed many qualities that could reasonably be expected of all effective teachers, regardless of their teaching conditions. These teachers closely monitored student learning progress; when students did not learn, teachers used alternative strategies in teaching; they had high expectations for student learning; they were enthusiastic; they had a sense of humor that promoted learning; they had a love for children; they used a broad range of resources and activities; and they had excellent personal interactions with their students. Again, these are not phenomenal qualities for teachers, yet of fifty "effective" teachers, *only three had large classes.*

After more years of research on the question of whether small class size improves learning, class-size researchers Jeremy Finn and Michelle Shanahan concluded that the answer not only is "unequivocally yes," but long-term research confirms that small classes in the early grades produce learning and behavioral benefits that extend into high school and college, with "the benefits for minority students as much as three times greater than the benefits to whites." Furthermore, small class learning is associated in adulthood with "increased employment and reduced resources needed for unemployment, welfare and health benefits, and even the costs of incarceration."[61]

Multibillionaire Bill Gates was, however, nonetheless unconvinced, arguing that education budgets must be kept down. Instead of trying to reduce class size, an erroneous policy "belief" that "has driven school budget increases for more than 50 years," he insisted that school systems should employ large classes instructed by very competent, well-paid teachers.[62] This alternative, Gates advised, would produce comparable, if not better, outcomes than in small classes. Gates appeared either not to know or to ignore the extensive research on the issue. He seemed ignorant of the conclusion that no evidence exists for claims that academic benefits are achieved through "exceptional teachers and large classes," and that three decades of studies document the gains and benefits from small-class instruction and learning. Regardless, laments the world's richest man and self-styled educational researcher, whose company, Microsoft, moves its vast profits offshore to avoid paying U.S. taxes, "You can't fund reforms without money and there is no more money."[63]

Corporate Tears but No Taxes

Parallel with corporate America's complaints about the failures of U.S. schools to meet business needs are the numerous corporate schemes that underfund U.S. education and thereby impair schools' ability to meet these purported needs. An analysis by Citizens for Tax Justice (CTJ) of 2008–10 state taxes found that the 265 largest companies, after raking in "a combined $1.33 trillion in profits," paid an average of 3 percent in state taxes, less than half the average state tax rate. Moreover, sixty-eight of the companies had paid no state corporate income tax in at least one of the three years studied, and twenty of the corporations averaged a tax rate of zero or less during this time period. In all, this corporate tax dodging came to $42.7 billion in lost state revenue over these three years.[64]

Extending its analysis from 2008 to 2012, CTJ found that the tax dodging continued, with these corporations depleting funds for education, among other public needs, by paying state income taxes of about 3.1 percent of their U.S. profits, again less than half the average statutory state corporate tax rate of about 6.25 percent. As CTJ explains, "At 6.25 percent average state corporate tax rate on the $2.3 trillion in U.S. profits that they reported to their shareholders, they would have paid $143 billion in state taxes. Instead, they paid $70.2 billion, thereby avoiding paying $73.1 billion over the five years."[65] Over this extended period even more corporations—ninety of the 269—were able, for at least one year, to avoid paying any state taxes.

While states across the nation are running deficits for education, public services, infrastructure and similar costs, the amount of taxes corporations avoid paying represent almost twice the total of reported state deficits. Though California, for example, has been cutting educational spending, "three of the largest and most visible companies (Google, Intel, Wells Fargo) paid just 1.6 percent of their profits in state taxes, less than 1/5 of the required rate." While the Chicago schools are firing teachers and support staff, "10 companies underpaid Illinois $1.4 billion in 2014, more than the entire 2016 Chicago school system deficit."[66]

For corporate America, state budgets are a genuine, hard-nosed issue. Again, quoting its chief corporate representative on educational matters, Bill Gates: "We need to care about state budgets," because "the bottom line is . . . they're critical for our kids and our future." But what is the underlying problem? It is unbalanced "state budgets," he explains, states not taking in as much money as they are spending, that are "breaking U.S. schools."[67] Nowhere in his rebuke does he mention corporate dodging of state income taxes. Nor does he have anything to say about the tax dodging of Microsoft, in which Gates continues to play a prominent role in steering the company as "founder and technology advisor" on Microsoft's board of directors.[68]

Microsoft's estimated tax contribution to schooling and related social needs, were the company's profits not placed in low-tax havens, would be approximately $35 billion.[69]

Corporate Helpers

Corporate tax dodgers do not work alone. Rather, they require a helping hand—a BIG helping hand—from government, the societal entity with which capitalism has a love-hate relationship. While business think tanks such as the Heritage Foundation rail against "big government," the reality is that capitalism and its corporate tax dodgers depend heavily on, and in fact, love "big government." With respect to the "global economy," for example, as economists Leo Panitch and Sam Gindin explain, government is in the center of global capitalism, as it has been for the operation of capitalism generally. Whether the issue is "maintaining property rights, overseeing contracts, reproducing class relations, or containing crises," government "has always been central to the operation of capitalism." For U.S. multinational companies, the U.S. government "has played an exceptional role in creating a fully global capitalism, coordinating its management" and fashioning the assistance of other governments.[70]

Corporate tax dodging doesn't come cheap, but compared with what corporations save in taxes, the millions corporations spend on getting legislators to craft tax-dodging legislation, they are amply repaid with vastly greater millions and billions in financial returns. For example, the *Boston Globe* calculated:

> By investing just $1.8 million over two years in payments for Washington lobbyists, Whirlpool secured the renewal of lucrative energy tax credits for making high-efficiency appliances that it estimates will be worth a combined $120 million for 2012 and 2013. Such breaks have helped the company keep its total tax expenses below zero in recent years. The return on that lobbying investment: about 6,700 percent.[71]

Other multinational companies and banks successfully lobbied for and "won tax breaks collectively worth $11 billion—a return on their two-year lobbying investment of at least 8,200 percent." Among these major corporations, Bill Gates's Microsoft leads all others with tax lobbying efforts that were enough, in the words of the Center for Responsive Politics, to make an "accountant's head spin."[72]

Whether corporate tax lobbyists represent specific companies or business associations, such as the U.S. Chamber of Commerce, their donation pockets are deeper and their numbers far greater than those of representatives of organizations promoting tax reform bills to stop corporate tax abuses. Consequently, legislation in Congress that would address tax loopholes and raise revenue, and thereby provide more potential funding for education, are subject to lobbying efforts that are overwhelmingly lopsided in favor of industry's interests.[73]

"Corporate Citizenship"

Between 2008 and 2012, 288 major corporations paid an effective federal income tax rate of just 19.4 percent, a bit more than half of the statutory 35 percent tax rate. This represents a significant average evasion rate, but many corporations did much better than that. For example, despite Boeing's claims in its *Corporate Citizenship Report* that the company is "investing in access to quality" education, Boeing, along with twenty-five other major corporations, such as General Electric and Verizon, paid no federal income tax at all over the five-year period. Behind them were 111—nearly 40 percent—that had at least one good year in which they paid zero or less in federal income taxes. Corporate citizenship was slightly better for about one-third (ninety-three), who paid a tax rate of a bit under ten percent, but of course still much closer to zero than to the 35 percent statutory corporate tax rate.[74]

These tax rates are similar to the average federal taxes of 12.6 percent that corporations as a whole actually pay, according to the U.S. Government Accountability Office (GAO). Looking at tax evasion another way, while U.S corporate profits as a share of the economy have been at a fifty-year high, the federal taxes corporations paid as a share of the economy have been at a fifty-year low. Corporations argue that they pay taxes throughout the world, but the GAO found that "even when foreign, state, and local taxes were included, the tax rate of large companies rose only to 16.9 percent of total income, still well below the official 35 percent."[75]

Criticize Here, but Keep Money Over There

As corporations criticize U.S. public education a common method of corporate tax evasion contributes mightily to inadequate funding of schools and ameliorating child poverty. This is the stashing of corporate profits overseas in no-tax or very-low-tax places like Bermuda, the Cayman Islands, and the Bahamas, where a U.S. corporation's purported subsidiary company often is no more than a post office box. CTJ reported that the top U.S. corporations in the Fortune 500 have avoided paying "up to $695 billion in U.S. federal income taxes by holding $2.4 trillion" of profits in various offshore tax havens, where tax rates are 10 percent or less. Examination of corporate tax filings in these countries showed that the reported U.S. corporate earnings were an outrageous "16 times the gross domestic product of each of those countries, which is clearly impossible."[76]

At the same time, right-wing think tanks like the Heritage Foundation charge that U.S. businesses are overtaxed compared with businesses in other countries in the "developed world," and that this excessive taxation has been costing America "jobs and higher wages."[77] Ignored by Heritage are the tax facts, such as those contained in a study by the Organization for Economic Cooperation and Development. Rather than being ground down by a tax millstone, U.S. businesses pay the eighth-lowest corporate taxes among thirty-three developed countries as measured by taxes paid as a share of the countries' Gross Domestic Product (the total value of a country's total yearly economic output of final goods and services). For example, while the U.S. corporate taxes are 2.0 percent of GDP, Norway's are

8.5 percent, Australia's are 5.2 percent, and the average of all the countries is 2.9 percent, a third higher than those paid by the "overtaxed" U.S. corporations.[78]

Charter School Funders: Spend Some, Hoard a Lot

In addition to corporations avoiding paying taxes and thereby withholding funds needed to improve U.S. schools and student achievement, another way to look at corporate indifference to the well-being of U.S. schools and youth is through corporate funding of charter schools, which claim to prove poverty cannot be an excuse for academic failure. No doubt, these certainties impel corporate funders to give to charters while withholding money from the public treasury that could go for public schools and alleviating child poverty.

A prominent example of corporate so-called good works is funding of the KIPP (Knowledge Is Power Program) charter schools. Enroll students from economically impoverished backgrounds in a no-excuses charter like one of KIPP's nearly two hundred schools and, say KIPP advocates, their chances of academic success will soar. In a KIPP school, hunger, poor health, relentless stress, lack of access to educationally enriching experiences, and many other harmful effects of poverty are rejected as impediments to learning and the attainment of good test scores. Given that poor youngsters in KIPP schools are supposed to flourish academically, it follows that if all economically poor students were in no-excuses KIPP and similar charter schools and not in every-kind-of-excuse-for-failure public schools, educational success would be theirs.

At least that is what corporate funders of charters maintain. However, if we step away from the clamor to a quiet reading of the research, we find no evidence that KIPP students or other charter school students perform any better than public school students.[79] Supporting this conclusion is research purportedly documenting KIPP's superior outcomes. These investigations have been funded by corporate funders of KIPP schools and therefore, from the start, raise serious issues of conflict of interest and objectivity. I will put this issue aside, however, when examining what the research tells us about KIPP versus public school funding. Education policy researcher Bruce Baker and colleagues, who have closely reviewed the comparisons between the two kinds of schools, are dubious about outcomes because KIPP schools have considerably greater financial resources than do public schools—thanks to corporate funders—financial resources that translate into "lots of additional time (and time is money) and reasonable class sizes."[80]

Supporting the conclusion about funding differences is the work of Matthew Di Carlo of the Albert Shanker Institute, who calculated the differences in middle school (grades 6–8) spending between public and charter schools, and concluded that to achieve comparable funding, New York City middle school students would require an additional $688 million ($4,300 per pupil x 160,000 pupils) to equal funding for their charter middle school peers. Similarly, in Houston, the 36,000 middle school students would need to receive about $2,000 per pupil, requiring an additional $72 million in the public school budget.[81]

Yet even with additional spending, KIPP schooling has been far from uniformly beneficial to students. As education researcher Jim Horn notes, the KIPP-funded studies found that of thirty-seven KIPP middle schools, just a little less than half (49 percent, eighteen schools) had "positive and statistically significant impacts in both math and reading"; approximately 25 percent (nine schools) had a "positive and statistically significant impact" *in just one (not both) of the subjects; 22 percent (8 schools) had no statistically significant impacts in either subject*; and two schools *had negative impacts in one or both subjects.* These are not exactly stellar outcomes. Similarly, Horn explains, of the eight KIPP elementary schools studied, *just three of the schools had a "positive and statistically significant impact" over public schools in "at least one measure of academic achievement"; two schools had marginally significant positive impacts on one subject; and three schools had "no statistically significant impacts" in either subject* (my emphases). Furthermore, attrition rates were high: over half of the students who started KIPP in 5th grade never finished 8th grade at KIPP. Nor has the achievement trajectory kept pace with the growth of KIPP schools. For example, Horn found that as the number of KIPP middle schools expanded between 2005 and 2014, test scores in reading and math had "a decidedly downward trend in KIPP's ability to raise test scores." In other words, KIPP schools' academic impact, especially for reading, has declined inversely with the increased number of KIPP schools from about 40 to 140. All of KIPP's underachievement has occurred despite KIPP's contrivances to encourage the enrollment of more promising students, such as the use of lotteries that, in turn, reflect parental self-selection associated with familial influences that promote better academic achievement.[82]

Finally, these research findings reveal that KIPP's academic outcomes are similar to the findings from other comparisons of charter and public schools. That is, ample evidence supports the conclusion that there is no difference in academic outcomes between the two forms of schooling, with some research concluding that public schools have better standardized test results.[83]

Corporate Supporters of KIPP

While corporations blame U.S. public schools for not supplying enough skilled workers to meet their new workforce needs, and concomitantly blame public schools for the low pay, unemployment, and difficult lives of purportedly underskilled workers, U.S. corporations evade, in every way possible, paying taxes essential for adequately supporting schools and bolstering academic outcomes. As part of this corporate hocus-pocus, charter schools have been an essential part of a corporate scheme that (a) criticizes public education; (b) praises charter schools as effective free-market alternatives and answers to business and worker needs; and (c) provides millions for the charters, formidable amounts of corporate money in the eyes of most people, but chump change for the donors who withhold billions in taxes from reaching schools, children and their families. The following review of prominent KIPP donors provides a graphic illustration of this strategy, as well as the morality associated with amassing of these billions, a morality not likely discussed in the KIPP curriculum.

Doris and Donald Fischer Fund

In the top group of KIPP donors ($60 million and above) is the initial funder of the schools, the Doris and Donald Fischer Fund, run by founders of The Gap clothing store chain. Although their philanthropy has been directed at the "underserved," neither the Fischers nor KIPP administrators and supporters appear to have any concern about how these philanthropic billions have been immorally amassed on the backs of the underserved in various parts of the world. In Gap sweatshop factories in Bangladesh, workers, many of whom are parents trying to care for their own children, "earn just 20 to 24 cents per hour, are routinely forced to work 14- to 17-plus-hour shifts, seven days a week, often putting in workweeks of over 100 hours, while being shortchanged of their legal wages—which are already well below subsistence levels."[84] KIPP philanthropy money for youngsters has also been accumulated in India, where child workers, some as young as ten, have produced Gap clothing in textile factories "in conditions close to slavery."[85]

Expressing a key motivation of many philanthropists, Donald Fischer wrote in his 2002 memoir, "Philanthropy is a good investment, as far as taxes are concerned" because philanthropic foundations provide tax shelters.[86] Serving as an example of how to keep money away from the public good, except as he defines the latter, the Fischers, in 2004, transferred half their stock to their son, in order to lower paying estate taxes through a method the IRS opposes.[87]

Walmart

Alongside the Fischer Fund in the top KIPP donors group, called "National Partners," is the Walmart Family Foundation, representing the six Walmart heirs who compose the wealthiest family in America, with a net worth of $130 billion in 2016. Collectively, these six Waltons have more wealth than 40 percent of American families. From these many billions, the foundation has, over several years, given KIPP a few million a year. As of 2018, this adds up to more than $60 million (the KIPP website provides donation ranges, not specific amounts.). Helping the Waltons make this contribution has been their tax avoidance at the state and local level through various tax abatements and economic development schemes.[88]

In turn, not only does Walmart avoid paying taxes, its "army of lawyers and consultants [who] systematically challenge property tax assessments to chip away at its property tax bills" costs taxpayers large amounts of legal expenses trying to combat the Walmart challenges. Taxpayers have also given the Waltons much more than the family has given to taxpayers or KIPP. Walmart has had to fund its tax avoidance efforts, but the approximately $10 million spent each year to lobby Congress is well worth it. In return, Americans for Tax Fairness calculated that Walmart and the Walton family have been avoiding paying taxes of about $1 billion a year through various tax breaks and loopholes, and have obtained more than $7.8 billion a year through taxpayer subsidies coming from public assistance programs, such as the food stamp program, which low-wage Walmart workers need to survive and support children.[89]

Broad Foundation

Back in 1996, Eli Broad, a $10–$25 million KIPP donor, whose current net worth is $7.7 billion, displayed his acumen for keeping profits away from the onerous tax collector.[90] Working with Wall Street bankers, Broad "lock[ed] in $194 million in profits on some of his SunAmerica stock" and contrived not to "owe a penny" of an "estimated $54 million in taxes" (worth about $85 million in 2018). When concluding the deal, Broad said "with a chuckle . . . 'We have our cake and are eating it too.'" This gastronomical-like tax manipulation, as one tax analyst put it, was not unusual, but was available not to the average citizen but "only to the wealthy few."[91]

Broad's anti-tax chuckles have continued into the twenty-first century. In 2013, he was identified as one of a group of "campaign donors who secretly . . . opposed a desperately needed tax increase on . . . the California ballot."[92] Rather than contributing tax money for the public good, Broad prefers philanthropy because, he maintains, philanthropic billionaires know best what will benefit the public: "Smart, entrepreneurial philanthropists," Broad insisted, are the preferred vehicle for providing the public good much better than if their money went to taxes for publicly elected officials (i.e., the "government") to spend, because these philanthropists know how to "get greater value for how they invest their money than if the government were doing it."[93]

On the other hand, Broad is not opposed to billionaires such as himself benefiting mightily from public taxes obtained when government knows what it's doing to serve the rich. For example, he was able to obtain $52 million from the Los Angeles Community Redevelopment Agency (CRA) for a parking lot for one of his buildings that will serve both as a museum to house his art collection and as office space for his foundation. While Broad obtained these millions, the *L.A. Weekly* calculated[94] that the public good, in comparison, did not do so well:

- "All of South Los Angeles, population 550,000, where unemployment among young minorities is said to exceed 30 percent, would get just $32 million from the CRA—$20 million less than Broad would get for his garage."
- "Watts, devastated by the recession, would get only $5.5 million from the CRA."
- "Eli Broad's $52 million could pay for health insurance for 52,000 California children who do not qualify for Medi-Cal. Run that math past a parent who doesn't have insurance for a sick kid."
- While Los Angeles contributed millions for the parking lot, the "cash-strapped"[95] city was "having trouble hiring cops and keeping fire stations manned."

Dell Foundation

The Dell computer company is owned by Michael Dell, whose

estimated wealth of $20.3 billion in 2017 put him at No. 46 in the *Forbes* list of "richest people,"[96] thereby making his KIPP donation of $10–$25 million quite affordable. Like many other corporations, Dell is skilled at stashing billions in profit out of public reach. By claiming that the company had "earned only 11 percent of its pretax profits in the U.S.," even though Dell reported that its U.S. revenues were "more than half of its worldwide total," Dell was able to pay just 6.9 percent in taxes for its purported "foreign" profits.[97]

One might think that Michael Dell, with his many billions and apparent interest in education, would not try to avoid paying taxes related to funding schools. But not Dell, who avoided California taxes by using a commercial property loophole in the state's Proposition 13, a property tax amendment supposedly meant to protect home-owners from skyrocketing tax increases, but which had the effect of cutting school funding nearly in half.[98] After buying a California hotel in 2006 and figuring out that Proposition 13 allowed "businesses to sidestep reassessment if no one acquires a majority stake in a com-pany that owns the property," Dell used the loophole to split the sale with his wife and two investment advisors, "so that no one owned more than 49 percent of the property." This kept the property taxed on its 1999 property value, resulting in a savings of about $1 million a year in state taxes. In recognition of this slick financial manipulation, *Los Angeles Times* reporter Jon Healey suggested that Proposition 13 should be called "Michael's Law."[99] Cleverly avoiding these state taxes that could have gone to California schools, Dell helped ensure that in 2006 there was no dip in his wealth of $17.1 billion.[100]

Robertson Foundation

KIPP contributions from hedge fund manager Julian H. Robertson, Jr.'s foundation are in the $10 million to $25 million range.[101] In its concern for a wide range of issues, the foundation's focus has included "solutions," but it is not clear how Robertson felt about having an assistant employ dazzling STEM skills in math, computer use, and spatial reasoning to prevent New York City from collecting $27 million in foundation taxes in 2000.

Robertson's scheme was this: after buying an apartment in the city in 1996, advisors warned him that to prevent being taxed as a resident, he should not spend more than 183 days there. To do so, Robertson assigned his "executive assistant to track his days and warn him when [Robertson] was using up days too quickly or nearing the 183-day limit."[102] The assistant scheduled Robertson's appointments and maintained a computerized record of Robertson's whereabouts, carefully distinguishing between "NYC days" and "non-NYC days."[103] For this head-spinning assignment, different colored boxes distinguished between confirmed and anticipated non-New York City days. Whenever the combined number of days fell below 183, the assistant advised Robinson to add more non-New York City days to his schedule. On Friday nights, Robertson usually left the city before midnight to avoid "wasting," that is, earning a tax day on Saturday. If his driver or limousine service could not be scheduled to get him out of the city before the Witching Hour, Robertson would hail a cab for his escape.

A court decision in 2010 hinged on a dispute over whether he was technically "in" the city when his private jet landed at LaGuardia Airport—late at night one day versus early morning the following day, and whether he was "in" the city if his plane was just passing through LaGuardia—with two of three judges ruling in his favor. Following the legal victory, Robertson's lawyer proclaimed his client "a man of great integrity," who would not pay the taxes as a matter of principle.[104] That integrity contributed to the underfunding of the city's schools and other public services at the time, but by running in and out of New York City throughout the year, Robertson helped expand his net worth to $3.8 billion in 2017 and raise his rank to 174 on *Forbes*'s list of the top 400 billionaires.[105]

Atlantic Foundation

"Chuck hates taxes. He believes people can do more with money than governments can." So said a friend of billionaire Charles Feeney, creator of the Atlantic Foundation, which has contributed to KIPP in the $10–$25 million range. In accord with his alleged hatred, Feeney made his billions by running duty-free shops that enable shoppers to avoid paying billions in taxes. Back in 1964, Feeney ran into tax laws that threatened his business and risked putting him in jail. To beat the tax laws and taxes, he and his partner transferred ownership to their foreign-born wives. A decade later, Feeney adroitly avoided taxes by stashing his money in the tax havens of Saipan and Bermuda, and further escaped U.S. taxes by keeping everything registered in his wife's name.[106]

Citi Foundation

The Citi Foundation, part of Citigroup, a multinational investment banking and financial services corporation formerly known as Citigroup, has given KIPP between $5 million and $10 million, a sum which, thanks to public taxpayers and corporate tax-dodging, it could easily afford. The taxpayer contributions came in 2008 through a publicly funded bailout of $2.5 trillion, following the start of the financial crisis. Indicating a pleasure in taxes flowing in one direction, parallel with and following the bailout, Citigroup employed a variety of tax avoidance schemes for itself and its clients. Unfortunately for Citigroup, these efforts were hindered in 2009 when it was fined $600,000 after the Financial Industry Regulatory Authority, a regulator of U.S. broker dealers, determined that Citigroup had helped clients "avoid paying billions of dollars of U.S. taxes."[107] Undeterred and continuing to look out for itself, Citigroup spent $6 million lobbying Congress and succeeded in 2012 in getting tax-evading legislation passed that benefited Citigroup by enabling the bank to hold more than $42 billion offshore,[108] thereby avoiding paying about $11.5 billion in taxes.[109]

In 2014, the federal government finally appeared to catch up to Citigroup's previous banking criminality by imposing a $7 billion penalty for the bank's mortgage practices that helped cause the 2008 financial collapse and recession. Of the $7 billion, $2.5 billion went toward "consumer relief," that is, toward helping homeowners with refinancing, loan modification, and principal reduction. Though the penalty was a large amount, within the context of the profits Citigroup made from those whom it bilked the sum was modest and insufficient, particularly because it was tax deductible. As the *Wall Street Journal* put it, "Citigroup to Get Tax Silver Lining in $7 Billion Settlement."[110] Moreover, Wall Street watchdog groups judged the terms of the settlement as falling short in the government's effort to hold banks accountable because "neither Citigroup nor any of its executives ha[d] been criminally charged for the bank's mortgage problems." With respect to the impact of Citigroup's illegal actions on well-being of American families and children, one member of an organization opposing home foreclosure observed, "Seven billion sounds like a lot, but compared to the number of families that lost their homes, it is not very much at all."[111]

Gates Foundation

The final example of KIPP donors is the Gates Foundation, whose cumulative donations range between $5 million to $10 million and whose tax avoidance has been extraordinary. For example, a U.S. Senate report documented a sophisticated Microsoft tax evasion system that reduced the company's taxes by billions. In 2011, it avoided paying $2.43 billion, which amounted to 44 percent of its legitimate tax bill, "by using a wide, international network of controlled foreign corporations and various loopholes in the U.S. corporate tax code."[112]

Though Bill Gates claims he pays all his personal taxes, Microsoft, "like other tax-avoiding technology giants such as Amazon, Facebook and Google, uses sophisticated systems to shift paper profits around the planet and evade the designs of governments." Remarkably, profits from Microsoft goods sold in the United States through a small office in Puerto Rico was then transformed into offshore profits, thereby saving the company $4.5 billion in taxes over three years. A Securities and Exchange Commission (SEC) study reported that Microsoft, by using this kind of offshore subsidiary manipulation, was holding "almost $29.6 billions it would owe in U.S. taxes if it repatriated the billions of earnings it is keeping offshore."[113]

Seattle Times reporter Matt Day outlined one of the transcontinental routes taken by money spent for a Microsoft product, a route that could serve as the basis for a good classroom geography lesson.[114] Following a purchase in a Microsoft store in Seattle, the money for the purchase took a short trip to Microsoft's company headquarters in nearby Redmond, Washington, after which the money went to a Microsoft sales subsidiary in Nevada. From there, the money zigzagged across the Atlantic through tax havens, finally arriving in sunny Bermuda where it joined Microsoft's $108 billion in offshore income. This kind of tax-avoidance arrangement was devised while Gates was the head of Microsoft and the company's largest individual stockholder, and the scheme has continued while Gates, although no longer officially running Microsoft, has approximately $13 billion in stock.[115]

Along with the classroom geography lesson that could be created by following the course of Microsoft's tax manipulation, the observation of business ethics professor Jeffrey Smith suggests Microsoft could also serve as a case study in standards of citizenship: One of the things we think of when we hear the word "citizenship" is meeting certain basic obligations. You could make a pretty tight case that if you're going to consider yourself a good citizen, you make sure you contribute your due to the system. Add to this the critique of tax scholar David Shaviro: "I don't think the people doing this [tax evasion] should be proud of themselves.[116]

Does Tax Avoidance Create Jobs?

I noted above that an argument made for lowering corporate taxes, such as that of the business coalition Reform America's Taxes Equitably (RATE) and of Donald Trump, is that lower business taxes would increase employment and, in turn, living standards for Americans. As RATE proclaims: "For more jobs, fix the corporate tax code" by cutting it in half.[117] Similarly, the Tax Foundation, a corporate organization that includes a Microsoft Director of Tax Affairs, asserted that cutting corporate taxes would "lead to higher wages."[118] Consequently, according to these and similar business groups, corporate tax reductions would translate into more financially thriving families.

Unfortunately for the job applicants, families, and children who purportedly are to benefit from lower corporate taxes, these self-serving claims of business organizations have never been supported by evidence. For example, in 2004 a "tax holiday" promisingly named the American Job Creation Act temporarily lowered corporate taxes on offshore profits.[119] Under the program, fifty-eight corporations saved $64 billion on their taxes while bringing $218 billion in profits back to the United States. Tax holiday supporters argued that the U.S. economy would increase by hundreds of billions of dollars which, in turn, as Verizon wrote to Congress, would lead to economic growth and "help create new jobs in the U.S." Regrettably for many workers and their families, that's not what happened. Instead, these fifty-eight companies eliminated 600,000 jobs! Among the companies that fired thousands of workers were those that supposedly made up the new "high-skills" global economy, such as Honeywell, Hewlett-Packard, General Electric, IBM, Microsoft, Intel, Eli Lilly, and Boston Scientific.

Further evidence on corporate tax reduction and job creation came from a study by the Center for Effective Government, which examined large corporations with the "highest and lowest effective tax rates between 2008 and 2012 to see how many jobs they created."[120] The fourteen corporations with the lowest tax rates eliminated "more than 63,000 jobs altogether, a 10.8 percent decline in their workforce over the five-year period." The term "lowest" is misleading because "these low-tax firms collectively reported $107 billion in pre-tax profits, yet none of them paid federal income taxes between 2008 and 2012." In contrast, the fourteen corporations that paid a third or more of their profits in taxes between 2008 and 2012 expanded their workforce by 12.7 percent.

A Canadian study drew similar conclusions about taxes and jobs.[121]

The country's corporate tax rate in recent years has been in the mid to low 20 percent range, down from 42 percent in the 1950s. These corporate tax cuts were supposed to free money for investment, but the opposite happened. "Despite several rounds of cuts in corporate income taxes, employment growth remained anemic" and low-paying jobs accounted for major proportion of Canadian job creation. What did the corporations that benefited most from the tax cuts do? Like their U.S. counterparts, they "increasingly stockpiled cash."

So much for the argument that low corporate taxes will lead to more jobs, which will lead to family well-being, which, in turn, will foster children's better engagement in and success from classroom teaching. Using the array of tax figures and corporate claims, educators could have considerable empirical material for critical thinking lessons in which students learn to distinguish between fact and fiction.

Get School Budget Money from the Poor

Finally, if money for public education is not coming from U.S. corporations in sufficient amounts, from where will it come? One answer across the nation has been to rely on a state lottery to help fund schools and to hail lottery spenders not as unwise, pie-in-the-sky gamblers but as noble societal participants benefiting schooling.[122] For example, the New York Lottery's mission statement asserts that its "sole mission is to earn revenue for education," suggesting that from the lottery players' pockets the revenue moves along to the education department. where it is added to the department's budget.[123]

Playing the lottery may appear to the lottery player to be like a contribution to a school bake sale, in which one's money is spent to supplement the school budget. However, money from a lottery is frequently used deceptively by state legislatures not as additional funding for education, but simply to pay for the education budget. In other words, lottery dollars substitute for "the money that would have been used had there been no lottery cash. . . . Public school budgets, as a result, haven't gotten a boost because of the lottery funding."[124]

According to O. Homer Erekson, dean of the business school at the University of Missouri in Kansas City and co-author of a study on lottery money and school financing, "Legislators merely substitute general revenue funds with lottery dollars so the schools don't really gain any additional funding."[125] Similarly, political scientist Patrick Pierce explains that even though there is a dramatic increase in education spending in the first year of a lottery, in subsequent years states without lotteries increase education spending more than states with lotteries.[126]

As everyone who has walked into a convenience store with a lottery counter knows, most lottery patrons do not come from the nation's 1 percent.[127] Rather, playing the lottery is a regressive form of funding mostly paid for by the poor, whose lottery spending often constitutes a disproportionately large part of their incomes, financed "primarily by a reduction in non-gambling expenditures," such as food, rent, mortgage payments, and other bills.[128] A national investigation found that adults who lived in communities with the highest economic "disadvantage had the highest number of days gambling on the lottery."[129] A Cornell University study found that "individuals falling just below the poverty line" make up the largest proportion of lottery sales because the economic anxiety created by poverty often translates to a desperate turning to lotteries in an effort to escape that poverty.[130]

Consequently, poor parents, who most need their meager incomes to support and advance their children's educational preparation and achievement, are enticed to become gamblers—all, according to lottery hype, in the cause of children's schooling—and thereby have even fewer funds for their children's well-being and education. When we compare this desperate spending with the many billions U.S. corporations hoard through an array of tax-dodging that avoids contributing to students' lives and education, the juxtaposition reveals that rather than "Mega-Millions," as state lotteries often are named, the better description would be "Mega-Macabre."

7. Fighting Back

Businesses feeding and profiting at the public tax trough have been a significant incentive driving the corporate attack on public education. Diane Ravitch, an admirable leading opponent of this attack, has rightly targeted educational "entrepreneurial opportunities,"[1] such as schools obtaining taxpayer money to purchase corporate-produced electronic and conventional instructional and testing materials, and taxpayer money providing the profits of business-run charter schools. Nonetheless, while moneymaking has been an important driver of the corporate attacks on and intrusions into schooling, the primary corporate impetus of this attack on the public schools, as argued throughout this book, has been to blame the nation's schools for the deteriorating lives and futures of many Americans. Consequently, when Ravitch identifies "poverty and racial segregation" and "inequitably resourced schools" as "root causes"[2] of educational underachievement, she is pointing to critical mediating, not root, causes. Similarly, the variety of "solutions" she cites, such as providing prenatal care, reducing class size, and eliminating high-stakes testing, racial segregation, and poverty, though all important issues to address, nonetheless fails to identify the root cause generating these problems.

That root cause is an economic system that has been profitable for corporations and the wealthy, but has decreased employment opportunities, income, and general well-being for vast numbers of Americans. As capitalism's profits have accelerated and the movement of wealth has steadily shifted upward, employment has grown increasingly precarious for U.S. workers.[3] While two-thirds believe their jobs are secure, approximately the same percentage is dissatisfied with the amount of money they earn, feel considerable on-the-job-stress, and are fearful about their future financial security. Beyond these full-time workers are millions working part-time because that is the only work they can obtain.[4]

This economic system continues to diminish its concern for the well-being of most Americans and people throughout the world, as demonstrated by the global outsourcing of production to obtain cheap labor; increased worker productivity alongside stagnant wages and expanded business profits; employment schemes that reduce job security and benefits; and corporate tax avoidance that harms education and reduces the number of good-paying government jobs—from road repair to firefighting—that contribute to public well-being.

In the United States, who is to blame for these deteriorating employment and living conditions? From the perspective of the businesses and financial institutions, it certainly is not them! Rather, it is the schools. Blame them for not preparing Americans for the new economy filled with well-paying STEM jobs that are unfilled because schools have not educated enough skilled applicants for these jobs.

A key corporate objective is to keep that refrain going while rejecting the reality that U.S. schools on the whole have been doing a very good job serving U.S. capitalism. As discussed in chapter 6, this multi-tiered school system, producing varied student outcomes that reflect the economic conditions in which the respective schools are located, provides enough STEM, middle, low, and unskilled workers for the economy's needs. Yes, the nation's schools serve capitalism quite well! Especially with respect to STEM employer needs, as noted in chapter 2, numerous studies have documented that the nation has no fundamental STEM worker shortage. The "shortages" businesses complain about have more to do with salary levels, geographic location, job security, and corporations wanting to employ H-1B workers at lower cost. There is no "shortage" due to U.S. job applicants lacking abilities to do skilled work. The reality for corporations is this: with enough applicants for the relatively minor numbers of STEM jobs and with non-STEM work projected to be the overwhelming U.S. employment for at least the next decade, why should capitalism fix what isn't broken?

Were the schools as a whole not serving the economy well, we can be certain that the nation's major corporations, such as Walmart, Dow Chemical, Goldman Sachs, Chevron, Microsoft, IBM, and Apple, would be focused on duplicating the best educational outcomes in STEM education by providing schools with additional tax funds from the more than a trillion dollars these corporations have stashed in offshore tax havens.[5] Similarly, were these corporations concerned that not enough poor children were being properly educated to meet employment needs, we should not doubt that some of these unpaid taxes would have made their way into these children's lives.

Given U.S. capitalism's control of the American economy, capitalism's educational needs are similarly served by ensuring that the nation's school achievement does not get out of hand; that is, schools become too successful in producing well-educated graduates for purported but nonexisting vast number of STEM jobs in the global economy. The corporate answer is simple. Just provide enough funds to maintain the educational system that currently serves the economy well; ensure that taxpayers fund most of the schooling serving businesses; do not fully fund schooling for those poor or marginally poor American youth whose futures will fit well with the present and future jobs that will be predominant in the economy, namely, fast food, simple service, basic health care, low-skilled factory work; maximize profit by not contributing more to the public good than is absolutely necessary for business needs; and pay workers as little as possible, maintaining that the work and wages are commensurate with their educational levels and skills. Finally, while withholding billions in taxes, corporations increasingly obtain the gratitude of many educators and parents by making financial contributions that, for these corporations, are a pittance compared with the taxes they keep from the public treasury.

Just as magicians accomplish their feats by misdirecting spectators' perception, attention, reasoning, and memory away from the cause of a magic effect, so too corporate ideological manipulations misdirect understanding of the predominant causes of people's occupational and financial problems. The corporate "weapon of mass distraction," one that has been ingrained in various national educational policies over recent decades, entices viewers to focus not on why the corporate-dominated economy has failed vast numbers of Americans, but on why the nation's schools are at fault.

Businesses Didn't Always Bash Schools

It is important to recognize that corporate bashing of schools is fairly new. Through most of the twentieth century, schools served capitalism well as "sorters" whose varying academic achievement outcomes explained the concomitant varying distribution of work, earnings, and class differences. As education historian Jeannie Oakes explained, in her 1985 book *Keeping Track: How Schools Structure Inequality*, the organization of schools from the early twentieth century onward was grounded in "curriculum differentiation—tracking and [IQ] ability grouping—with markedly different learnings for what were seen as markedly different groups of students."[6] During these decades, businesses did not blame schools for issuing the raw material for the distribution of work, earnings, and class outcomes within capitalism; rather, the distribution businesses regarded as making perfect sense.

However, as school tracking continued to be challenged and exposed as invalid, racist, and classist, sorting took another direction, one that has turned the IQ mental ability explanation on its head, with a new ideology known as "no excuses." Varying mental capacity is not the cause of varying academic achievement; rather, the variation derives from the excuses educators use to explain underachievement, particularly the excuse that poverty conditions adversely affect students' learning. Orchestrating much of the recent debate over student achievement and subsequent employment opportunities, "no excuses" posits rhetorical questions and answers for public school education, particularly the question, "Is poverty an 'excuse' for academic underachievement that actually is the fault of teachers?" For the corporate criticism of public schools, the answer is a loud, decisive "yes."

Educators Answer Back

Responding to these corporate attacks, educational organizations have maintained that the "no excuses" ideology actually excuses insufficient corporate support of public schools and indifference to poverty's effects on educational achievement. The National Education Association (NEA), for example, whose "3 million members work at every level of education—from pre-school to university graduate programs," making it the largest teacher organization, has taken on the corporate attack on schools by denouncing corporate tax avoidance schemes that hurt schools and "defund the American Dream."[7] Underscoring the plight of poor people and poverty's effects on child development and educational success, the NEA has called for "policies that offer affordable housing, food assistance, economic security" and "investing more money into policies that help people work and make a living wage with those that ensure the basic needs of children" and "help break the cycle of poverty."[8]

Similarly, the American Federation of Teachers, with its 1.6 million members, has fired back at the corporate assault on education. Its 2014 "State of the Union" report, for example, highlighted "the right-wing corporate and anti-union interests that want to eviscerate the power of American workers [and] use all means available to strip us and our members of rights." Making this connection was especially important, the AFT explained, because the corporate attack on public workers' unions has been framed for the public as "Why should your taxes go to pampering these indulged workers?" By linking the national corporate attack on teachers' organizations with the broader attack on working people's efforts to increase their united strength, the AFT stressed the importance of rejecting the corporate divide and conquer attack. The AFT has also criticized the corporate-backed politicians who work "to eviscerate unions" as part of their legislative efforts to preserve "a rigged, trickle-down economic system" that enables corporations to amass ever-greater wealth.

The attack on public education also has been opposed by grassroots organizations. Save Our Schools, for example, has called for equitable funding of schools, an end to high-stakes testing, "teacher, family, and community leadership in forming public education policies," and curricula "responsive to and inclusive of local school communities."[9] Similarly, Parents Across America has criticized school privatization, mass school closings, and "the deprofessionalism of teaching," while advocating for "child-centered" curricula, smaller class size, "a strong parent voice in school decision making, quality multiple assessments, adequate social services, and reduced class sizes."[10] Finally, there is the Network for Public Education, co-founded by educators Diane Ravitch and Anthony Cody, "an advocacy group whose mission is to preserve, promote, improve and strengthen public schools for both current and future generations of students." Like other grassroots organizations, the Network supports "a full, rich curriculum," resources for students' needs, "equitable funding of schools, with extra resources for those students with the greatest needs," small class size, early childhood education, and other reforms that would improve teaching and learning.[11]

Accepting and Supporting the Dominant Explanation

Organizational responses have demanded reforms that, if implemented, would substantially improve the educational outcomes of many students. The problem with these demands, however, as I underscored at the beginning of this chapter, is not that they are invalid, but that they fail to address two fundamental issues for U.S. capitalism: first, that U.S. schools are definitely meeting the employment needs of U.S. capitalism and, second, even if large numbers of students were to attain STEM educations, corporate America's inability to provide work for them would be revealed. Therefore, maintaining a vision of a national twenty-first-century occupational meritocracy, part of a global occupational meritocracy, in which schools are failing to provide the education that would prepare graduates for good-paying twenty-first-century STEM jobs is exactly what U.S. corporations require to divert understanding of what they will not provide. Regrettably, although educators are being blamed for failing the future of countless American youth, educators also have provided credence to the corporate narrative. AFT president Randi Weingarten summed it up in her pronouncement, "Today's public school teachers are on the front lines of our collective efforts to compete in a global economy."[12]

Describing the link between schooling and work, the AFT has employed the phrase "ladder of opportunity," conjuring an image of a connection between the economy's step-after-step employment "opportunities" and students' educational attainment that will place them on one ladder step or another. For example, criticizing inadequate state funding of education, the AFT has argued: "When school funding is truly equitable and provides disadvantaged students with the resources . . . to overcome the consequences of poverty, then we can say a state is doing all it can to help ensure a ladder of opportunity for all children."[13] Or, "Too many obstacles still stand in the way" of "children's health, safety and well-being" as the AFT fights "to ensure everyone can climb the ladder of opportunity."[14] Or, providing "all children with a high-quality public education" is a critical step for rebuilding the "ladder of opportunity to the middle class."[15] The image contains enough truth to seem valid because an upward progression of educational attainment can be conceived as rungs alongside a structure extending to ever-better occupational and income opportunities. Even if a person does not climb to the top, the ascent can be high enough to attain a decent occupational and material life.

Despite the AFT's good intention in using the phrase to criticize the corporate attack on schools for keeping many youngsters from climbing high on "the ladder," the term ignores how those who dominate the economy construct the actual conditions available at each rung, the economic levels of the rungs themselves, and the meaning of "opportunity." If, for example, someone gets only to the middle rungs or ascends beyond them to the top rungs, what work income, benefits, and security will be associated with the economic structural level alongside these rungs? "Opportunity" does not portray, for example, the increasing number of poorly paid, insecure jobs or the structures associated with ever-higher rungs, especially illustrated by the number of young college graduates who are stuck on levels of the economic structure considerably below the work and income to which they expected to ascend. Nor does "opportunity" help describe the too few jobs actually available for those who have ascended further up the ladder. The image is especially lacking in explaining that the rulers of the economy need to impede widespread educational acquisition precisely because the vast amount of work and income they associate with the ladder's upper rungs simply does not exist.

The NEA similarly reinforces the dominant corporate ideology about preparing students to compete for work in the global economy, explaining that "if the United States is to hold a competitive edge in a rapidly changing global workforce, bolstering the nation's science, technology, engineering and math (STEM) workforce is essential" and that the "NEA leads the way" with the expansion of its STEM education teaching program.[16]

Every Student Succeeds Act

Another example of NEA and AFT promotion of the corporate claim that schooling is the paramount determinant of well-being in the new economy is their support of the Obama administration's 2015 Every Student Succeeds Act (ESSA), legislation also supported by the Trump administration. The chief purpose of this law is to transfer education policy control to states to ensure that children, "regardless of race, income, background, or where they live, have the *chance* to make of their lives what they will" (my emphasis). However, the

Trump administration's version differs from Obama's by putting more policy power in the hands of governors and less in stakeholders, such as school boards, parents, and educators. Remarkably, the legislation is described not as aimed at helping ensure, but solely "to ensure" achieving the goal of giving all children "the chance to make of their lives what they will."[17] A serious reading of this legislative aim makes evident its total blather. Even with more years of schooling and study of certain courses, considering the varied and commonly bleak occupational conditions around the country, what "chance" is there that these youngsters will go on "*to make of their lives what they will*"? 2 percent? 15 percent? 80 percent? As for transferring educational policy power to states, what is the historical evidence for the educational and social benefits that are derived from that change?

Less enthralled with the act are educators Mary Battenfeld and Felicity Crawford, who applaud ESSE's corrections of some problems of No Child Left Behind (NCLB), such as ending yearly testing that requires schools to show test score gains or be penalized, and ESSE also providing grants for preschool programs for poor children. Nonetheless, Battenfeld and Crawford conclude, ESSE does not "vary radically from the accountability through testing' mandates that have marked federal education policy for the last 14 years." Most important, the legislation offers no anti-poverty legislation aimed at closing the achievement gap. An appeal of the legislation for many educators is the transfer of oversight of testing accountability from the federal government to the states, possibly making it easier for educational organizations to influence testing legislation. However, although this move to relatively more local oversight might seem appealing, Battenfeld and Crawford contend that the long history of the failure of many states to address educational inequality for "vulnerable children" suggests otherwise. Finally, the law will likely expand the number of charter schools, despite their failure to show superior academic outcomes compared with public schools. By supporting this legislation, the AFT and NEA support the prevailing corporate ideological assumption that schools are the institution that will "ensure" that all children have "the chance to make of their lives what they will."[18] Conversely, these educator organizations fail to explain to the public the relationship between the economy, work, and schooling, and where the onus for dim occupational futures of vast numbers of Americans should be placed.

Combatting the Corporate Attack

Educational organizations have an admirable record of fighting for school and classroom conditions that promote teaching and learning, and of combatting corporate-led attacks on teachers' salaries, working conditions, and purportedly cushy jobs funded by hardworking taxpayers. However, why have these organizations not confronted the reality that schooling is an institution within an economic system not run to provide for the well-being of all and that those ruling that economic system have made schooling the villain responsible for people's occupational and income problems? Why have these organizations allowed this corporate duplicity to occur without identifying, explaining, and denouncing it to Americans? Why have teacher organizations allowed their members to be identified as the chief villains harming their fellow workers and those aspiring to be workers? Unlike all other unions, educational organizations have had to contend not simply with accusations and attacks accusing teachers, especially those teaching poor children, of being incompetent and overpaid, but also of poorly serving the nation's workforce. Unfortunately, like other unions, the NEA and AFT have largely abandoned a broad class politics in favor of representing employees.

Similar to the rest of organized labor, teachers' organizations also have long accepted the economic system as a given and have functioned within it as agents negotiating wages, benefits, and working conditions. The latter, as I have discussed, have included calls for increased school funding, effective class size and teaching load, adequate curricula materials, and classroom infrastructure (room temperature, lighting, teaching equipment, furniture, etc.). However, teachers' organizations, by accepting capitalism as a given, cannot find a way to confront head-on the corporate attack in which schools are scapegoated for the failures of the economic system. Among labor unions they are not alone. As labor organizer Andrew Tillett-Saks has noted, the union strategy of accepting a fundamental bond with corporate overseers has been "self-defeating" for many decades and "it's unclear how bad it must get for labor [and educational organizations] to recognize the strategy's emptiness."[19]

In the 2016 presidential campaign, both the AFT and the NEA endorsed early in the 2015 Democratic primaries pro-charter schools candidate Hillary Clinton over anti-corporate, pro-labor, anti-charter schools candidate Bernie Sanders. With respect to the corporate "education to compete in the global economy" ideology, Clinton called for investment in computer science and STEM education that is "critical to our nation's success" and for "reducing economic and social inequality." "Strong STEM programming in every public school" is critical, she said, both "to our nation's success, and to reducing economic and social inequality." The United States needs to build a "human talent pipeline" for twenty-first-century jobs. This economy demands "more agile, adaptable, and technologically literate workers than ever before," she continued, workers who, whether in "early career, mid-career, and even late-career . . . can keep up with changes in technology and industry, and shift fields or move up in their fields." Hundreds of thousands of high-tech jobs, such as in computer science will be unfilled because the schools are not graduating enough young people with the "cutting-edge skills" to do this work, she emphasized. Sadly, the teachers' organizations stood ready to build the pipeline for the twenty-first-century jobs. Neither major education organization had anything to say about the fact that the nation's schools are already serving capitalism's employment needs.[20]

Were teachers' organizations to take the leadership in combating the corporate criticism of schools not producing the workforce needed in the global economy, they might put forth some of the arguments in the following sections.

The Worth of a Degree in STEM and Non-STEM Work

A common image conjured when schools are attacked for not providing students with the education that would ensure secure and comfortable future income levels is one comparing the earnings associated with a "professional degree" against earnings correlated with a high school diploma in 2016 ($1,730 versus $678) and the inverse unemployment rates (1.5 percent vs. 5.4 percent).[21] The comparison of the different schooling levels appears compelling, but educational organizations need to pose this question: If schools were to enable every student to graduate and get a professional degree would that mean there would be enough advanced skilled jobs to provide every college graduate with $1,730 a week? Of course not, and, additionally, an increasing pool of skilled applicants would inevitably result in decreasing wages. Educational organizations would also have to explain that, at present, even for college graduates in STEM areas, remuneration continues to decline because of crowdsourcing, employment available only to "independent contractors," and the use of outsourcing employment firms.

Schooling and Societal Needs

Educational organizations also need to raise the issue of the use and worth of education with respect to societal needs. For example, students skilled in music and other arts cannot find work, but not because there is no societal or individual need for these arts. In the past—for example, in the 1960s and 1970s—there was a fair amount of public money to fund the arts and the humanities because work in these areas was recognized as a fulfillment of personal and social needs. The elimination of this funding, in the name of building a society grounded in products and a narrow assemblage of business "services," was a policy choice made through narrow, profit-driven decisions about what counts in a society, not through full, ongoing discussions of human needs. Educational organizations must spearhead discussions around the full needs of individuals and society, and the work that nourishes these needs, such as aesthetic enrichment, which certainly should stand side by side with STEM-work satisfaction.

What Has Been Responsible for Good-Paying Jobs?

Educational organizations also need to explain that good-paying jobs are not solely a consequence of advanced education. Although skilled jobs (medicine. engineering, legal service) are associated with higher incomes, the large number of what have historically been called "good-paying jobs" associated with the middle class were largely a consequence of labor union organization and power, not advanced degrees or skills.

Looking back once more to the 1950s, one-in-three private-sector workers were in unions, a ratio that has dropped to one-in-twenty today, a decline in labor power that has been accompanied by a decline in wages and benefits for both unionized and non-unionized labor. Union workers help non-union workers, because businesses pay non-union workers more to keep unions out of their workplace. Again, this history reveals that it is the decline in labor's organized power, not insufficient STEM education, that has been the primary reason for the overall shrinkage of middle-class jobs in both size and pay over the last decades,[22] even in the manufacturing sector.[23] The decline of unions was not a natural phenomenon; it "did not just happen," economist Dean Baker stresses. Rather, it occurred through a "deliberate effort" by business interests to reduce the power of labor. We need only look at "Canada, a country with a very similar economy and culture," which has not experienced a comparable corporate attack and, therefore, has had "no comparable decline in unionization rates. Almost 30 percent of its labor force is still represented by unions."[24]

Considering this history, educational organizations must emphasize that unionized labor power is a major creator of *jobs that pay well*. This causation is, of course, the reason for the corporate attack to eliminate that power. The Economic Policy Institute calculates that when private-sector male union membership "fell from 34 percent in

1979 to just 10 percent in 2013," (in 2015 for all private sector workers it declined to 6.6 percent), wages and benefits declined for both
unionized and non-unionized male workers. For businesses, money
went in the opposite direction, with an annual gain of $109 billion![25]
(Comparable calculations for women are not available because they
were less unionized in 1979.)

Explain the U.S. Economy's Skilled and Other Labor

Meanwhile, U.S. corporations have little to say about the income,
benefits, and working conditions of non-STEM work done by an
increasing number of Americans. Home health care workers, representing "one of the nation's fastest-growing occupations," for example,
are "mostly women, mostly minorities," who had earned an average
of $10.11 an hour in 2015, *a 10-cent loss over the $10.21 per hour they
earned in 2005.*[26] With national surveys reporting that older people
overwhelmingly say they want to remain at home as they age, the
country will need at least 600,000 more home care workers by 2024,
almost double the 820,000 health aides currently employed. As one
New York Times economics reporter quipped, "As baby-boomers fade
into old age, we will be living in the United States of Home Health
Aides."[27] It is up to education organizations to highlight the reality
of the composition of the entire workforce, as suggested by the size
and employment conditions of this group of workers and the need to
provide good incomes for this essential, growing work.

Blaming Schools as Work Disappears

A close look at projections of the impact automation will have on
creating "extraneous" workers underscores why educational organizations cannot be timid in pushing back firmly against the criticism
about the failure of U.S. schools in the twenty-first-century economy.
Boston Consulting Group, a business and management research
organization, projects an accelerated advancement in manufacturing technologies—autonomous robots, digital manufacturing,

manufacturing machines that can communicate with one another—"making production systems more intelligent and highly networked" and thereby "reducing production costs."[28] As a consequence, these technologies could bring manufacturing back to the United States from overseas. This possible transfer home, however, *will not mean additional jobs* because the various technologies will have replaced much human labor.[29] The United States is not yet at the point where robots compose the majority of the blue-collar workforce, but as media professor Robert McChesney and journalist John Nichols project in their book, *People Get Ready*, the nation is moving toward an economy with more automation and fewer jobs of all kinds.[30] No doubt that as the nation moves toward this future, educational organizations will need to counter greater corporate criticism of schools for insufficiently educating the workforce that businesses need.

The Loss of Twentieth-Century Jobs

Moving away from a focus on twenty-first-century jobs, educational organizations must also stress the loss of twentieth-century jobs. These comprise police officers, teachers, firefighters, safety inspectors, and infrastructure maintenance workers, and similar other workers who have been and will remain critical to individual, family, and community health and happiness. The schools have been abundantly successful in educating for these jobs, which have declined largely because of the corporate attack on the public sphere. Not surprisingly, corporations have little to say about the success of the nation's schools in educating for jobs for the public good.

Corporate America's Worst Nightmare: Universal School Success

From my discussion of what is purported to be the chief aim of contemporary education—educating potential workers fully equipped to meet the needs of U.S. and global capitalism—it should be clear that the worst nightmare for corporate leaders and the rich would be universal school success, in which vast numbers of graduates were fully able to do the purported extraordinary number of STEM jobs said to be awaiting them in the grand global economy. Educational organizations must explain that, given the actual number of STEM jobs that presently exist and are projected for the future, if the schools were to produce qualified applicants to meet U.S. businesses' alleged employment needs, the job-seeking lines of qualified applicants would be stalled, and growing longer. In turn, other long lines would evolve for middle- and low-level jobs for which these overqualified STEM graduates would be forced to apply. These are the educational-economic realities that organizations must confront and help Americans transcend.

Study the Global Economy/Global Capitalism

Responding to the corporate attack on teachers and schools for failing to prepare a twenty-first-century workforce, educational organizations also must insist that if schools are charged with preparing students for work in the global economy, students should have to study the whole of that economy, its workings and impacts. Doing so, students need to go beyond an amorphous conception of businesses, inventions, product manufacturing and distribution, occupations, communication, and similar aspects contained within the boundaries of conventional definitions of the global economy.

Global economy curricula will differ among school districts, given the varied politics across the nation, with many states and communities adhering to conventional definitions, such as one devised by the Ohio Center for History, Art and Technology, whose corporate-friendly curriculum outline of "globalization" contains the following objective: "Students will understand the need for businesses to work globally and how product development and marketing may need to differ from region to region." Activities include having students

> visit the McDonald's and Coca-Cola Company websites . . .
> have students observe the changes that must be made to those
> brands when they are marketed overseas. . . . Give students

time to browse other companies that work globally and afterward discuss other products that could go global. . . . Place
students in groups and have them pick a product that they
would like to market globally. . . . Ask students if they can
think of any other products/companies working globally and
discuss how this might affect their branding and marketing.[31]

Alternatively, course curricula could and should include much
more, such as the global economy's distribution of wealth, its impact
on people around the world, especially on young people the same age
as the U.S. students studying the economy, and the global economy's
environmental effects. An array of classroom materials on globalization are readily available from human rights organizations, such as
Oxfam, which provides lesson plans on global manufacturing, the
beneficiaries of globalization, global working conditions, human
rights, wages and sweatshops, and similar topics on what is behind a
manufacturer's label.[32]

Another curriculum source is Cultural Connection, a "transdisci-
plinary and transnational team of educators," from the United States to
West Africa, that explores "the consequences of economic globalization on educational, health, food, linguistic, and economic systems."[33]
Based at Western Michigan University, Cultural Connection offers
curricula on globalization that includes student research and discussion on commodities that students own. Topics include:

- What do we know about each of the countries/regions where these
  objects were made?
- For those not made in the United States, why do you think these
  objects were made overseas?
- Who profits from these objects being made in another country
  but sold here?
- Who suffers or is exploited?
- Why do you think our economy is set up in this way?

Focusing on Senegal, for example, the Cultural Connection

curriculum helps students explore how, on the one hand, globalization has helped the poor make worldwide connections and increase
their knowledge through the accessibility of the Internet, newspapers,
and radio programming. On the other hand, students examine how
neoliberal financial institutions, such as the World Bank, through
loans to Senegal, have acquired considerable power in determining
and damaging Senegal's food production and market trade. More
broadly, other curricula units include the effect of globalization on
food access and security, hunger and malnutrition.[34]

Curricula on global capitalism can also draw on "the *New York
Times* Learning Network, which focuses on working conditions
in the Third World." Included in the Learning Network's lessons is
the classroom study question about the factory building collapse in
Bangladesh: "Do American companies have a responsibility to ensure
the health and safety of the workers who manufacture the clothing
they sell?" Another lesson asks students to pick and research a clothing manufacturer's record of labor and safety practices.[35]

As discussed in chapter 1, an exemplary curriculum text is
Rethinking Globalization: Teaching for Justice in An Unjust World,
"an extensive collection of readings and source material on critical
global issues." A publication of the teachers' activist group Rethinking
Schools, and edited by social studies teacher Bill Bigelow and fifth-
grade teacher Bob Peterson, the book is a collection of "background
readings, lesson plans, teaching articles, role plays and simulations,
student handouts, interviews, poems, cartoons, annotated resource
lists, and teaching ideas. It is curricular [material] without being a
curriculum." Readings span from the "history of colonial domination of much of the world," to current free trade agreements and
bank loans, such as from the World Bank, that have forced massive debt and external economic domination on poor countries.
Specific readings include "Debt: The New Colonialism," "The Lives
Behind the Labels," "Declaration of the Rights of the Child," "Oil,
Rainforests and Indigenous Cultures: A Role Play," "Global Warming:

The Environmental Issue from Hell," and Martin Luther King Jr.'s "A Revolution of Values."[36]

Rethinking Schools followed *Rethinking Globalism* with *A People's Curriculum for the Earth*, a volume of readings on the connection between the global environmental crisis and the global economy. As in the first volume, the editors acknowledge that this text is not "neutral." Addressing the issue of why "the future of life on Earth has been put at risk," they provide classroom readings and exercises that explore the connections between the "free market, the fossil fuels industries, and privatized decisions that affect life on Earth." While the volume enables students to "encounter and wrestle with multiple views," the study materials are grounded in a view of the general inseparability between Earth's climate and the "global economy," and the specific connection between the global environmental crisis and "the nature of global capitalism."[37]

Studying *about* the global economy would seem to be an obvious imperative for curricula aimed at educating *for* the global economy, a goal upon which educational organizations must insist. Of course, studying the global economy—global capitalism—is the last topic corporate powers governing that economy want in the curriculum, unless, as in the Ohio Center for History, Art and Technology activities, classroom work focuses narrowly and positively on capitalist production and marketing. This kind of curriculum constriction is a central reason for the corporate intrusion into schools that I discussed in chapter 4. In his book *Who Rules the World?* Noam Chomsky poses a question he maintains should be "foremost in the minds" of Americans: "What principles and values rule the world?"[38] For corporate "education benefactors" like *Project Lead the Way* and *Change the Equation*, or corporate "supporters" of schooling, like IBM, Chevron, and Dow Chemical, the question "What principles and values rule the world?" is precisely the topic their curriculum intrusions seek to prevent students from thoroughly exploring. To repeat Maxine Greene's observation quoted in chapter 5, the corporate mission is to derail students from imagining *"alternative visions of the world—visions of what might be, what ought to be."*

Conclusion

Will educational organizations take the leadership in explaining and confronting the fiction that "education to compete in the global economy" is the answer to the well-being of the American workforce and that corporations and the economic system, not schools, are responsible for the bleak futures of today's youth and the occupational and financial difficulties of an increasing number of Americans? And will these educational organizations also expose the reality that, because of the aforementioned fiction, corporations cannot possibly support the reforms that educational organizations demand?

Underscoring the need for funding that will provide schools with the best teachers, 2016 National Teacher of the Year Jahana Hayes rightly called for investment in education that will "give teachers the resources they need, to pay teachers the salaries they deserve because they are professionals; until that happens, we're not going to attract the best teachers."[39] Will educational organizations explain to Americans why these legitimate demands do not meet corporate interests and needs and, therefore, will never obtain corporate support?

A 2016 poll by the educational organization Phi Delta Kappan (PDK), asking adult Americans about the main goal of a public school education, found that adults were most concerned about their children's occupational futures and saw schooling as a chief path for that goal. While just 25 percent were extremely job focused, believing that "the main purpose of public schools is to prepare students for work," the majority of adults—68 percent—supported broader educational goals, but nevertheless thought public schools should "focus more on career-technical or skills-based classes" than on "more honors or advanced academic classes." Only 26 percent identified "citizenship" as schools' primary purpose.[40] Given the problematic reality of work in the United States, these parental concerns and desires are understandable, and are further reasons educational organizations must explain the realities of schooling and future work.

A measure of the need to expose the refashioning and deteriorating relationship between schooling and work can be seen in a comment made over fifty years ago by the radical college students who began Students for a Democratic Society. In its founding political declaration, known at the Port Huron Statement, adopted at SDS's first convention in 1962, the students observed, "The real function of the educational system—as opposed to its more rhetorical function of 'searching for truth'—is to impart the key information and styles that will help the student get by, modestly but comfortably, in the big society beyond." This association between schooling and the future is worth repeating: radical students in 1962 took for granted that schooling, narrow and indoctrinating as it was, would lead to good-paying, fairly secure jobs. Compared with today, the bleak educational perspective of young 1960s radicals, with its assumption of a post-school future of work availability and steady, decent incomes, now seems like nirvana.

Three years later, SDS leader Paul Potter, at an anti-Vietnam War demonstration in front of the Washington Monument, spoke more broadly about the system from which the immoral U.S. war was being waged. Potter exclaimed, "We must name that system. . . . We must name it, describe it, analyze it, understand it and change it."[41] Since then, that "system" has been named, sometimes with considerable praise and minor criticism, as by Bill Gates, and often very critically, as by non-Marxist economist Thomas Piketty, who documents in his *Capital in the Twenty-First Century* contemporary capitalism's return to the stunning levels of inequality in wealth of the 1890s and 1920s, and a continuously increasing and immoral distribution of wealth.[42] The trajectory Piketty describes and the harsh lives this maldistribution creates for billions of people, Americans included, is a distribution that will not be altered by expanding educational achievement to "compete in the global economy." Accepting and giving credence to this phony claim only serves corporate power and wealth, and destroys the futures of today's youth. The reality behind "education for the global economy" is one that educational organizations, unions, and activist organizations must analyze, explain, and unrelentingly help change.

NOTES

Introduction

1. Curtis Mayfield, "Choice of Colors," http://www.lyricsfreak.com/c/curtis+mayfield/choice+of+colors_20668501.
2. Catherine Gewertz, "Little Progress Seen in Student Results on Reading NAEP," March 30, 2010, http://www.edweek.org/ew/articles/2010/03/31/27naep-2.h29.html.
3. Gerald Coles, *Reading the Naked Truth: Literacy, Legislation, and Lies* (Portsmouth, NH: Heinemann, 2003).
4. Elizabeth Goldbaum, "President Signs Successor to No Child Left Behind Act into Law," Geological Society of America, December 11, 2015, https://speakingofgeoscience.org/2015/12/11/president-signs-successor-to-no-child-left-behind-act-into-law/.
5. Vince M. Bertram, "Secretary DeVos's Most Important Task," FoxNews.com, March 19, 2017.http://www.foxnews.com/opinion/2017/03/19/secretary-devos-most-important-task.html.
6. Stem Education Coalition, "Secretary-Designate DeVos Answers STEM Education Questions," Stemedcoalition.org, February 2, 2017.
7. Ibid.
8. Edward Burtynsky, *Manufacturing Landscapes*, http://www.edwardburtynsky.com/site_contents/Films/Manufactured_Landscapes_Film.html.

Chapter 1. Educating for the Global Economy

1. Obama's Remarks on Education, CBS News, March 10, 2009, http://www.cbsnews.com/news/obamas-remarks-on-education/.
2. John McCain, Key Issues, Education, http://www.mccain.senate.gov/public/?p=Education.

3.   Mitt Romney's Plan to Restore the Promise of America's Education System, http://www.edweek.org/media/romney-ed_plan.pdf.

4.   American Federation of Children, "AFC and ExcelinEd Encourage RNC and DNC Platforms to Embrace School Choice," January 27, 2016, http://www.federationforchildren.org/afc-excelined-encourage-rnc-dnc-platforms-embrace-school-choice/.

5.   David Harvey, *A Brief History of Neoliberalism* (New York: Oxford University Press, 2007), 65.

6.   Randi Weingarten, "Public Schools Are Cornerstone of Strong Economy, Strong Democracy, Strong Middle Class," January 24, 2012, http://www.aft.org/press-release/public-schools-are-cornerstone-strong-economy-strong-democracy-strong-middle.

7.   "U.S. Chamber Welcomes Secretary Duncan's Remarks on Education Reform Funding," March 4, 2009, https://www.uschamber.com/press-release/us-chamber-welcomes-secretary-duncans-remarks-educa-tion-reform-funding.

8.   Lauren Camera, "Tennessee on Dogged Path to Race to Top Finish," *Education Week*, July 9, 2014. http://www.edweek.org/ew/articles/2014/07/09/36tennessee_ep.h33.html.

9.   Bill Gates, "How to Keep America Competitive," *Washington Post*, February 25, 2007, http://www.washingtonpost.com/wp-dyn/content/article/2007/02/23/AR2007022301697.html.

10.   Common Core Standards Mission Initiative, http://www.corestandards.org/.

11.   Council on Competitiveness, *Innovate America* (Washington, D.C.: U.S. Council on Competitiveness, 2005).

12.   Ibid.

13.   Tapping America's Potential, http://www.tapcoalition.org/.

14.   Tapping America's Potential, *Gaining Momentum, Losing Ground: Progress Report 2008*, http://www.tapcoalition.org/resource/pdf/tap_2008_prog-ress.pdf.

15.   Tapping America's Potential, *The Education for Innovation Initiative*, 2005. http://www.tapcoalition.org/resource/pdf/TAP_report2.pdf.

16.   Joseph Stiglitz and Bruce Greenwald, *Creating a Learning Society: A New Approach to Growth, Development, and Social Progress* (New York: Columbia University Press, 2014).

17.   Cornel West and Christa Buschendorf, *Black Prophetic Fire* (Boston: Beacon Press, 2015), 59.

18.   Pablo Neruda, *United Fruit Company*. https://www.poemhunter.com/poem/the-united-fruit-co/.

19.   William Blum, "United States Bombings of Other Countries," http://williamblum.org/chapters/rogue-state/united-states-bombings-of-other-countries.

20.   Garry Leech, "Revolution in the United States," *Counterpunch*, November 7, 2014. http://www.counterpunch.org/2014/11/07/revolution-in-the-united-states/.

21. National Priorities Project, "Discretionary Spending 2015: $1.16 Trillion," https://static.nationalpriorities.org/images/charts/2015/discretionary-desk.png.

22. Robert Pollin and Heidi Garrett-Peltier, "The U.S. Employment Effects of Military and Domestic Spending Priorities," 2011, Political Economy Research Institute, https://www.peri.umass.edu/media/k2/attachments/PERI_military_spending_2011.pdf.

23. Jacob Gardenswartz, "Does President Trump Still Believe Climate Change Is a Hoax?," *Vox*, March 28, 2017.

24. Naomi Klein, *This Changes Everything: Capitalism vs. the Climate* (New York: Simon & Schuster, 2014), 21.

25. Ibid., 76, 79.

26. Ibid., 21.

27. Jay Richards, "Phelps: The Moral Superiority of Dynamic Capitalism," American Enterprise Institute, May 3, 2010, http://www.aei.org/publication/phelps-the-moral-superiority-of-dynamic-capitalism/.

28. Mark J. Perry, "Note to Pope from Professor Walter E. Williams: Profits and capitalism have improved the human condition," American Enterprise Institute, December 18, 2013, http://www.aei.org/publication/note-to-pope-from-professor-walter-e-williams-profits-and-capitalism-have-improved-the-human-condition/.

29. Edwin J. Feulner, "Capitalism's Carping Critics," Heritage Foundation, December 16, 2013, http://www.heritage.org/trade/commentary/capitalisms-carping-critics.

30. Fred L. Smith, Jr., "Valentine for Capitalism," Competitive Enterprise Institute, February 13, 2013, https://cei.org/content/valentine-capitalism.

31. Bill Gates, "A New Approach to Capitalism in the 21st Century," World Economic Forum, January 24, 2008, https://news.microsoft.com/speeches/bill-gates-world-economic-forum-2008/.

32. Randall Lane, "Bill Gates: My New Model for Giving," *Forbes*, September 18, 2012. http://www.forbes.com/sites/randalllane/2012/09/18/bill-gates-my-new-model-for-giving /#72bac4687d9f.

33. Ibid.

34. "Bill Moyers Interviews Bill Gates," PBS, May 9, 2003, http://www.pbs.org/now/printable/transcript_gates_print.html.

35. BBC. "Bill Gates: Capitalism a 'phenomenal system,' " *BBC Today*, January 25, 2012, http://news.bbc.co.uk/today/hi/today/newsid_9686000/9686095.stm.

36. Bill Gates, "I wrote Steve Jobs a letter as he was dying. He kept it by his bed," *The Telegraph*, January 27, 2012, http://www.telegraph.co.uk/technology/bill-gates/9041726/Bill-Gates-I-wrote-Steve-Jobs-a-letter-as-he-was-dying.-He-kept-it-by-his-bed.html.

37. Olivia Solon, "Bill Gates: Capitalism means male baldness research gets more funding than malaria," *Wired*, March 14, 2013, http://www.wired.co.uk/article/bill-gates-capitalism.

38. Ibid.

39. Barbara Kiviat and Bill Gates, "Making Capitalism More Creative," *Time*, July 31, 2008, http://content.time.com/time/magazine/article/0,9171,1828417,00.html.

40. https://www.brainyquote.com/

41. Hurst-Euless-Bedford Independent School District, "Curriculum Overview: Preparing for the Global Challenge," http://www.hebisd.edu/page.cfm?p=510.

42. Minnesota Department of Education, "Goal: Improve student achievement/prepare students to compete in a global economy, 2010," https://www.leg.state.mn.us/docs/2010/other/100424/www.departmentresults.state.mn.us/mde/DeptDetail.htm.

43. National Education Association, "An Educator's Guide to the Four Cs: Preparing 21st Century Students for a Global Society," http://www.nea.org/assets/docs/A-Guide-to-Four-Cs.pdf.

44. BBC World Service, "Economic System Seen as Unfair: Global Poll," *Globescan*, April 25, 2012, http://www.globescan.com/images/images/pressreleases/bbc2012_economics/BBC12_Economics.pdf.

45. Bill Bigelow and Bob Peterson (eds.), *Rethinking Globalization: Teaching for Justice in an Unjust World* (Milwaukee, WI: Rethinking Schools Press, 2002).

46. Amanda Ripley, *The Smartest Kids in the World: And How They Got That Way* (New York: Simon and Schuster, 2013).

47. Ibid., 98–99.

48. Ibid., 192.

49. Ibid .

50. Ibid., 193.

51. International Labour Organization, "The Hidden Face of Youth Unemployment," May 17, 2012, http://www.ilo.org/global/research/global-reports/youth/2012/WCMS_181063/lang--en/index.htm.

52. Yojana Sharma, "What do you do with millions of extra graduates?," BBC News, July 1, 2014. http://www.bbc.com/news/business-28062071.

53. Isil Kurnaz, "High unemployment among young college graduates in Turkey," *Steuerberatung-Turkei*, September 26, 2014, http://www.steuerberatung-tr.com/en/high-unemployment-among-young-college-graduates-turkey/.

54. Juan Dolado, "Europe: No Country for Young People," *Vox Europe*, February 9, 2015, http://voxeu.org/article/europe-no-country-young-people.

55. Jaison R. Abel and Richard Deitz, "Are Job Prospects of Recent College Graduates Improving?," Federal Reserve Bank of New York, September 4, 2014.

56. Catherine Dunn, "U.S. Jobs Report: Unemployment for College Grads Up Slightly," *International Business Times*, September 5, 2014. http://www.ibtimes.com/us-jobs-report-unemployment-college-grads-slightly-1679888.

57. Bureau of Labor Statistics, "Employment Projections: Occupations with the Most Job Growth," *United States Department of Labor: Bureau of Labor Statistics*, April 18, 2016. https://www.bls.gov/emp/ep_table_104.htm.

58. Michael S. Teitelbaum, *Falling Behind: Boom, Bust & the Global Race for Scientific Talent* (Princeton: Princeton University Press, 2014), 21–22.

59. Matthew Kish, "How Much Do Nike Contract Workers Get Paid" (Database), *Portland Business Journal*, May 20, 2014, http://www.bizjournals.com/portland/blog/threads_and_laces/2014/05/how-much-do-nike-contract-factory-workers-get-paid.html.

60. Mbiyimoh Ghogomu, "U.S. Factory Workers Make 76 Times More per Hour Than Workers In Indonesia," *The Higher Learning*, April 9, 2015. http://thehigherlearning.com/2015/04/09/u-s-factory-workers-make-76-times-more-per-hour-than-workers-in-indonesia/.

61. Kathy Marks, "Nike Supplier 'Resisting Pay Rises' in Indonesia," *Independent*, January 15, 2013, http://www.independent.co.uk/news/world/asia/nike-supplier-resisting-pay-rises-in-indonesia-8452946.html.

62. China Labor Watch, "Apple's Unkept Promises: Cheap Iphones Come at High Costs to Chinese Workers," July 29, 2013. http://www.chinalaborwatch.org/upfile/2013_7_29/apple_s_unkept_promises.pdf.

63. China Labor Watch, "Analyzing Labor Conditions of Pegatron and Foxconn: Apple's Low Cost Reality," February, 2015. http://www.chinalaborwatch.org/upfile/2015_02_11/Analyzing%20Labor%20Conditions%20of%20Pegatron%20and%20Foxconn_vF.pdf.

64. Emma Brown and Danielle Douglas-Gabriel, "Trump seeks to slash Education Department but make big push for school choice," *Washington Post*, March 16, 2017.

65. Oxfam, "Just 8 Men Own Same Wealth as Half the World," January 16, 2017. https://www.oxfam.org/en/pressroom/pressreleases/2017-01-16/just-8-men-own-same-wealth-half-world.

66. Worldwatch Institute, "The State of Consumption Today," February 12, 2017. http://www.worldwatch.org/node/810.

67. United Nations Environmental Programme, "Global Material Flow and Resource Productivity," Assessment Report of the UNEP International Resource Panel, 2016. http://unep.org/documents/irp/16-00169_LW_GlobalMaterialFlowsUNEReport_FINAL_160701.pdf.

68. Tom Lehrer, "Wernher von Braun," *lyricsfreak.com*. http://www.lyricsfreak.com/t/tom+lehrer/wernher+von+braun_20138402.html.

Chapter 2. The Flat World and the Education Needed for It

1. Lamar Alexander, *America 2000: An Education Strategy* (Washington, D.C.: Department of Education, 1991), http://files.eric.ed.gov/fulltext/ED327009.pdf.

2. Thomas L. Friedman, *The World Is Flat: A Brief History of the Twenty-First Century* (New York: Farrar, Straus and Giroux, 2005), 305.

3. Ibid., 7.

4. Thomas L. Friedman, "It's a Flat World, After All," *New York Times*, April 3, 2005, http://www.nytimes.com/2005/04/03/magazine/its-a-flat-world-after-all.html.

5. Forbes, "India's 100 Richest People (Nandan Nilekani)," February 13, 2017, http://www.forbes.com/profile/nandan-nilekani/.

6. Forbes, "India's 100 Richest People (Mukesh Ambani)," February 13, 2017, http://www.forbes.com/profile/mukesh-ambani/.

7. Jim Yardley, "Soaring Above India's Poverty, a 27-Story Home," *New York Times*, October 28, 2010, http://www.nytimes.com/2010/10/29/world/asia/29mumbai.html.

8. Arundhati Roy, "Capitalism: A Ghost Story," *Outlook*, March 26, 2012, http://www.outlookindia.com/magazine/story/capitalism-a-ghost-story/280234.

9. Mark Garrison, "New York's New Billionaire Street," *Marketplace*, June 4, 2013. http://www.marketplace.org/2013/06/04/economy/new-yorks-new-billionaire-street.

10. Tara Loader Wilkinson, "The World's Most Lavish High-Rise Apartments," *Billionaire*, April 7, 2014, http://www.billionaire.com/luxury-real-estate/790/the-worlds-most-lavish-highrise-apartments.

11. Andrew Malone, "The GM Genocide: Thousands of Indian Farmers Are Committing Suicide After Using Genetically Modified Crops," *Daily Mail*, November, 2008, http://www.dailymail.co.uk/news/article-1082559/The-GM-genocide-Thousands-Indian-farmers-committing-suicide-using-genetically-modified-crops.html.

12. Ibid.

13. Christy Rodgers, "A 'Seminar' Organized by the Zapatistas Draws Over a Thousand Participants in Chiapas: Letter from Mexico: Part Two," *Dissident Voice*, May 7, 2015.

14. ABC News, "What We Know About the 43 Missing Mexican Students," October 24, 2014, http://abcnews.go.com/International/43-missing-mexican-students/story?id=26423875.

15. David Agren, "Mexico: Burned Bodies Likely of 43 Missing Students," *USA Today*, November 7, 2014, http://www.usatoday.com/story/news/world/2014/11/07/mexico-missing-students/18669187/.

16. Friedman, *The World Is Flat*, 384.

17. Faiza Mawjee, "Compassion Capitalism for the Developing World," *Asia Society*, May 19, 2010, http://asiasociety.org/asia21-young-leaders/compassionate-capitalism-developing-world.

18. Vivian Stewart, *A World-Class Education: Learning from International Models of Excellence and Innovation* (Alexandria, VA: ASCD, 2012), 9.

19. Ibid., 10.

20. Ibid., 17.

21. Linda Darling-Hammond, *The Flat World and Education: How America's Commitment to Equity Will Determine Our Future* (New York: Teachers College Press, 2009).

22. Ibid., 3.

23. Ibid., 328.

24. Ibid., 54.

25. Howard Zinn, *A People's History of the United States* (New York: Harper's, 2015), 1–7.

26. Hugh Thomas, *The Slave Trade: The Story of the Atlantic Slave Trade:1440–1870* (New York: Simon and Schuster, 1999).

27. Michael Parenti, *Against Empire* (San Francisco: City Lights Books, 1995).

28. Ibid., see chaps. 1–2.

29. U.S. Department of State, *Right to Protect Citizens in Foreign Countries by Landing Forces*, Memorandum of the Solicitor for the Department of State, October 5, 1912 (Washington, D.C.: Government Printing Office, 1929), https://babel.hathitrust.org/cgi/pt?id=mdp.39015062380293;view=1up;seq=5.

30. Barbara Salazar Torreon, *Instances of Use of United States Armed Forces Abroad, 1798–2016* (Washington, D.C.: Congressional Research Service, 2016), https://fas.org/sgp/crs/natsec/R42738.pdf.

31. Ibid., 4.

32. Stephanie Rosenbloom, "Apple Watch: A Test Run for Travelers," *New York Times*, May 5, 2015, https://www.nytimes.com/2015/05/10/travel/apple-watch-a-test-run-for-travelers.html.

33. Farhad Manjoo, "Apple Watch Review: Bliss, but Only After a Steep Learning Curve," *New York Times,* April 8, 2015.

34. World Health Organization, "Lack of Sanitation for 2.4 Billion People is Undermining Health Improvements," June 30, 2015. http://www.who.int/mediacentre/news/releases/2015/jmp-report/en/.

35. Worker Rights Consortium, "Global Wage Trends for Apparel Workers, 2001–2011," *Center for American Progress*, July 11, 2013, https://www.americanprogress.org/issues/economy/reports/2013/07/11/69255/global-wage-trends-for-apparel-workers-2001-2011/.

36. Bangladesh Institute of Labour Studies, *Bangladesh: Labour Market Profile, 2014*, http://www.ulandssekretariatet.dk/sites/default/files/uploads/public/PDF/LMP/lmp_bangladesh_2014_final_version.pdf.

37. Syed Zain Al-Mahmood, "Bangladesh's Garment Industry Still Offers Women Best Work Opportunity," *Guardian*, May 23, 2013, https://www.theguardian.com/global-development/2013/may/23/bangladesh-garment-industry-women-opportunity.

38. Worker Rights Consortium, "Made in Vietnam: Labor Rights Violations in Vietnam's Export Manufacturing Sector," May 2013, http://www.workersrights.org/linkeddocs/WRC_Vietnam_Briefing_Paper.pdf.

39. Damien Cavemay, "As Ties With China Unravel, U.S. Companies Head to Mexico," *New York Times*, May 31, 2014.

40. Nick Miroff, "With Mexican Auto Manufacturing Boom, New Worries," *Washington Post*, July 1, 2013, https://www.washingtonpost.com/world/the_americas/with-mexican-auto-manufacturing-boom-new-worries/2013/07/01/10dd57e8-d7d9-11e2-b418-9dfa095e125d_story.html.

41. Peter Coy, "Four Reasons Mexico Is Becoming a Global Manufacturing

Power, *Bloomberg*, June 27, 2013. https://www.bloomberg.com/news/articles/2013-06-27/four-reasons-mexico-is-becoming-a-global-manufacturing -power.

42. George Friedman, "The PC16: Identifying China's Successors," *Stratfor*, July 30, 2013. https://www.stratfor.com/weekly/pc16-identifying-chinas-successors.

43. National Labor Committee, "Microsoft Supplier in China Forces Teenagers to Work 15-Hour Shifts Under Sweatshop Conditions," Institute for Global Labour and Human Rights, April 13, 2010, http://www.globallabourrights.org/alerts/microsoft-supplier-in-china-forces-teenagers-to-work-15-hour-shifts-under-sweatshop-conditions.

44. Reuters, "Foxconn Says Underage Workers Used in China Plant," October 17, 2012. http://www.reuters.com/article/us-foxconn-teenagers-idUS-BRE89F1U62 0121017.

45. Charles Riley, "HP to Limit Student Labor in China," CNN Tech, February 8, 2013, http://money.cnn.com/2013/02/08/technology/hp-china-student-labor/index.html.

46. China Labor Watch, "Samsung, HEG, and Vocational School Cover Up Truth about Child Labor," December 3, 2014, http://www.chinalaborwatch.org/report/106.

47. Liyan Chen, "The World's Largest Tech Companies: Apple Beats Samsung, Microsoft, Google," *Forbes*, May 11, 2015, http://www.forbes.com/sites/liyanchen/2015/05/11/the-worlds-largest-tech-companies-apple-beats-samsung-microsoft-google/#15015c53415a.

48. China Labor Watch, "An Investigation of Eight Samsung Factories in China," September 4, 2012, http://www.chinalaborwatch.org/report/64.

49. Enough Project, "Conflict Minerals Company Rankings," *Raise Hope for Congo*.2012, http://www.raisehopeforcongo.org/content/conflict-minerals-company-rankings-0.

50. Bet DiPietro, "Appeals Court Hears Conflict Minerals Arguments," *Wall Street Journal*, January 7, 2014, http://blogs.wsj.com/riskandcompliance/2014/01/07/appeals-court-hears-conflict-minerals -arguments/.

51. Cydney Posner, "Will Congress Revisit the Conflict Minerals Rule?," *Cooley*, March 5, 2015, https://www.youtube.com/watch?v=Nuw8GJbqx94 https://cooleypubco.com/2015/03/05/will-congress-revisit-the-conflict -minerals-rule/.

52. Bullion Street, "Electronics Industry Uses 320 Tons of Gold, 7500 Tons of Silver Annually," *BullionStreet*, July 9, 2015, http://www.bullionstreet.com/news/electronics-industry-uses-320-tons-of-gold7500-tons-of-silver-annually/2255.

53. Zama Coursen-Neff, "Africa's Child Mining Shame," Human Rights Watch, September 11, 2013, https://www.hrw.org/news/2013/09/11/africas-child-mining-shame.

54. Bureau of Gender Equality, "Girls in Mining: Research Findings from Ghana, Niger, Peru and the United Republic of Tanzania," International Labour Organization, January 1, 2007, http://www.ilo.org/ipecinfo/product/viewProduct.do?productId=5304.

55. Human Rights Watch, *Toxic Toil: Child Labor and Mercury Exposure in Tanzania's Small-Scale Gold Mines*, August 28, 2013, https://www.hrw.org/report/2013/08/28/toxic-toil/child-labor-and-mercury-exposure-tanzanias-small-scale-gold-mines.

56. Beth Hoffman, "How Can We End Child Labor In the Fields?: Pay Farmers Better," *Forbes*, April 8, 2014, http://www.forbes.com/sites/bethhoffman/2014/04/08/how-can-we-end-child-labor-in-the-fields-pay-farmers-better/#d555cb36e8fa.

57. "The World's Next Great Leap Forward: Towards the End of Poverty," *The Economist*, June 1, 2013, http://www.economist.com/news/leaders/21578665-nearly-1-billion-people-have-been-taken-out-extreme-poverty-20-years-world-should-aim.

58. Michael Yates, *The Great Inequality* (New York: Routledge, 2016), chap. 7.

59. *The Economist*, "The World's Next Great Leap Forward: Towards the End of Poverty." 60. RT News, "World Bank Estimate of 1BN People in Poverty 30% 'Too Low,' April 11, 2014.

60. Christopher Deeming and Bina Gubaju, "The Mis-Measurement of Extreme Poverty: A Case Study in the Pacific Islands," *Journal of Sociology*, September 2015, 689–706, https://www.ncbi.nlm.nih.gov/pmc/articles/PMC4547200/.

61. Economic Commission for Latin America and the Caribbean, "Poverty and Indigence Reduction Stalls in Most of Latin American Countries," January 26, 2015, http://www.cepal.org/en/comunicados/se-estanca-la-reduccion-de-la-pobreza-y-la-indigencia-en-la-mayoria-de-paises-de-america.

62. Jason Hickel, "Exposing the Great Poverty Reduction Lie," Aljazeera, August 21, 2014, http://www.aljazeera.com/indepth/opinion/2014/08/exposing-great-poverty-reductio-201481211590729809.html.

63. Peter Edward, "The Ethical Poverty Line as a Tool to Measure Global Absolute Poverty," *Third World Quarterly* 27/2, 377–93. http://courses.arch.vt.edu/courses/wdunaway/gia5524/edward06.pdf.

64. Bill and Melinda Gates, "Our Big Bet for the Future; 2015 Gates Annual Newsletter," *Gatesnotes*, 2015, https://www.gatesnotes.com/2015-annual-letter?page=0&lang=en&WT.mc_id=01_21_2015_AL2015-BG_YT_BMGvideo_Top_12.

65. Sindhu Kashyap, "Skill Up India Takes PM's Dream of Skilled Indian Manpower a Step Ahead," *Your Story*, May 14, 2015, https://yourstory.com/2015/05/skill-up-india-code-for-india/.

66. "North Must Wake Up to STEM Education Opportunities," *Newry Times News*, January 13, 2015, http://newrytimes.com/2015/01/13/north-must-wake-up-to-stem-education-opportunities-rogers/.

67. "Nigeria: Vocation and Technical Education—A Key to Improving Nigeria's Development," *Allafrica*, 2015, http://allafrica.com/stories/201501120436.html.

68. Thompson Morrison, "Why Oregon Tech Leaders Will Take Aim at

Education," *Portland Business Journal*, April 20, 2015, http://www.bizjournals.com/portland/blog/techflash/2015/04/why-oregon-tech-leaders-will-take-aim-at-education.html.

69. Chaim Potok, *The Chosen* (New York: Ballantine, 1967).

Chapter 3. The U.S. Economy, Schooling, and Knowledge

1.   "Local Company Tackles Skills Gap Issue," *News8000.com*. 2015, http://www.news8000.com/news/local-news/local-company-tackles-skills-gap-issue_20161118084031504/169449769.

2.   Madeline J. Goodman, Anita M. Sands and Richard J. Coley, *America's Skills Challenge: Millennials and the Future* (Princeton: Educational Testing Service, 2015), http://www.ets.org/s/research/30079/asc-millennials-and-the-future.pdf.

3.   Stephen S. Tang and Darren A. Spielman, "It's Time to Get Serious About STEM Education," *Philadelphia Business Journal*, June 9, 2015, http://www.bizjournals.com/philadelphia/blog/guest-comment/2015/06/tang-and-spielman-its-time-to-get-serious-about.html.

4.   "Former Baltimore Mayor: City Must Confront the 'Rot Beneath the Glitter,' " *National Public Radio*, June 5, 2015, http://www.npr.org/sections/codeswitch/2015/06/05/412063621/former-baltimore-mayor-city-must-confront-the-rot-beneath-the-glitter.

5.   Norm Heikens, "New Workforce Thrust Aims to Boost Indy Tech Expertise," *Indiana Business Journal* April 30, 2015, http://www.ibj.com/articles/52979-new-workforce-thrust-aims-to-boost-indy-tech-expertise.

6.   "JPMorgan Chase Releases Skiils Gap Report in Chicago," *Webwire*, June 10, 2015, http://www.webwire.com/ViewPressRel.asp?aId=198217.

7.   Theresa Seiger, "Governor: Fairhope Aviation Academy Focused on Coveted, High-Demand Skills," *AL.com*, May 2, 2015, http://www.al.com/news/mobile/index.ssf/2015/05/govenor_training_at_fairhope_a.html.

8.   John Guenther, "Task Force: Future of California Economy Depends on Funding Middle-Skill Job Education," *California Economic Summit*, June 12, 2015, http://www.caeconomy.org/reporting/entry/task-force-future-of-california-economy-depends-on-funding-middle-skill-job.

9.   Allison Barber, "Companies Growing in Indiana, but Skills Gap Persists," *Chicago Tribune*, June 9, 2015, http://www.chicagotribune.com/suburbs/post-tribune/opinion/ct-ptb-jobs-gap-in-indiana-ptb-0610-20150609-story.html.

10. "Closing the Job Skills Gap with New York Workers," *Ready Nation: Council for a Strong America*, n.d., http://readynation.s3.amazonaws.com/wp-content/uploads/RN-NY-Skills-Brief.pdf.

11. Yi Xue and Richard C. Larson, "STEM Crisis or STEM Surplus? Yes and Yes," *Monthly Labor Review*, Bureau of Labor Statistics, May 2015, https://www.bls.gov/opub/mlr/2015/article/pdf/stem-crisis-or-stem-surplus-yes-and-yes.pdf.

12. David Langdon, George McKittrick, David Beede, Beethika Khan and

Mark Doms, *STEM: Good Jobs Now and for the Future*, U.S. Department of Commerce, July 2011, http://www.esa.doc.gov/sites/default/files/stemfinalyjuly14_1.pdf.

13. William Butz et al., *Will the Scientific and Technology Workforce Meet the Requirements of the Federal Government?* (Santa Monica, CA: Rand Corporation), 2004, 17, http://www.rand.org/content/dam/rand/pubs/monographs/2004/RAND_MG118.pdf.

14. Ibid., 18.

15. Robert N. Charette, "The STEM Crisis Is a Myth: Forget the Dire Predictions of a Looming Shortfall of Scientists, Technologists, Engineers, and Mathematicians," *IEEE Spectrum*, August 30, 2013, http://spectrum.ieee.org/at-work/education/the-stem-crisis-is-a-myth.

16. Hal Salzman, Daniel Kuehn, and B. Lindsay Lowell, "Guestworkers in the High-Skill U.S. Labor Market: An Analysis of Supply, Employment, and Wage Trends," Economic Policy Institute, April 24, 2013, http://www.epi.org/publication/bp359-guestworkers-high-skill-labor-market-analysis/.

17. Anthony Carnevale and Ban Cheah, *Hard Times: College Majors, Unemployment and Earnings* (Georgetown, VA: Georgetown Policy Institute, 2013), https://cew.georgetown.edu/wp-content/uploads/2014/11/HardTimes.2013.2.pdf.

18. Heidi Shierholz, "Is There Really a Shortage of Skilled Workers?" Economic Policy Institute, January 23, 2014, http://www.epi.org/publication/shortage-skilled-workers/.

19. Ibid.

20. Michelle Davidson, "Is there a shortage of skilled IT workers in the U.S.?" *TechTarget*, May 2005, http://search400.techtarget.com/feature/Is-there-a-shortage-of-skilled-IT-workers-in-the-US.

21. Adam Davidson, "Skills Don't Pay the Bills," *New York Times*, November 20, 2012, http://www.nytimes.com/2012/11/25/magazine/skills-dont-pay-the-bills.html.

22. Boston Consulting Group, "Skills Gap in U.S. Manufacturing Is Less Pervasive Than Many Believe," *Marketwired*, October 15, 2012, http://www.marketwired.com/press-release/skills-gap-in-us-manufacturing-is-less-pervasive-than-many-believe-1713071.htm.

23. "The Low-Wage Recovery: Industry Employment and Wages Four Years into the Recovery," *National Employment Law Project*, April 2014, http://www.nelp.org/content/uploads/2015/03/Low-Wage-Recovery-Industry-Employment-Wages-2014-Report.pdf.

24. Amy K. Glasmeier, "The Living Wage Calculator," Massachusetts Institute of Technology, 2017, http://livingwage.mit.edu/.

25. Bureau of Labor Statistics, U.S. Department of Labor, "Occupational Employment and Wages Summary," March 30, 2016, https://www.bls.gov/news.release/ocwage.nr0.htm.

26. Michael Clemens, "More Unskilled Workers, Please," *Foreign Policy*, July 8, 2013. http://foreignpolicy.com/2013/07/08/more-unskilled-workers-please/.

27. "Realities of the Working World" Classes of 2014–2016 Reports, *Accenture,* www.accenture.com/collegegradresearch.

28. Jaison R. Abel, Richard Deitz, and Yaqin Su, "Are Recent College Graduates Finding Good Jobs?," Federal Reserve Bank of New York, 2016, https://www. accenture.com/t20160512T073844__w__/us-en/_acnmedia/PDF-18/ Accenture-Strategy-2016-Grad-Research-Gig-Experience-Unleash- Talent.pdf#zoom=50.

29. Burning Glass Technologies, *Moving the Goalposts: How Demand for a Bachelor's Degree Is Reshaping the Workforce,* 2014, http://burning-glass. com/wp-content/uploads/Moving_the_Goalposts.pdf.

30. Catherine Rampell, "It Takes a B.A. to Find a Job as a File Clerk," *New York Times,* February 19, 2013,http://www.nytimes.com/2013/02/20/business/ college-degree-required-by-increasing-number-of-companies.html.

31. Richard Vedder, Christopher Denhart, Matthew Denhart, Christopher Matgouranis and Jonathan Robe, *From Wall Street to Wal-Mart: Why College Graduates Are Not Getting Good Jobs,* Center for College Affordability and Productivity, 2010, http://www.centerforcollegeaffordability.org/uploads/ From_Wall_Street_to_Wal-Mart.pdf.

32. Gus Lubin, "A Staggering Look at the Rise of College Underemployment," *Business Insider,* August 22, 2013, http://www.businessinsider.com/ rise-of-college-student-underemployment-2013-8.

33. Barbara A. Butrica, Howard M. Iams, Karen E. Smith, and Eric J. Toder, "The Disappearing Defined Benefit Pension and Its Potential Impact on the Retirement Incomes of Baby Boomers," *Social Security Bulletin* 69/3 (2009), https://www.ssa.gov/policy/docs/ssb/v69n3/v69n3p1.html.

34. Heidi Shierholz, Alyssa Davis, and Will Kimball, "The Class of 2014: The Weak Economy Is Idling Too Many Young Graduates," *EPI Briefing Paper #377,* Economic Policy Institute, May 1, 2014.

35. Phil Izzo, "Congratulations to Class of 2014, Most Indebted Ever," *Wall Street Journal,* May 16, 2014, http://blogs.wsj.com/numbers/ congatulations-to-class-of-2014-the-most-indebted-ever-1368/.

36. Federal Reserve Bank of St. Louis, *All Employees:Manufacturing,* January 2017. https://fred.stlouisfed.org/series/MANEMP.

37. Catherine Ruckelshaus and Sarah Leberstein, "Manufacturing Low Pay: Declining Wages in the Jobs That Built America's Middle Class," National Employment Law Project, November 2014, http://www.nelp.org/content/ uploads/2015/03/Manufacturing-Low-Pay-Declining-Wages-Jobs-Built- Middle-Class.pdf.

38. Robert Reich, "The 'Paid-What-You're-Worth' Myth," *Robert Reich.org,* March 13, 2014. http://robertreich.org/post/79512527145.

39. Livia Gershon, "No, manufacturing jobs won't revive the econ- omy," *Salon,* June 29, 2013. https://www.salon.com/2013/06/29/ no_manufacturing_jobs_wont_revive_the_economy.

40. Ruckelshaus and Leberstein, "Manufacturing Low Pay," 15.

41. Bureau of Labor Statistics, "Union Members Summary," January 26, 2017, https://www.bls.gov/news.release/union2.nr0.htm.

42. Ronil Hira, "Immigration Reforms Needed to Protect Skilled American Workers," Testimony in Hearing Before the Judiciary Committee, U.S. Senate, March 17, 2015, https://www.judiciary.senate.gov/imo/media/doc/Hira%20Testimony.pdf.

43. Ronil Hira, "The Impact of High-Skilled Immigration on U.S. Workers," Testimony Before Subcommittee on Immigration and the National Interest of the Judiciary Committee, U.S. Senate, February 25, 2016, https://www.judiciary.senate.gov/imo/media/doc/02-25-16%20Hira%20Testimony.pdf.

44. Julia Preston, "Pink Slips at Disney, but First, Training Foreign Replacements," *New York Times*, June 3, 2015.

45. Ron Hira, "Et Tu, Mickey Mouse? Disney Pads Record Profits by Replacing U.S. Workers with Cheaper H-1B Guestworkers," Economic Policy Institute, June 5, 2015, http://www.epi.org/blog/et-tu-mickey-mouse-disney-pads-record-profits-by-replacing-u-s-workers-with-cheaper-h-1b-guestworkers/.

46. Shirin Jaafari, "Senator: Investigate Disney for Firing Americans, Using US Visa Program to Bring in Foreign Replacements," Public Radio International, June 5, 2015, https://www.pri.org/stories/2015-06-05/senator-calls-probe-after-disney-fires-american-workers-uses-h-1b-visas-fly.

47. Kevin Fogarty, "Pfizer Accused of Using U.S. Workers to Train Foreign Replacements," *eweek,* November 5, 2008, http://www.eweek.com/c/a/IT-Management/Pfizer-Accused-of-Using-US-Workers-to-Train-Foreign-Replacements.

48. Patrick Thibodeau, "Southern California Edison IT Workers 'Beyond Furious' Over H-1B Replacements: About 500 IT jobs are cut at utility through layoffs and voluntary departures," *Computerworld*, February 4, 2015, http://www.computerworld.com/article/2879083/it-outsourcing/southern-california-edison-it-workers-beyond-furious-over-h-1b-replacements.html.

49. Patrick Thibodeau, "Northeast Utilities creates STEM jobs—in India," *Computerworld*, April 23, 2014, http://www.computerworld.com/article/2476210/it-management/northeast-utilities-creates-stem-jobs-in-india.html.

50. Mike Hughlett, "Cargill to outsource IT services; 900 jobs affected," *Star Tribune*, March 27, 2014, http://www.startribune.com/cargill-to-outsource-it-services-900-jobs-affected/252483851/.

51. Thibodeau, "Southern California Edison IT Workers 'Beyond Furious' Over H-1B Replacements."

52. Susan Hall, "Harley-Davidson Cuts IT Staff; Shifts Some to Infosys," *Dice*, July 30, 2012, http://insights.dice.com/2012/07/30/harley-davidson-infosys/.

53. Hal Salzman, Daniel Kuehn, and B. Lindsay Lowell, "Current and proposed high-skilled guestworker policies discourage STEM students and grads from entering IT," Economic Policy Institute, May 30, 2013. http://www.epi.org/publication/current-proposed-high-skilled-guestworker/.

54. "The Roar of the Crowd," *The Economist*, May 2, 2012, http://www.economist.com/node/21555876.

55. Eric Simonson and Sarthak Brahma, "Every Crowd Has a Silver Lining: Crowdsourcing Is Gaining Traction Despite Inherent Challenges," Everest Group, 2011, http://www.everestgrp.com/wp-content/uploads/2012/02/EGR-2011-2-V-0602-Crowdsourcing.pdf.

56. Haydn Shaughnessy, "Work Without Jobs: A Trend for the Educated Elite," *Forbes*, May 10, 2012, http://www.forbes.com/sites/haydnshaughnessy/2012/03/10/a-little-more-on-work-without-jobs-for-the-educated-elite/#17a5939f33aa.i.

57. Louisa Peacock, "IBM crowdsourcing could see employed workforce shrink by three quarters," *Personnel Today*, April 23, 2010, http://www.personneltoday.com/hr/ibm-crowd-sourcing-could-see-employed-workforce-shrink-by-three-quarters/.

58. Moshe Z. Marvit, "How Crowdworkers Became the Ghosts in the Digital Machine," *The Nation*, February 5, 2014.

59. Miriam Cherry, "Working the Crowd," *Concurring Opinions*, July 18, 2012, https://concurringopinions.com/archives/2012/07/working-the-crowd.html.

60. Ibid.

61. Simonson and Brahma, "Every Crowd Has a Silver Lining," 3.

62. Marvit, "How Crowdworkers Became the Ghosts in the Digital Machine."

63. Ryan Kim, "By 2020, Independent Workers Will Be the Majority," *Gigaom*, December 8, 2011, https://gigaom.com/2011/12/08/mbo-partners-network-2011/.

64. Simon Head, *Mindless: Why Smarter Machines Are Making Dumber Humans* (New York: Basic Books, 2014), 19.

65. Ibid., 44.

66. Spencer Soper, "Amazon Warehouse Workers Fight for Unemployment Benefits," *The Morning Call*, December 17, 2012.

67. Angelo Young, "Amazon.com's Workers Are Low-Paid, Overworked and Unhappy; Is This the New Employee Model for the Internet Age?," *International Business Times*, December 19, 2013, http://www.ibtimes.com/amazoncoms-workers-are-low-paid-overworked-unhappy-new-employee-model-internet-age-1514780.

68. David Weil, *The Fissured Workplace: Why Work Became So Bad for So Many and What Can Be Done To Improve It* (Cambridge, MA: Harvard University Press, 2014), 77.

69. Robert Reich, "Why We're All Becoming Independent Contractors," *RobertReich.org*, February 22, 2015, http://robertreich.org/post/111784272135.

70. Oxford Economics, *Workforce 2020: The Looming Talent Crisis*, 2014, http://www.oxfordeconomics.com/workforce2020/reports/.

71. Elise Gould and Alyssa Davis, "Public Sector Employment Is Stuck in the Doldrums," Economic Policy Institute, July 2, 2015, http://www.epi.org/blog/public-sector-employment-is-stuck-in-the-doldrums/.

72. Ibid.
73. Jocelyn Fong, "Think Government Job Losses Don't Hurt Us? Think Again Research," *Media Matters*, June 10, 2012, http://mediamatters. org/research/2012/06/10/think-government-job-losses-dont-hurt-us -think/186250.
74. Adam Looney, Michael Greenstone, and Michael Greenstone and Adam Looney, "A Record Decline in Government Jobs: Implications for the Economy and America's Workforce," Brookings Institution, August 3, 2012, https://www.brookings.edu/blog/jobs/2012/08/03/a-record-decline-in-gov-ernment-jobs-implications-for-the-economy-and-americas-workforce/.
75. Ben Adler, "California Teacher Layoffs Up Slightly This Year," Capital Public Radio, March 13, 2015, http://www.capradio.org/articles/2015/03/13/ california-teacher-layoffs-up-slightly-this-year/.
76. Kay Steiger, "Teachers Face Layoffs Around the Country," *Raw Story*, September 7, 2012, http://www.rawstory/2012/09/teachers-face-layoffs-around -the-country/.
77. Editors, "Even well-off Michigan districts can't avoid layoffs," *Detroit Free Press*, July 9, 2015, http://www.freep.com/story/opinion/ editorials/2015/07/09/school-funding-layoffs/29933495/.
78. Allison Kilkenny, "Anchorage School District Plans to Cut 219 Positions, Including 159 Teachers," *The Nation*, January 27, 2014, https://www. thenation.com/article/anchorage-school-district-plans-cut-219-positions-including-159-teachers/.
79. State of New Jersey, "Christie Administration Takes Action to Implement Building Block of High Academic Standards in New Jersey Schools," September 13, 2011, http://www.state.nj.us/governor/news/news/552011/ approved/20110913a.html.
80. Caryn Shinske, "NJ AFL-CIO claims Chris Christie cut educa-tion funding by $1.6B while giving out $2B in corporate tax breaks," *PolitiFact:New Jersey*, May 23, 2013, http://www.politifact.com/ new-jersey/statements/2013/may/23/new-jersey-state-afl-cio/ afl-cio-claims-chris-christie-cut-ed-funding-16b-w/.

Chapter 4. Corporate "Support" of Schooling and Protecting Corporations

1. "School That Will Get You a Job," *Time*, February 14, 2014, http://naf.org/ news_articles/the-school-that-will-get-you-a-job.
2. Ibid.
3. Al Bakeroct, "At Technology High School, Goal Isn't to Finish in 4 Years," *New York Times*, October 21, 2012, http://www.nytimes.com/2012/10/22/ nyregion/pathways-in-technology-early-college-high-school-takes-a-new-approach-to-vocational-education.html.
4. Ibid.
5. Craig Wolf, "IBM Jobs Cuts Hit; Hudson Valley Numbers Unclear," *Poughkeepsie Journal*, February 28, 2014, http://www.lohud.com/story/ money/2014/02/28/ibm-jobs-cuts-hit-valley-numbers-unclear/5889559/.

6.   "IBM Starts Job Cuts; Most Lay-Offs Outside U.S.," *The Hindu*, June 16, 2013, http://www.thehindu.com/business/Industry/ibm-starts-job-cuts-most-layoffs-outside-us/article4820411.ece.

7.   Julie Bort, "It Sounds Like IBM Layoffs Are Still Going On," *Business Insider*, June 18, 2015, http://www.businessinsider.com/ibm-watchdog-more-layoffs-this-month-2015-6?op=1.

8.   C. J. Arlotta, "IBM Layoffs 2015: Here's What You Need to Know," *Talkin Cloud*, January 29, http://talkincloud.com/cloud-companies/01282015/ibm-layoffs-2015-heres-what-you-need-know.

9.   Eric DuVall, "IBM Continues Layoffs That Could Top 14,000 Job Cuts, *UPI Business News,*May 21, 2016, https://www.upi.com/Business_News/2016/05/21/IBM-continues-layoffs-that-could-top-14000-job-cuts/8041463860302/.

10. Kevin McLaughlin, "IBM Has Started to Lay Off Thousands of Workers Worldwide," *Business Insider*, June 12, 2013, http://www.businessinsider.com/ibm-begins-layoffs-2013-6.

11. Paul McDougall, "Amid Global Push, IBM Has Shrunk Its U.S. Workforce by Half since 2000," *International Business Times*, October 2, 2014, http://www.ibtimes.com/amid-global-push-ibm-has-shrunk-its-us-workforce-half-2000-1698785.

12. Jia Lynn Yang, "IBM Is Cutting Jobs Across the Country This Week, but One State Is Being Spared," *Washington Post*, February 28, 2014, https://www.washingtonpost.com/news/wonk/wp/2014/02/28/ibm-is-cutting-jobs-across-the-country-this-week-but-one-state-is-being-spared/.

13. Ibid.

14. Project Lead the Way (PLTW), https://www.pltw.org/.

15. PLTW, "About Us," 2017, https://www.pltw.org/about-us.

16. PLTW, "Chevron and PLTW Announce National Partnership," *PLTW*, November 11, 2013, https://www.pltw.org/news/chevron-and-pltw-announce-national-partnership.

17. Jeb Blount, "Chevron Brazil Faces Criminal Oil-Spill Charges, Reinstated on Appeal," Reuters, April 4, 2014, http://www.reuters.com/article/chevron-brazil-idUSL1N0MW05720140404.

18. Will Bunch, "The Chevron Guarantee: Our well won't explode . . . or your pizza is free!," *The Inquirer*, February 17, 2014, http://www.philly.com/philly/blogs/attytood/Chevron-Endure-our-fracking-fire-and-the-pizzas-on-us.html.

19. Ibid.

20. "Dow and Project Lead the Way Partner to Grow STEM Skills in Key Dow Communities: Partnership to help build the pipeline for a skilled workforce," *Business Wire*, February 24, 2015, http://www.businesswire.com/news/home/20150224006258/en/Dow-Project-Lead-Partner-Grow-STEM-Skills#.VbaQNvm5XIU.

21. Anna Lappe, "What Dow Chemical Doesn't Want You to Know About Your Water," *CSRWire*, May 7, 2011, http://www.csrwire.com/csrlive/

commentary_detail/4646-What-Dow-Chemical-Doesn-t-Want-You-to-Know-About-Your-Water.

22. Environmental Protection Agency, "Dow Chemical Company Settlement," July 29, 2011, https://www.epa.gov/enforcement/dow-chemical-company-settlement.

23. Project Lead the Way, "D.C. Public Schools Expand STEM Curriculum through Multi-Million Dollar Investment from Lockheed Martin," *PR Newswire*, November 7, 2014, http://www.prnewswire.com/news-releases/dc-public-schools-expands-stem-curriculum-through-multi-million-dollar-investment-from-lockheed-martin-281976461.html.

24. Project on Government Oversight, "Top 10 Contractors by total FY15 contract awards," http://www.contractormisconduct.org/misconduct.

25. Pratap Chatterjee, "Meet the New Interrogators: Lockheed Martin," *CorpWatch*, November 4, 2005, http://www.corpwatch.org/article.php?id=12757.

26. William D. Hartung, "Prophets of War: How Defense Contractor Lockheed Martin Dominates the Military Establishment," *Alternet*, January 11, 2011, http://www.alternet.org/story/149492/prophets_of_war:_how_defense_contractor_lockheed_martin_dominates_the_military_establishment/.

27. "Billings Schools Focus on STEM Subjects," *KULR8News*, June 19, 2014. http://www.kulr8.com/story/25707841/billings-schools-focus-on-stem-subjects.

28. Monica Mainland and John Brewer, "U.S. Business Depends on Solid STEM Education," *Billings Gazette*, August 24, 2014, http://billingsgazette.com/news/opinion/guest/guest-opinion-u-s-business-depends-on-solid-stem-education/article_8789893e-a630-588c-b2ad-8ba6f271b656.html.

29. Matthew Brown, "$1.7M penalty proposed for ExxonMobil oil spill into Yellowstone River," Associated Press, March 25, 2013, http://billingsgazette.com/news/state-and-regional/montana/m-penalty-proposed-for-exxonmobil-oil-spill-into-yellowstone-river/article_5a611f71-1127-5857-937e-29b7705a6abc.html.

30. Marybeth Holleman, "After 25 years, *Exxon Valdez* oil spill hasn't ended," CNN, March 25, 2014, http://www.cnn.com/2014/03/23/opinion/holleman-exxon-valdez-anniversary/.

31. Ewen MacAskill, "18 years on, *Exxon Valdez* oil still pours into Alaskan waters," *The Guardian*, February 1, 2007, https://www.theguardian.com/business/2007/feb/02/oil.pollution.

32. William Yard, "Recovery Still Incomplete after *Valdez* Spill," *New York Times*, May 5, 2010, http://www.nytimes.com/2010/05/06/us/06alaska.html.

33. Eli Clifton, "The Secret Foreign Donor Behind the American Enterprise Institute," *The Nation*, June 25, 2013, https://www.thenation.com/article/secret-foreign-donor-behind-american-enterprise-institute/.

34. "Global Warming Skeptic Organizations," *Union of Concerned Scientists*, 2013, http://www.ucsusa.org/global_warming/solutions/fight-misinformation/global-warming-skeptic.html#.VcvERvm5XIU.

35.   I. S. Hall, "How Kern Family Foundation Approaches STEM Funding," *Inside Philanthropy*, December 10, 2014, http://www.insidephilanthropy.com/higher-education/2014/12/10/how-kern-family-foundation-approaches-stem-funding.html.

36.   Tim McDonnell, "Scott Walker Is the Worst Candidate for the Environment, *Mother Jones,* March 11, 2015.

37.   Wisconsin Democracy Campaign, "10 Million in 10 Years Drives School Agenda," April 15, 2013, http://www.wisdc.org/pr040513.php.

38.   Union of Concerned Scientists, *The Climate Deception Dossiers: Internal Fossil Fuel Industry Memos Reveal Decades of Corporate Disinformation*, 2015, http://www.ucsusa.org/sites/default/files/attach/2015/07/The-Climate-Deception-Dossiers.pdf.

39.   Ibid.

40.   Change the Equation, "President Obama Launches Change the Equation," September 16, 2010, http://changetheequation.org/press/president-obama-launches-change-equation.

41.   "Fulbright Speech Charges: Defense Contracts Subvert University Services," *Stanford Daily*, January 31, 1968. http://stanforddailyarchive.com/cgi-bin/stanford?a=d&d=stanford19680131-01.2.11&e=-------en-20--1--txt-txIN.

42.   Katie Valentine, "Telecom Company to Pay $52 Million for Illegally Dumping Electronic Waste," *Think Progress*, November 21, 2014, https://thinkprogress.org/telecom-company-to-pay-52-million-for-illegally-dumping-electronic-waste-ec90b44ce19e#.se3xuqsm7.

43.   Steve Gorman, "ATT to pay California $52 million in hazardous waste disposal settlement," Reuters, April 22, 2013, http://www.reuters.com/article/us-usa-at-t-california-idUSKCN0J50AG20141121.

44.   Elizabeth Weise, "DuPont Settles Water Pollution Case for $300M," *USA Today*, September 9, 2004, http://usatoday30.usatoday.com/money/industries/manufacturing/2004-09-09-dupont-teflon-settlement_x.htm.

45.   Environmental Working Group, "DuPont Hid Teflon Pollution For Decades," December 13, 2002, http://www.ewg.org/research/dupont-hid-teflon-pollution-decades.

46.   Joseph Popiolkowski, "DuPont to pay $440,000 fine in pollution settlement linked to town of Tonawanda plant," *Buffalo News*, July 22, 2014, http://buffalonews.com/2014/07/22/dupont-to-pay-440000-fine-in-pollution-settlement-linked-to-town-of-tonawanda-plant/.

47.   U.S. Environmental Protection Agency, "DuPont Fined for Air Pollution at Deepwater, New Jersey," January 8, 2015, https://www.epa.gov/newsreleases/dupont-fined-air-pollution-deepwater-new-jersey.

48.   Allyson Siwik, "Freeport-McMoran Fined $276,000 for Million-Gallon 2007 Chino Acid Spill," *Gila Resources Information Project*, April 21, 2009, http://gilaresources.info/wp/blog/2009/04/21/freeport-mcmoran-fined-276000-for-million-gallon-2007-chino-acid-spill/.

49.   "Freeport McMoRan slapped with $6.8 million fine," *Mining.com*, April 26, 2012, http://www.mining.com/freeport-slapped-with-6-8-million-fine/.

50. Jane Perlez and Raymond Bonnerdec, "Below a Mountain of Wealth, a River of Waste, *New York Times*. December 27, 2005, http://www.nytimes.com/2005/12/27/world/asia/below-a-mountain-of-wealth-a-river-of-waste.html.

51. Freeport-McMoran, *Transforming Tomorrow Together*, 2017, http://www.freeportinmycommunity.com/communities/indonesia.

52. Andy Giegerich, "Intel Agrees to $143K Fluoride Fine," *Portland Business Journal*, April 25, 2014, http://www.bizjournals.com/portland/morning_call/2014/04/intel-agrees-to-143k-fluoride-fine.html.

53. "Intel Reports Full-Year Revenue of $52.7 Billion, Net Income of $9.6 Billion, *Intel Newsroom*, January 16, 2014, https://newsroom.intel.com/news-releases/intel-reports-full-year-revenue-of-52-7-billion-net-income-of-9-6-billion/.

54. Mike Rogoway, "Oregon Embraces Intel, but in New Mexico Environmental Doubts Persist," *The Oregonian*, December 11, 2010, http://www.oregon-live.com/business/index.ssf/2010/12/oregon_embraces_intel_but_in_n.html.

55. Barbara Rockwell, "Boiling Frogs—Intel vs. the Village," May 21, 2015, http://boilingfrogs-intelvsthevillage.blogspot.com/.

56. Ibid.

57. Gerry Mullanymay, "Carly Fiorina on the Issues," *New York Times*, May 4, 2015, https://www.nytimes.com/2015/05/05/us/politics/carly-fiorina-on-the-issues.html.

58. William A. Jacobson, "Carly Fiorina at Her Absolute Best," *Legal Insurrection*, July 17, 2015, http://legalinsurrection.com/2015/07/carly-fiorina-at-her-absolute-best/.

59. Joseph Romm, "The Dumbing Down of Carly Fiorina," *Salon*, June 4, 2010. http://www.salon.com/2010/06/04/global_warming_carly_fiorina/.

60. Hewlett-Packard, "Sustainability-Environment," 2017, http://www8.hp.com/us/en/hp-information/environment/ecosolutions.html.

61. Phil Trounstine and Jerry Roberts, "Meg Whitman's Climate Change Strategy," *Los Angeles Times*, January 11, 2010, http://articles.latimes.com/2010/jan/11/opinion/la-oe-robertstrounstine11-2010jan11.

62. Margot Roosevelt, "Meg Whitman Wants to Fix California's Global Warming Law," *Los Angeles Times*, October 13, 2010, http://latimesblogs.latimes.com/greenspace/2010/10/meg-whitman-global-warming-ab-32-prop-23.html.

63. Trounstine and Roberts, "Meg Whitman's Climate Change Strategy."

64. Devin Connors, "HP Confirms It's Splitting in Two, Results in 55,000 Layoffs," *Escapist Magazine,* October 6, 2014, http://www.escap-istmagazine.com/news/view/137858-HP-Spinoff-Meg-Whitman-55000-Layoffs-Hewlett-Packard.

65. Julie Bort, "HP CEO Meg Whitman Will Get a Monstrous Payout If She's Ever Fired," *Business Insider*, March 31, 2015.

66. Dwight D. Eisenhower, "Military-Industrial Complex Speech, *Public*

Papers of the Presidents, 1961, http://coursesa.matrix.msu.edu/~hst306/documents/indust.html.

67. Allen McDuffee, "Killer Robots with Automatic Rifles Could Be on the Battlefield in 5 Years," *Wired*, October 18, 2013, https://www.wired.com/2013/10/weaponized-military-robots/.

68. Human Rights Watch, *Campaign to Stop Killer Robots*, 2017, http://www.stopkillerrobots.org/coalition/

69. Mary Wareham, "Banning Killer Robots in 2017," *Human Rights Watch*, January 15, 2017, https://www.hrw.org/news/2017/01/15/banning-killer-robots-2017.

70. Human Rights Watch, *Losing Humanity: The Case Against Killer Robots*, International Human Rights Watch Clinic, November, 2012. https://www.hrw.org/sites/default/files/reports/arms1112_ForUpload.pdf.

71. "Autonomous Weapons: An Open Letter from AI & Robotics Researchers," *Future of Life Institute*, July 28, 2015, https://futureoflife.org/open-letter-autonomous-weapons#signatories.

72. Chalmers Johnson, "The Rand Corporation: America's University of Imperialism," *Alternet*, April 29, 2008, http://www.alternet.org/story/83910/the_rand_corporation%3A_america%27s_university_of_imperialism/.

73. Abigail Fielding-Smith and Crofton Black, "Revealed: The Private Firms Tracking Terror Targets at Heart of US Drone Wars," *Bureau of Investigative Journalism*, July 30 2015, https://www.thebureauinvestigates.com/stories/2015-07-30/revealed-the-private-firms-tracking-terror-targets-at-heart-of-us-drone-wars.

74. "SAP North America Corporate Social Responsibility," *SAP*, 2017. http://www.sap.com/about/social-responsibility.html#.

75. "SAP and New York City Education Partners Open Six-Year High School in New York Focused on STEM," *MarketWatch*, September 4, 2014, http://www.marketwatch.com/story/sap-and-new-york-city-education-partners-open-six-year-high-school-in-new-york-focused-on-stem-2014-09-04?reflink=MW_news_stmp.

76. Barry Grey, "Standard and Poor's Credit Rating Agency Charged with Fraud in Sub-Prime Mortgage Ratings," *Global Research*, February 6, 2013, http://www.globalresearch.ca/sp-charged-with-fraud-in-mortgagen-ratings/5322037.

77. Paul Davidson , Kaja Whitehouse, and Kevin Johnson, "S&P Paying $1.4B over Crisis-Era Ratings," *USAToday*, February. 3, 2015, http://www.usatoday.com/story/money/markets/2015/02/03/standard-poors-settlement-fcc/22788653/.

78. Ibid.

79. "Goldman Sachs STEM Symposium," Bucknell University, September 30, 2014, http://careerinsider.blogs.bucknell.edu/2014/09/30/goldman-sachs-stem-symposium/.

80, Goldman Sachs, "Engineering at GS," 2016, https://goldman-sachs.tal.net/vx/mobile-0/brand-2/candidate/so/pm/1/pl/3/

opp/11706-Firmwide-2016-Summer-Analyst-STEM-GS-University-of-Michigan/en-GB.

81. Goldman Sachs, "Citizenship," 2017, http://www.goldmansachs.com/citizenship/index.html.

82. "Goldman Sachs Nearing $1.1 Billion Settlement with U.S. Housing Regulator," *Huffington Post*, August 22, 2014, http://www.huffingtonpost.com/2014/08/22/goldman-sachs-fhfa-settlement_n_5701510.html.

83. Arthur MacEwan and John Miller, *Economic Collapse, Economic Change: Getting to the Roots of the Crisis* (New York: Routledge, 2011), 114.

84. "Discovery Place Education Studio at Bank of America STEM Center for Career Development Officially Opens," *Discovery Place*, May 19, 2014, https://www.discoveryplace.org/about/press/releases/discovery-place-education-studio-at-bank-of-america-stem-center-for-career-development-officially-opens.

85. Kevin McCoy, "Bank of America Fined $1.3B for Bad Mortgages," *USA TODAY*, July 30, 2014, http://www.usatoday.com/story/money/business/2014/07/30/bank-of-america-countrywide-mortgage-fines/13366837/.

86. Doug G. Ware, "Bank of America Fined $30M for Violations Involving U.S. Service Members," UPI, May 30, 2015, http://www.upi.com/Business_News/2015/05/30/Bank-of-America-fined-30M-for-violations-involving-US-servicemembers/1221433022297/.

87. Alanna Petroff, "Bank of America Fined $2 Million for Race Discrimination," CNN, September 24, 2013, http://money.cnn.com/2013/09/24/news/companies/bofa-racial-discrimination/.

Chapter 5. Constructing the Curriculum

1. Randolph S. Bourne, *War and the Intellectuals* (New York: Harper, 1964) 71–72.

2. Samuel Bowles and Herbert Gintis, *Schooling in Capitalist America* (Chicago: Haymarket Books, 2011).

3. David J. Blacker, *The Falling Rate of Learning and the Neoliberal Endgame*, (Wnchester, UK: Zero Books, 2013), 99.

4. Allen Graubard, *Free the Children: Radical Reform and the Free School Movement* (New York: Pantheon, 1972), 262–63.

5. Michael J. Crozier, Samuel Huntington, Joji Watanuki, *The Crisis of Democracy: Report on the Governability of Democracies to the Trilateral Commission* (New York: New York University Press, 1975), http://trilateral.org/download/doc/crisis_of_democracy.pdf#page=108&zoom=auto,-152,662.

6. James Rothenberg, "The Open Classroom Reconsidered," *Elementary School Journal*, 1989, 90, 69–86.

7. Carol Edelsky, *Making Justice Our Project* (Urbana, IL: National Council of Teachers of English, 1999) 29.

8. Jeanne Chall, *Learning to Read: The Great Debate* (New York: McGraw-Hill, 1967).

9. The Commission on Reading of the National Academy of Education, *Becoming a Nation of Readers* (Washington, D.C.: National Institute of Education, 1985).

10. William Bennett, *A Report on Elementary Education in America* (Washington, D.C.: U.S. Department of Education, 1986).

11. Ira Shor, *Empowering Education: Critical Teaching for Social Change* (Chicago: University of Chicago Press, 1992).

12. Robert W. Sweet, Jr., *Illiteracy: An Incurable Disease or Education Malpractice?* (Washington, D.C.: U.S. Senate Republican Policy Committee, 1996).

13. "An Injustice to Juveniles," *Boston Sunday Globe*, February 25, 1990.

14. Gerald Coles, *Reading the Naked Truth: Literacy, Legislation, and Lies*, 2003, (Portsmouth, NH: Heinemann, 2003). The book provides a thorough examination of the Report.

15., B.C. Gamse, H.S. Bloom, J.J. Kemple, R.T. Jacob, *Reading First Impact Study: Interim Report* (NCEE 2008-4016) (Washington, D.C.: National Center for Education Evaluation and Regional Assistance, Institute of Education Sciences, U.S. Department of Education, 2008).

16. George N. Schmidt, "Duncan Boosts Controversial Science Claim about Early Reading Instruction," *Substance*, October 29, 2002, http://substance-news.com/archive/Nov02/duncanboosts.htm.

17. Kenneth Goodman, "Whose Knowledge Is Worth What?," *National Literacy Policies: The View From the Classroom*, November 4, 2010, http://readinghalloffame.org/node/287.

18. Jennifer McMurrer, "NCLB Year 5: Choices, Changes, and Challenges: Curriculum and Instruction in the NCLB Era," *Center on Education Policy*, 2007, http://www.cep-dc.org/displayDocument.cfm?DocumentID=312.

19. Steve Goldberg, "The Essential Role of Social Studies: Reflections on Arne Duncan's Article," National Council for the Social Studies, 2011, http://connected.socialstudies.org/socialeducation/communityhome/duncan_mj2011.

20. Ilene Berson, Linda Bennett, and Dorothy Dobson, "Powerful and Purposeful Teaching and Learning in Elementary School Social Studies," *Task Force on Early Childhood/Elementary Studies: National Council for the Social Studies*, 2009, http://www.socialstudies.org/positions/powerfulandpurposeful.

21. Bill of Rights Institute, "2011–2012 'Being an American' Essay Contest Winners," 2012, http://billofrightsinstitute.org/2011-2012-being-an-american-essay -contest-winner-announced-2/.

22. Bill of Rights Institute, "Our Story," 2017, http://billofrightsinstitute.org/about-us/institute/story/.

23. Bill of Rights Institute, "Occupy Protests and the Bill of Rights," 2017, http://billofrightsinstitute.org/educate/educator-resources/lessons-plans/current-events/occupy-protests/.

24. Ibid.

25. Clare O'Connor, "Occupy Movement Wants Koch Brothers Out of Politics, Marches

on Georgia-Pacific HQ," *Forbes*, October 25, 2011, https://www.forbes.com/sites/clareoconnor/2011/10/25/occupy-movement-wants-koch-brothers-out-of-politics-marches-on-georgia-pacific-hq/#584e72bf162d.

26. Caitlin MacNeal, "The Conservative Ideas the Koch Brothers Want to Sneak Into Schools," *Talking Points Memo*, December 10, 2014, http://talkingpointsmemo.com/dc/koch-brothers-north-carolina-history-class.

27. Center for Media and Democracy, "ALEC Exposed," 2017, http://www.alecexposed.org/wiki/ALEC_Exposed.

28. General Assembly of North Carolina, *Founding Principles Course*, North Carolina State Board of Education, 2017, http://ssnces.ncdpi.wikispaces.net/The+Founding+Principles.

29. U.S. Department of Education, "Use of Technology in Teaching and Learning," 2016, https://www.ed.gov/oii-news/use-technology-teaching-and-learning.

30. Michael Noer, "One Man, One Computer, 10 Million Students: How Khan Academy Is Reinventing Education," *Forbes*, November 2, 2012, https://www.forbes.com/sites/michaelnoer/2012/11/02/one-man-one-computer-10-million-students-how-khan-academy-is-reinventing-education/#46553a3c44e0.

31. Vanessa Romo, "The Khan Academy Takeover: Inside the New Classroom Revolution," *TakePart*, September 4, 2013, http://www.takepart.com/article/2013/08/27/the-khan-academy-teachers-stories/.

32. Robert Murphy, Larry Gallagher, Andrew Krumm, Jessica Mislevy, Amy Hafter, "Research on the Use of Khan Academy in Schools," *SRI Education*, 2014, https://www.sri.com/sites/default/files/publications/khan-academy-implementation-report-2014-04-15.pdf.

33. Khan Academy Press Release, 2017, https://khanacademy.zendesk.com/hc/en-us/articles/202483630-Press-Releases-and-Other-Resources-.

34. CBS, "Khan Academy: The Future of Education?," *60 Minutes*, March 11, 2012, http://www.cbsnews.com/videos/khan-academy-the-future-of-education-4/.

35. Frank Newport, "Americans Continue to Say U.S. Wealth Distribution Is Unfair," Gallup, May 4, 2015, http://www.gallup.com/poll/182987/americans-continue-say-wealth-distribution-unfair.aspx.

36. Michael Parenti, *Contrary Notions* (San Francisco: City Lights Books, 2007), 312–18.

37. Eva Golinger, "US Aggression Against Venezuela," *Counterpunch*, February 26, 2015 http://www.counterpunch.org/2015/02/26/us-aggression-against-venezuela/.

38. William Blum, "US coup Against Hugo Chavez of Venezuela," *WilliamBlum.org*, 2002, https://williamblum.org/chapters/freeing-the-world-to-death/us-coup-against-hugo-chavez-of-venezuela-2002.

39. William Blum, *Killing Hope: U.S. Military and CIA Interventions since World War II* (Monroe, ME: Common Courage Press, 2014).

40. Tara Kangarlou, "South Africa Since Apartheid: Boom or Bust?," CNN, November 27, 2013, http://www.edition.cnn.com/2013/11/27/business/south-africa-since-apartheid/index.html.

41. Haroon Bhorat, "Economic Inequality Is a Major Obstacle to Growth in South Africa," *New York Times*, December 6, 2013, http://www. nytimes.com/roomfordebate/2013/07/28/the-future-of-south-africa/ economic-inequality-is-a-major-obstacle-to-growth-in-south-frica.

42. Ronnie Kasrils, "How the ANC's Faustian Pact Sold out South Africa's Poorest," *Guardian*, June 24, 2013, https://www.theguardian.com/ commentisfree/2013/jun/24/anc-faustian-pact-mandela-fatal-error.

43. John Pilger, "South Africa: Twenty Years of Apartheid by Another Name," *Global Research*, April 12, 2014, http://www.globalresearch.ca/ south-africa-twnety-years-of-apartheid-by-another-name/5377555.

44. Vijay Prashad, *The Poorer Nations: A Possible History of the Global South* (New York: Verso, 2014), 170–72.

45. John Pilger, "Apartheid Never Died in South Africa. It Inspired a World Order Upheld by Force and Illusion," *JohnPilger.com*, September 19, 2012, http://johnpilger.com/articles/apartheid-never-died-in-south-africa-it- inspired-a-world-order-upheld-by-force-and-illusion.

46. Statistics South Africa, "South Africa's Young Children: Their Family and Home Environment," 2012, http://us-cdn.creamermedia.co.za/assets/arti- cles/attachments/47023_stats_sa_report-03-10-072012.pdf.

47. CIA, "Country Comparison: Distribution of Family Income—Gini Index," *World Factbook*, 2017, https://www.cia.gov/library/publications/the- world-factbook/rankorder/2172rank.html.

48. Andrew Ross Sorkin, "So Bill Gates Has This Idea for a History Class," *New York Times*, September 5, 2014, https://www.nytimes.com/2014/09/07/ magazine/so-bill-gates-has-this-idea-for-a-history-class.html.

49. David Stannard, *American Holocaust: The Conquest of the New World* (New York: Oxford University Press), 1992.

50. R. J. Rummel, "Pre-Twentieth-Century Democide," *Death by Government* (New Brunswick, NJ: Transaction Publishers, 1994), chap. 3, http://www. hawaii.edu/powerkills/DBG.CHAP3.HTM.

51. Iraq Body Count.org, "Documented Civilian Deaths From Violence," 2017, https://www.iraqbodycount.org/database/.

52. Dane Farsetta, "How Many Iraqis Have Really Died?," *Alternet*, March 1, 2008, http://www.alternet.org/story/77992/how_many_iraqis_have_really_died.

53. Bill Gates, "Vision of the Future, 10.2," *Big History*, 2014, https:// s3.amazonaws.com/KA-share/BigHistory/10.2_Transcript_Visions_of_ the_Future_2014.pdf.

54. Bolivia Ministerio de Relaciones Exteriores, "Statement of the World's Peoples' Conference on Climate Change and the Defense of Life," 2016, http://www.cancilleria.gob.bo/webmre/node/1115.

55. Scott Jaschik, "Obama vs. Art History: President Joins the Ranks of Politicians Who Suggest Liberal Arts Disciplines Don't Lead to Jobs," *Inside Higher Ed*, January 31, 2014, https://www.insidehighered.com/news/2014/01/31/ obama-becomes-latest-politician-criticize-liberal-arts-discipline.

56. Aamer Madhani, "Obama Apologizes for Joking about Art History Majors," *USA Today*, February 19, 2014, http://www.usatoday.com/story/theoval/2014/02/19/obama-apologizes-to-texas-art-history-professor/5609089/.

57. Basmat Parsad and Maura Spiegelman, *Arts Education in Public Elementary and Secondary Schools: 1999–2000 and 2009–10*, National Center for Education Statistics, 2012, https://nces.ed.gov/pubsearch/pubsinfo.asp?pubid=2012014rev.

58. Jackie Zubrzycki, "Testing Encroaches on Arts Time, New Jersey Educators Report," *Education Week*, October 1, 2015. http://blogs.edweek.org/edweek/curriculum/2015/10/testing-encroaches-on-arts-time-report.html?cmp=eml-enl-cm-news3.

59. "A Snapshot of State Policies for Arts Education," *Arts Education Partnership*, March 2014, http://www.aep-arts.org/wp-content/uploads/2014/03/A-Snapshot-of-State-Policies-for-Arts-Education.pdf.

60. Tim Walker, "The Testing Obsession and the Disappearing Curriculum," National Education Association, September 2, 2014, http://neatoday.org/2014/09/02/the-testing-obsession-and-the-disappearing-curriculum-2/.

61. Valeriya Metla, "School Art Programs: Should They Be Saved?, *Law Street*, May 14, 2015, https://lawstreetmedia.com/issues/education/cutting-art-programs-schools-solution-part-problem/.

62. Tyleah Hawkins, "Will Less Art and Music in the Classroom Really Help Students Soar Academically?," *Washington Post*, December 28, 2012, https://www.washingtonpost.com/blogs/therootdc/post/will-less-art-and-music-in-the-classroom-really-help-students-soar-academically/2012/12/28/e18a2daUseful.

63. James S. Catterall, Susan A. Dumais, and Gillian Hampden-Thompson, *The Arts and Achievement in At-Risk Youth: Findings From Four Longitudinal Studies*, National Endowment for the Arts, 2012. https://www.arts.gov/sites/default/files/Arts-At-Risk-Youth.pdf.

64. National Performing Arts Convention, "Quotes for Arts Advocates," 2012, http://performingartsconvention.org/advocacy/id=28.

65. Maxine Greene, "Democratic Vistas; Renewing a Perspective," 2007, *maxinegreene.org*, https://maxinegreene.org/uploads/library/democratic_v.pdf.

66. Maxine Greene, "On One Side, Horror," 2007, *maxinegreene.org*.

67. Carol S. Jeffers, "On Empathy: The Mirror Neuron System and Art Education," *International Journal of Education & the Arts*, 2009, http://www.ijea.org/v10n15.

68. Candice Jesse Stout, "The Art of Empathy: Teaching Students to Care," *Art Education*, March 1999, http://www.tandfonline.com/doi/abs/10.1080/00043125.1997.11650892?journalCode=uare20.

69. Vicki L. Baker, Roger G. Baldwin, and Sumedha Makker, "Where Are They Now? Revisiting Breneman's Study of Liberal Arts Colleges," *Liberal Education*, 2012, http://www.aacu.org/publications-research/periodicals/where-are-they-now-revisiting-brenemans-study-liberal-arts.

70. Victor E. Ferrall Jr., "Valediction for the Liberal Arts," *Inside Higher Ed,* January 27, 2015, https://www.insidehighered.com/views/2015/01/27/ essay-offers-valediction-liberal-arts.

71. Ibid.

72. Valerie Strauss, "N.C. Governor Attacks Higher Ed, Proposes Funding Colleges by Graduates' Jobs," *Washington Post,* February 7, 2013, https:// www.washingtonpost.com/news/answer-sheet/wp/2013/02/07/n-c-gover-nor-attacks-higher-ed-proposes-funding-colleges-by-graduates-jobs/.

73. Zac Anderson, "Rick Scott Wants to Shift University Funding Away From Some Degrees," *Herald-Tribune,* October 10, 2011, http://politics.herald-tribune.com/2011/10/10/rick-scott-wants-to-shift-university-funding -away-from-some-majors/.

74. Tracy Jan, "GOP Pushes Funding Cuts for Social Science Work," *Boston Globe,* April 14, 2014, http://www.bostonglobe.com/news/ nation/2014/04/14/gop-pushes-funding-cuts-for-social-science-work/5q4mMRROhWuwHaC46lW23N/story.html.

75. Lamar Smith, "Research in the National Interest," *The Hill,* November 5, 2014, http://thehill.com/blogs/congress-blog/education/222810-research-in -the-national-interest.

76. Vivek Ranadivé, "A Liberal Arts Degree Is More Valuable than Learning Any Trade," *Forbes,* November 13, 2012, https://www.forbes.com/sites/ vivekranadive/2012/11/13/a-liberal-arts-degree-is-more-valuable-than-learning-any-trade/#5e231c7f6d01.

77. Jon Marcus, "The Unexpected Schools Championing the Liberal Arts," *The Atlantic,* October 15, 2015, https://www.theatlantic.com/educa-tion/archive/2015/10/the-unexpected-schools-hampioning-the-liberal -arts/410500/.

78. American Academy of Arts and Sciences, "Commission on the Humanities and Social Sciences, Established by American Academy of Arts and Sciences, Responds to Congressional Request," *National Humanities Center,* February 17, 2011.

79. Public Citizen Texas, "Exelon's History of Radiation Leaks and Hiding It from the Public," *nukefreetexas,* 2008, http://nukefreetexas.org/proposed-nukes/ exelon-victoria/.

80. Michael Hawthorne, "Exelon to Pay $1 Million to Settle Suits Over Leaks at Power Plants," *Chicago Tribune,* March 12, 2010. http://articles. chicagotribune.com/2010-03-12/business/ct-biz-0312-exelon-leak-settle-ment-20100312_1_exelon-nuclear-tritium-leaks.

81. Center for Climate and Energy Solutions, "John W. Rowe, Chairman and CEO, Exelon," 2017, https://www.c2es.org/energy-efficiency/conference/ speakers/john-w-rowe-chairman-and-ceo-exelon.

82. Illinois Institute of Technology, "Wanger Institute for Sustainable Energy Research (WISER)," 2017, http://web.iit.edu/wiser.

83. Commission on the Humanities and Social Sciences, *The Heart of the Matter*

(Cambridge, MA: American Academy of Arts and Sciences, 2013),http://www.humanitiescommission.org/_pdf/HSS_Report.pdf.

84. Annette Gordon-Reed, "Critics of the Liberal Arts Are Wrong," *Time*, June 19, 2013, http://ideas.time.com/2013/06/19/our-economy-can-still-support-liberal-arts -majors/.

85. Commission on the Humanities and Social Sciences, *The Heart of the Matter*.

Chapter 6. U.S. Capitalism's Pretense of Supporting Education for the Global Economy

1. J.P. Mangalindan, "A History of the iPhone," *Fortune*, September 26, 2013, http://fortune.com/2013/09/26/a-history-of-the-iphone/.

2. Hannes Sverrisson, "Innovation at Apple," *Seekingalpha*, January 2, 2015, http://seekingalpha.com/article/2794075-innovation-at-apple.

3. John Cox, "How Apple's Billion Dollar Sapphire Bet Will Pay Off," *NetworkWorld*, April 22, 2014, http://Www.Networkworld.Com/Article/2176241/Wireless/Wireless-How-Apple-S-Billion-Dollar-Sapphire-Bet-Will-Pay-Off.Html.

4. Sam Oliver, "Apple's R&D Spending Shoots Up 42% Year-over-year, hit new $1.9B record in Q1," *appleinsider*, January 28, 2015, http://appleinsider.com/articles/15/01/28/apples-rd-spending-shoots-up-42-year-over-year-hit-new-19b-record-in-q1.

5. Milton Schwebel, *Remaking America's Three School Systems: Now Separate and Unequal* (Lanham, MD: Rowman and Littlefield, 2003).

6. "A New Majority Research Bulletin: Low Income Students Now a Majority in the Nation's Public Schools," *Southern Education Foundation*, 2015, http://www.southerneducation.org/Our-Strategies/Research-and-Publications/New-Majority-Diverse-Majority-Report-Series/A-New-Majority-2015-Update-Low-Income-Students-Now.

7. Assistant Secretary for Planning and Evaluation, "2015 Poverty Guidelines," U.S. Department of Health & Human Services, 2015, https://aspe.hhs.gov/2015-poverty-guidelines.

8. Yang Jiang, Maribel R. Granja, and Heather Koball, "Basic Facts about Low-Income Children: Children Under 6 Years," National Center for Children in Poverty, 2016, http://nccp.org/publications/pdf/text_1145.pdf.

9. UNICEF Office of Research, *Child Well-Being in Rich Countries: A Comparative Overview* (Florence, IT: UNICEF Office of Research, 2013), https://www.unicef-irc.org/publications/pdf/rc11_eng.pdf.

10. Richard Rothstein, *Class and Schools: Using Social, Economic, and Educational Reform to Close the Black-White Achievement Gap* (Washington, D.C.: Economic Policy Institute, 2004).

11. Ibid.

12. Diane Ravitch, *Reign of Error: The Hoax of the Privatization Movement and the Danger to America's Public Schools* (New York: Vintage, 2014).

13. Council of the Great City Schools, *Reversing the Cycle of Deterioration in*

the *Nation's Public School Buildings*, 2014, http://www.bestfacilities.org/best-home/docuploads/pub/250_ReversingtheCycleofDeteriorationin theNationsPublicSchoolBuildings.pdf.

14. Ibid.

15. School Superintendents Association, *Education Cuts Have Yet to Heal: How the Economic Recession Continues to Impact Our Nation's Schools*, 2015, http://aasa.org/uploadedFiles/Policy_and_Advocacy/Resources/EducationCutsDontHeal_121515.pdf.

16. American Society of Civil Engineers, *2017 Infrastructure Report Card: Schools*. 2017, http://www.infrastructurereportcard.org/cat-item/schools/.

17. Emma Brown, "See the Roaches, Rats and Crumbling Ceilings That Detroit Teachers Are Protesting," *Washington Post*, January 20, 2016, https://www.washingtonpost.com/news/education/wp/2016/01/20/see-the-roaches-rats-and-crumbling-ceilings-that-detroit-teachers-are-protesting/.

18. Kristen Graham, "'Hazardous, Unsanitary' Conditions Inside City Schools," *The Inquirer*, July 1, 2015, http://www.philly.com/philly/blogs/school_files/Hazardous-and-.html.

19. Sun-Times Staff, "CPS Principals Say Schools Remain 'Filthy' Under $340M Janitorial Contracts," *Chicago Sun Times*, March 19, 2015, http://chicago.suntimes.com/news/cps-principals-say-schools-remain-filthy-under-340m-janitorial-contracts/.

20. Keri Brown, "As Education Spending Grabs Spotlight, Deteriorating Schools Get Little Aid," *88.8WFDD*, March 4, 2015, http://www.wfdd.org/story/education-spending-grabs-spotlight-deteriorating-schools-get-little-aid.

21. Chelsea Rarrick, "Mayor Jones: More Money for Schools Could Threaten City Services," *CBS6TV*, April 15, 2016, http://wtvr.com/2016/04/15/mayor-jones-richmond-schools/.

22. "Study: Virginia Corporations Stashing Profits Offshore to Avoid Taxes," *Augusta Free Press*, October 6, 2015. http://augustafreepress.com/study-virginia-corporations-stashing-profits-offshore-to-avoid-taxes/.

23. Jason Koebler, "280,000 Nationwide Teaching Jobs in Danger Following Senate Vote, *CBS6TV*, October 24, 2011, http://wtvr.com/2016/04/15/mayor-jones-richmond-schools/.

24. Motoko Richaug, "Teacher Shortages Spur a Nationwide Hiring Scramble," *New York Times*, August 9, 2015, https://www.nytimes.com/2015/08/10/us/teacher-shortages-spur-a-nationwide-hiring-scramble-credentials-optional.html.

25. Joe Bartels, "Teacher Shortage at 'Crisis' Levels Just Days Before Classes Resume," abc15arizona, July 24, 2015, http://www.abc15.com/news/state/teacher-shortage-at-crisis-levels-just-days-before-classes-resume.

26. Jennifer Johnson, "Why Are Arizona Teachers Leaving in Droves?," *AZ Central*, July 2, 2015, http://www.azcentral.com/story/opinion/op-ed/2015/07/02/arizona-teacher-turnover/29571171/.

27. Valerie Strauss, "Why Teachers Are Fleeing Arizona in Droves," *Washington Post*, June 19, 2015, https://www.washingtonpost.com/news/answer-sheet/wp/2015/06/19/why-teachers-are-fleeing-arizona-in-droves/.

28. Kay Steiger, "Teachers Face Layoffs Around the Country," *Raw Story*, September 7, 2012, http://www.rawstory.com/2012/09/teachers-face-layoffs -around-the-country/.

29. Rebecca Klein, "A Memo To States: This Is How You Create a Teacher Shortage," *Huffington Post*, August 6, 2015, http://www.huffingtonpost.com/ entry/kansas-teacher-shortage-recipe_us_55c28ce6e4b0f1cbf1e3a2d7.

30. Joseph Kolb, "New Mexico Faces Teacher Shortage Two Days before School Begins," Reuters, August 11, 2014. http://www.reuters.com/article/ us-usa-newmexico-teachers-idUSKBN0GB1P620140811.

31. Motoko Richaug, "Teacher Shortages Spur a Nationwide Hiring Scramble (Credentials Optional)," *New York Times*, August 9, 2015, https://www. nytimes.com/2015/08/10/us/teacher-shortages-spur-a-nationwide-hiring-scramble-credentials-optional.html.

32. Lisette Partelow, "You're Hired (to Teach, for the Right Reasons)," *U.S. News and World Report*, October 14, 2015. https://www.usnews.com/ opinion/knowledge-bank/2015/10/14/address-americas-teacher-shortage -the-right-way.

33. Jim Hull, Center, "Cutting to the Bone: How the Economic Crisis Affects Schools," Center for Public Education, 2010, http://www. centerforpubliceducation.org/Main-Menu/Public-education/Cutting-to-the-bone-At-a-glance/Cutting-to-the-bone-How-the-economic-crisis -affects-schools.html.

34. Leib Sutcher, Linda Darling-Hammond, and Desiree Carver-Thomas, "A Coming Crisis in Teaching? Teacher Supply, Demand, and Shortages in the U.S.," *Learningpolicyinstitute.org*, September 15, 2016, https://www.learningpolicyinstitute.org/product/coming-crisis-teaching.

35. Robert Reich, "The Shameful Attack on Public Employees Wednesday," *Robertreich.org*, January 5, 2011, http://robertreich.org/post/2615647030.

36. Ulrich Boser and Chelsea Straus, "Mid- and Late-Career Teachers Struggle with Paltry Incomes," *Center for American Progress*, July 23, 2014, https://cdn. americanprogress.org/wp-content/uploads/2014/07/teachersalaries-brief.pdf.

37. Mia Tuan, "Smart Investments Would Ease Chronic Teacher Shortage," *Seattle Times*, January 23, 2016, http://www.seattletimes.com/opinion/ smart-investments-would-ease-chronic-teacher-shortage/.

38. MetLife Inc., *The MetLife Survey of the American Teacher: Challenges for School Leadership*, 2013.

39. Motoko Richaug, "At Charter Schools, Short Careers by Choice," *New York Times*, August 26, 2013, http://www.nytimes.com/2013/08/27/education/ at-charter-schools-short-careers-by-choice.html.

40. Helen Zelon, "Why Charter Schools Have High Teacher Turnover," *Citylimits.org*. August 20, 2014, http://citylimits.org/2014/08/20/why-charter-schools -have-high-teacher-turnover/.

41. Matthew Di Carlo, "Teacher Turnover at Success Academy Charter Schools," Albert Shanker Institute, April 9, 2015, http://www.shankerinstitute.org/blog/teacher-turnover-success-academy-charter-schools.

42. Francisco Vara-Orta, "It's Harder for Charter Schools to Keep Teachers," *My San Antonio*, September 30, 2012, https://www.mysanantonio.com/news/education/article/It-s-harder-for-charter-schools-to-keep-teachers-3905914.php.

43. Alexandria Neason, "Charter Schools' Latest Innovation: Keeping Teachers Happy," *Slate*, April 27, 2015, http://www.slate.com/blogs/schooled/2015/04/27/charter_schools_and_churn_and_burn_how_they_re_trying_to_hold_on_to_teachers.html.

44. Jaclyn Zubrzycki, "More Colorado Teachers Left Their School Districts Last Year," *Chalkbeat*, May 28, 2015, http://www.chalkbeat.org/posts/co/2015/05/28/more-colorado-teachers-left-their-school-districts -last-year/.

45. Charles Boisseau, "UF Researchers Find High Teacher Attrition Rates at Charter Schools," University of Florida, January 5, 2016, https://education.ufl.edu/news/2016/01/05/uf-researchers-find-high-teacher -attrition-rates-at-charter-schools/.

46. Stephen Sawchuk, "Teacher-Retention Data for Charters Still Murky," *Education Week*, June 2, 2015, http://www.edweek.org/ew/articles/2015/06/03/teacher-retention-data-for-charters-still-murky.html.

47. Stephen Sawchuk, "Charters Look to Change Perceptions on Teacher Turnover," *Education Week*, June 2, 2015,,http://www.edweek.org/ew/articles/2015/06/03/charters-look-to-change-perceptions-on-teacher.html.

48. Alfred Chris Torres, "How Teacher Turnover, Burnout Can Impact 'No-Excuses' Charter Schools," *Journalist's Resource*, October 20, 2015. https://journalistsresource.org/studies/society/education/teacher-turn over-burnout -charter-schools.

49. Christine H. Roch and Na Sai, "Charter School Teacher Job Satisfaction," *Education Policy*, January 10, 2016, http://journals.sagepub.com/doi/abs/10.1177/0895904815625281.

50. Rebecca Karabus, "Charter School Teachers Report Satisfaction," *Yale News*, February 16, 2016, http://yaledailynews.com/blog/2016/02/16/charter-school-teachers-report-satisfaction/.

51. Akane Otani, "Most Teach For America Instructors Plan to Flee Teaching," *Bloomberg News*, March 9, 2015, https://www.bloomberg.com/news/articles/2015-03-09/most-teach-for-america-instructors -plan-to-flee-teaching.

52. Nat Malkus, "The Exaggerated Teacher Shortage," *U.S. News & World Report*, November 25, 2015, https://www.usnews.com/opinion/knowl edge-bank/2015/11/25/the-teacher-shortage-crisis-is-overblown-but -challenges-remain.

53. Andrew Biggs, "Is There Really a Teacher Shortage?," *Forbes*, August 13, 2015, https://www.forbes.com/sites/andrewbiggs/2015/08/13/is-there-really-a-teacher-shortage/ #7fa5c9256751.

54. "Teachers and Pupil/Teacher Ratios," *National Center for Education Statistics*, May 2016, https://nces.ed.gov/programs/coe/indicator_clr.asp.

55. National Education Association, "Rankings of the States 2013 and Estimates

of School Statistics 2014," *NEA*, 2014. http://www.nea.org/home/rankings-and-estimates-2013-2014.html.

56. Sam Dillon, "Tight Budgets Mean Squeeze in Classrooms," *New York Times*, March 6, 2011, http://www.nytimes.com/2011/03/07/education/07classrooms.html.

57. Angie Crouch and Heather Navarro, "Overcrowding, Classroom Size Outrage in LAUSD Schools May Force Parents to File Complaint Against District," October 19, 2015, http://www.nbclosangeles.com/news/local/class-size-lausd-overcrowding-complaint-district-334401371.html.

58. United Federation of Teachers, "UFT Survey Finds City Successful in Reducing Some Oversize Classes to Contract Limits," *UFT.org*, October 19, 2015, http://www.uft.org/press-releases/uft-survey-finds-city-successful-reducing-some-oversize-classes-contract-limits.

59. Gerald Coles, *Reading Lessons: The Debate Over Literacy* (New York: Hill & Wang, 1998).

60. Ibid.

61. Jeremy D. Finn and Michele E. Shanahan, "Does Class Size (Still) Matter?," in *Class Size: Eastern and Western Perspectives,* ed. Peter Blatchford et al. (New York: Routledge, 2016), 62–93.

62. Bill Gates, "How Teacher Development Could Revolutionize Our Schools," *Washington Post*, February 28, 2011, http://www.washingtonpost.com/wp-dyn/content/article/2011/02/27/AR2011022702876.html.

63. Sam Dillonov, "Gates Urges School Budget Overhauls," *New York Times*, November 19, 2010, http://www.nytimes.com/2010/11/19/us/19gates.html.

64. Citizens for Tax Justice, "Corporate Tax Dodging in the Fifty States, 2008–2010," *CTJ.org*, 2011, http://www.ctj.org/corporatetaxdodgers50states/CorporateTaxDodgers50StatesReport.pdf.

65. Robert S. McIntyre, Matthew Gardner, and Richard Phillips, "90 Reasons We Need State Corporate Tax Reform: State Corporate Tax Avoidance in the Fortune 500, 2008 to 2012," *Citizens for Tax Justice*, 2014, http://ctj.org/90reasons/90ReasonsFull.pdf.

66. Paul Buchheit, "The Painful Facts, State-by-State: How We're Victimized by Corporate State Tax Avoidance," *Common Dreams*, September 28, 2015, http://www.commondreams.org/views/2015/09/28/painful-facts-state-state-how-were-victimized-corporate-state-tax-avoidance.

67. Bill Gates, "How State Budgets Are Breaking U.S. Schools," *TED.com*, March 2011 https://www.nytimes.com/2018/03/03/style/olivia-de-havilland-fx-ryan-murphy-lawsuit.html?hp&action=click&pgtype=Homepage&clickSource=story-heading&module=second-column-region&region=top-news&WT.nav=top-news, https://www.ted.com/talks/bill_gates_how_state_budgets_are_breaking_us_schools/transcript?language=en#t-381000.

68. Microsoft, "Board of Directors," *Microsoft.com*, 2017, https://news.micro-soft.com/microsoft-board-of-directors/.

69. Citizens for Tax Justice, *Fortune 500 Companies Hold a Record $2.4 Trillion Offshore*, March 3, 2016, http://ctj.org/pdf/pre0316.pdf.

70. Leo Panitch and Sam Gindin, *The Making of Global Capitalism: The Political Economy of American Empire* (New York: Verso, 2012), 1.

71. Christopher Rowland, "Tax Lobbyists Help Businesses Reap Windfalls," *Boston Globe*, March 17, 2013, https://www.bostonglobe.com/news/politics/2013/03/16/corporations-record-huge-returns-from-tax-lobbying-gridlock-congress-stalls-reform/omgZvDPa37DNlSqi0G95YK/story.html.

72. Dave Levinthal, "Corporations, Special Interests Lobbying Taxes to Death," *OpenSecrets.org*, April 18, 2011, http://www.opensecrets.org/news/2011/04/businesses-may-hate-taxes-which/.

73. Public Citizen, *Lax Taxes: Industry Has Massive Resource Advantage in Fight Over Bills That Would Raise Revenue and Bring Fairness to Tax Code*, *Citizen.org*, 2013. http://www.citizen.org/documents/corporate-tax-lobbying-report.pdf.

74. Boeing, *Corporate Citizen Report*, 2015, http://www.boeing.com/resources/boeingdotcom/principles/community-engagement/pdf/reports/Boeing_2015_CitizenshipReport.pdf.

75. Nelson D. Schwartz, "Big Companies Paid a Fraction of Corporate Tax Rate," *New York Times*, July 1, 2013, http://www.nytimes.com/2013/07/02/business/big-companies-paid-a-fraction-of-corporate-tax-rate.html.

76. Citizens for Tax Justice, *Fortune 500 Companies Hold a Record $2.4 Trillion Offshore*.

77. Curtis Dubay and David Burton, "How Congress Should Reform Business Taxes," Heritage Foundation, June 4, 2015, http://www.heritage.org/taxes/report/how-congress-should-reform-business-taxes.

78. Citizens for Tax Justice, "The U.S. Collects Lower Level of Corporate Taxes than Most Developed Countries," *CTJ.org*, 2015, http://ctj.org/pdf/OECDcorp2015.pdf.

79. Gerald Coles, "KIPP Schools: Power Over Evidence," *Living in Dialogue*, August 15, 2012, http://blogs.edweek.org/teachers/living-in-dialogue/2012/08/gerald_coles_kipp_schools_powe.html.

80. Bruce D. Baker, Ken Libby, and Kathryn Wiley, "Spending by the Major Charter Management Organizations: Comparing Charter School and Local Public District Financial Resources," National Education Policy Center, May 5, 2012, http://nepc.colorado.edu/publication/spending-major-charter.

81. Bruce D. Baker, "The Non-Reformy Lessons of KIPP," *Schoolfinance101*, March 1, 2013, https://schoolfinance101.wordpress.com/2013/03/01/the-non-reformy-lessons-of-kipp/.

82. Jim Horn, "KIPP Study Shows Declining Test Performance and No Improvements in 'Character,' " *Schoolsmatter.info*, September 18, 2015, http://www.schoolsmatter.info/2015/09/kipp-study-shows-declining-test.html.

83. Grace Chen, "Charter Schools vs. Traditional Public Schools: Which One Is Under-Performing?," *Publicschoolreview*, February 27, 2017, https://

www.publicschoolreview.com/blog/charter-schools-vs-traditional-public-schools-which-one-is-under-performing.

84. Institute for Global Labour and Human Rights, "Gap and Old Navy in Bangladesh," 2013, http://www.globallabourrights.org/reports/document/1310-IGLHR-GapOldNavyinBangladesh.pdf.

85. Dan McDougall, "Indian 'Slave' Children Found Making Low-Cost Clothes Destined for Gap," *Guardian*, October 28, 2007, https://www.theguardian.com/world/2007/oct/28/ethicalbusiness.retail.

86. Matt Smith, "Filling the Civic Gap," *SF Weekly*, June 21, 2006, http://archives.sfweekly.com/sanfrancisco/filling-the-civic-gap/Content?oid=2160163&showFullText=true.

87. "Gap Founders Transfer Assets," *Los Angeles Times*, August 7, 2004, http://articles.latimes.com/2004/aug/07/business/fi-gap7.

88. Philip Mattera, "Shifting the Burden for Vital Public Services: Walmart's Tax Avoidance Schemes," *Goodjobsfirst.org*, 2011, http://www.goodjobsfirst.org/sites/default/files/docs/pdf/walmart_shiftingtheburden.pdf.

89. Americans for Tax Fairness, *Walmart on Tax Day: How Taxpayers Subsidize America's Biggest Employer and Richest Family*, 2014, https://americansfortaxfairness.org/files/Walmart-on-Tax-Day-Americans-for-Tax-Fairness-1.pdf.

90. "Forbes 400 List; Eli Broad," *Forbes*, 2017, https://www.forbes.com/profile/eli-broad/.

91. Diana B. Henriques, "Wealthy, Helped by Wall St., New Find Ways to Escape Tax on Profits," *New York Times*, December 1, 1996, http://www.nytimes.com/1996/12/01/business/wealthy-helped-by-wall-st-new-find-ways-to-escape-tax-on-profits.html.

92. "Eli Broad, Koch Brothers Funded Secret Anti-Prop 30/Anti-Prop 38 Effort in California," *Hemlock Rocks*, June 17, 2014, http://www.hemlockontherocks.com/2014/06/fwd-4lakids-some-of-news-that-doesnt.html.

93. Stephanie Stromsept, "Big Gifts, Tax Breaks and a Debate on Charity," *New York Times*, September 6, 2007, http://www.nytimes.com/2007/09/06/business/06giving.html.

94. Tibby Rothman and Jill Stewart, "Jerry Brown Redevelopment Alert: Wealthy Eli Broad Gets $52 Million for a Garage; the Entirety of South L.A. Gets $32 Million," *LA Weekly*, January 27, 2011.

95. Dennis Romero, "Eli Broad Gets $52 Million of Your Money for Parking Garage: Thanks, L.A. City Council," *LA Weekly*, May 11, 2011. http://www.laweekly.com/authors/dennis-romero-2126212.

96. "Forbes 400 List; Michael Dell," *Forbes,* 2017, https://www.forbes.com/profile/michael-dell/.

97. Matthew Gardner and Richard Phillips, "The Sorry State of Corporate Taxes: What Fortune 500 Firms Pay (or Don't Pay) in the USA and What They Pay Abroad—2008 to 2012," *Citizens for Tax Justice*, 2014, http://www.ctj.org/corporatetaxdodgers/sorrystateofcorptaxes.pdf.

98. Adrian Glick Kudler, "Dell Founder Using Prop. 13 Loophole to Save

Bundle on Fairmont Miramar Taxes," *Curbed Los Angeles*, May 6, 2013, http://la.curbed.com/2013/5/6/10246474/dell-founder-using-prop-13 -loophole-to-save-bundle-on-fairmont.

99.   Jon Healey, "Michael Dell: Poster Boy for a Proposition 13 U.S. Capitalism's Pretense of Supporting Education for the Global Economy Tweak," *L.A. Times*, May 15, 2014, http://www.latimes.com/opinion/opinion-la/la-ol-michael-dell-proposition-13-change-20140514-story.html.

100. "Tech Titans," *Forbes*, August 17, 2006, https://www.forbes.com/2006/08/17/cx_mn_0817techtitanslide_06egang.html.

101. Robertson Foundation, *Index*, 2017, http://www.robertsonfoundation.org/index.html.

102. Janet Novack, "Billionaire Julian Robertson Notches Tax Win for New York City Non-Residents, *Forbes*, October 27, 2010, https://www.forbes.com/sites/janetnovack/2010/10/27/billionaire-julian-robertson-notches-tax-win-for-new-york-city-non-residents/#6102a9578f00.

103. James B. Stewart, "Tax Me If You Can: The Things Rich People Do to Avoid Paying Up," *The New Yorker*, March 19, 2012, http://www.newyorker.com/magazine/2012/03/19/tax-me-if-you-can.

104. Ibid.

105. *Forbes* 400, "#174 Julian Robertson, Jr.," 2017, https://www.forbes.com/profile/julian-robertson-jr/.

106. Steven Bertoni, "Chuck Feeney: The Billionaire Who Is Trying To Go Broke," *Forbes*, September 18, 2012, https://www.forbes.com/sites/stevenbertoni/2012/09/18/chuck-feeney-the-billionaire-who-is-trying-to-go-broke/#37007a5f291c.

107. Lydie Pierre-Louis, "Citigroup Fined $600,000 for Implementing Tax Avoidance Strategies that Defrauded IRS of Billions in Taxes," *Corporate Justice Blog*, October 14, 2009, http://corporatejusticeblog.blogspot.com/2009/10/citigroup-fined-600k-for-employing-tax.html.

108. Scott Klinger, Sarah Anderson, and Javier Rojas, "Corporate Tax Dodgers: 10 Companies and Their Tax Loopholes," *American for Tax Fairness*, 2013, https://americansfortaxfairness.org/files/Corporate-Tax-Dodgers-Report-Final.pdf.

109. Ben Hallman, "Citigroup Avoided Paying $11.5 Billion in Taxes Thanks to Tax Shelters," *Huffington Post*, November 11, 2013, http://www.huffington-post.com/2013/07/31/citigroup-tax-shelters_n_3672029.html.

110. Michael Rapoport and Christina Rexrode, "Citigroup to Get Tax Silver Lining in $7 Billion Settlement," *Wall Street Journal*, July 14, 2014, http://blogs.wsj.com/moneybeat/2014/07/14/citigroup-to-get-tax-silver-lining -in-7-billion-settlement/.

111. Michael Corkery, "Citigroup Settles Mortgage Inquiry for $7 Billion," *New York Times*, July 14, 2014, https://dealbook.nytimes.com/2014/07/14/citigroup-and-u-s-reach-7-billion-mortgage-settlement/?_php=true&_type=blogs&_php=true&_type=blogs&_r=2.

112. Walter Hickey, "It's Not Just Apple: The Ultra-Complicated Tax Measures that Microsoft Uses to Avoid $2.4 Billion In U.S. Taxes,"

Business Insider, May 21, 2013, http://www.businessinsider.com/apple-microsoft-avoids-taxes-loopholes-irs-2013-1.

113. David Sirota, "Should Companies Have to Pay Taxes?" *Creators Syndicate*, September 25, 2015, https://www.creators.com/read/david-sirota/09/15/should-companies-have-to-pay-taxes.

114. Matt Day, "How Microsoft Moves Profits Offshore to Cut Its Tax Bill," *Seattle Times*, December 16, 2015, http://www.seattletimes.com/business/microsoft/how-microsoft-parks-profits-offshore-to-pare-its-tax-bill/.

115. Dan Alexander, "Bill Gates Now Owns Less of Microsoft than Steve Ballmer," *Forbes*, May 2, 2014, https://www.forbes.com/sites/danalexander /2014/05/02/bill-gates-now-owns-less-of-microsoft-than-steve-ballmer/#6aa428ba6a2d.

116. Day, "How Microsoft Moves Profits Offshore to Cut Its Tax Bill."

117. Yuri Vanetik, "For More Jobs, Fix the Corporate Tax Code," *Reform America's Taxes Equitability*, July 3, 2013, http://ratecoalition.com/2013/07/03/for-more-jobs-fix-the-corporate-tax-code/.

118. Scott A. Hodge, "The Economic Effects of Adopting the Corporate Tax Rates of the OECD, the UK, and Canada," *Tax Foundation*, August 20, 2015, https://taxfoundation.org/economic-effects-adopting-corporate-tax-rates-oecd-uk-and-canada/.

119. Scott Klinger, Sam Pizzigati, John Cavanagh, Chuck Collins, and Sarah Anderson, "America Loses: Corporations That Take 'Tax Holidays' Slash Jobs," *Institute for Policy Studies*, October 4, 2011. http://www.ips-dc.org/corporations_that_take_tax_holidays_slash_jobs/.

120. Scott Klinger, "Think Corporate Tax Cuts Create Jobs? Think Again," *Center for Effective Government*, February 25, 2015, http://www.foreffectivegov.org/blog/think-corporate-tax-cuts-create-jobs-think-again/.

121. Jordan Brennan, "Do Corporate Income Tax Rate Reductions Accelerate Growth?, " *Canadian Centre for Policy Alternatives*, November 30, 2015, https://www.policyalternatives.ca/publications/reports/do-corporate-income -tax-rate-reductions-accelerate-growth.

122. Valerie Strauss, "Mega Millions: Do Lotteries Really Benefit Public Schools?," *Washington Post*, March 30, 2012, https://www.washingtonpost.com/blogs/answer-sheet/post/mega-millions-do-lotteries-really-benefit-public-schools/2012/03/30/gIQAbTUNlS_blog.html.

123. New York Lottery, "Mission for Education," *NY.gov*, 2016, http://nylottery.ny.gov/wps/portal/Home/Lottery/About+Us/Mission+for+Education.

124. Strauss, "Mega Millions: Do Lotteries Really Benefit Public Schools?"

125. Ron Stodghill and Ron Nixonoct, "For Schools, Lottery Payoffs Fall Short of Promises, *New York Times*, October 7, 2007, http://www.nytimes.com/2007/10/07/business/07lotto.html.

126. Oliver Libaw, "Where Does Lottery Revenue Go?," ABC News, August 25, 2001, http://abcnews.go.com/US/story?id=92598&page=1.

127. John Wihbey, "Who Plays the Lottery, and Why: Updated Collection of Research," *Journalist's Resource*, July 27, 2016, https://journalistsresource.org/studies/economics/personal-finance/research-review-lotteries-demographics.

128. Sarah Ovaska-Few, "Hope and Hard Luck," *NC Policy Watch*, December 17, 2010, http://www.ncpolicywatch.com/2010/12/17/hope-and-hard-luck/#map.

129. Grace M. Barnes, John W. Welte, Marie-Cecile O. Tidwell, and Joseph H. Hoffman, "Gambling on the Lottery: Sociodemographic Correlates across the Lifespan," National Institutes of Health, July 18, 2014, https://www.ncbi.nlm.nih.gov/pmc/articles/PMC4103646/.

130. Garrick Blalock, David R. Just, and Daniel H. Simon, "Hitting the Jackpot or Hitting the Skids: Entertainment, Poverty, and the Demand for State Lotteries," *American Journal of Economics and Sociology*, 2007. http://stoppredatorygambling.org/wp-content/uploads/2014/07/Cornell-Univ-study-Entertainment-Poverty-and-the-Demand-for-State-Lotteries1.pdf

Chapter 7. Fighting Back

1. Diane Ravitch, *Reign of Error*, 12.

2. Ibid., 6.

3. Frank Newport and Jim Harter, "U.S. Workers' Satisfaction with Job Dimensions Increases," *Gallup*, August 29, 2016, http://www.gallup.com/poll/195143/workers-satisfied-job-dimensions.aspx?utm_source=alert&utm_medium=email&utm_content=morelink&utm_campaign=syndication.

4. Bureau of Labor Statistics, "The Employment Situation," *Department of Labor*, February 2017, https://www.bls.gov/news.release/pdf/empsit.pdf.

5. Oxfam Media Briefing, "Broken at the Top: How America's Dysfunctional Tax System Costs Billions in Corporate Tax Dodging," *Oxfam*, April 14, 2016, https://www.oxfamamerica.org/static/media/files/Broken_at_the_Top_4.14.2016.pdf.

6. Joanne Oakes, *Keeping Track: How Schools Structure Inequality* (New Haven: Yale University Press, 1985), 21.

7. Amanda Litvinov, "Activists Prompted Treasury to Curb Corporate Tax Avoidance Scheme that Hurts Schools," *Nea.org*, April 14, 2016, http://educationvotes.nea.org/2016/04/14/activists-prompted-treasury-to-curb-corporate-tax-avoidance-scheme-that-hurts-schools/.

8. Brenda Álvarez, " 'Everyone's Job to Help': Addressing Student Poverty Beyond the Schoolhouse," *NEA Today*, May 31, 2016, http://neatoday.org/2016/05/31/addressing-student-poverty/.

9. Save Our Schools, "Guiding Principles," 2016, http://saveourschoolsmarch.org/about/guiding-principles/.

10. Parents Across America, "What We Believe," http://parentsacrossamerica.org/.

11. Network for Public Education, "What We Do," 2017, https://networkforpubliceducation.org/.

12. Randi Weingarten, "President Obama Says We Need to Stop Teaching to the Test," *AFT.org*, January 24, 2012, http://www.aft.org/press-release/public-schools-are-cornerstone-strong-economy-strong-democracy-strong-middle#sthash.T8FBzmXL.dpuf.

13. Randi Weingarten, "AFT on Texas Supreme Court Ruling on School Funding," *AFT.org*, May 13, 2016, http://www.aft.org/node/11193.

14. American Federation of Teachers, *Helping Children Thrive: Child Health Survey Report*, 2015, http://www.aft.org/sites/default/files/wysiwyg/helpingchildrenthrive2015.pdf

15. American Federation of Teachers, "State of the Union, 2012-2014," 2014, http://www.aft.org/sites/default/files/wysiwyg/aft_sotu2014.pdf.

16. Tim Walker, "NEA to Expand STEM Teacher Training Program," October 2, 2012, http://neatoday.org/2012/10/02/nea-to-expand-stem-teacher -training-program-2/.

17. U.S. Department of Education, "Every Student Succeeds Act: Accountability and State Plans," *Federal Register*, May 31, 2016, https://www2.ed.gov/policy/elsec/leg/essa/nprmaccountabilitystateplans52016.pdf.

18. Mary Battenfeld and Felicity Crawford, "Why Every Student Succeeds Act Still Leaves Most Vulnerable Kids Behind," *The Conversation*, December 11, 2015, https://theconversation.com/why-every-student-succeeds-act-still-leaves-most-vulnerable-kids-behind-46247.

19. Andrew Tillett-Saks, "Labor's Stockholm Syndrome: Why Unions Must Stop Backing Anti-Labor Candidates in the Primaries," *Truthout*, August 03, 2016, http://www.truth-out.org/opinion/item/37081-labor-s-political-stockholm-syndrome-why-unions-must-stop-supporting-anti-labor-candidates-in-primaries.

20. Hillary Clinton, "Initiative on Technology & Innovation," 2016, https://www.hillaryclinton.com/briefing/factsheets/2016/06/27/hillary-clintons-initiative-on-technology-innovation/.

21. Bureau of Labor Statistics, U.S. Department of Labor, "Earnings and Employment Rates by Educational Attainment, 2015," March 2016, https://www.bls.gov/careeroutlook/2016/data-on-display/education-matters.htm.

22. Dionne Searcey and Robert Gebeloff, "Middle Class Shrinks Further as More Fall Out Instead of Climbing Up," *New York Times*, January 25, 2015.

23. Nelson D. Schwartz and Patricia Cohennov, "Falling Wages at Factories Squeeze the Middle Class," *New York Times*, November 20, 2014. https://www.nytimes.com/2014/11/21/business/falling-wages-at-factories-squeeze-the-middle-class.html.

24. Dean Baker, "Labor Day 2016: Moderate Progress in Last Year Monday," *Truthout*, September 05, 2016, http://www.truth-out.org/opinion/item/37491-labor-day-2016-moderate-progress-in-last-year.

25. Jake Rosenfeld, Patrick Denice, and Jennifer Laird, "Union Decline Lowers Wages of Nonunion Workers: The Overlooked Reason Why Wages Are Stuck and Inequality Is Growing," *Economic Policy Institute*, August 30, 2016, http://www.epi.org/publication/union-decline-lowers-wages-of-nonunion-workers-the-overlooked-reason-why-wages-are-stuck-and-inequality-is-growing/.

26. Paula Span, "Wages for Home Care Aides Lag as Demand Grows," *New York Times*, September 23, 2016, https://www.nytimes.com/2016/09/27/health/home-care-aides-wages.html.

27.   Binyamin Applelbaum, "Why Are Politicians So Obsessed with Manufacturing?," *New York Times*, October 4, 2016, https://www.nytimes.com/2016/10/09/magazine/why-are-politicians-so-obsessed-with-manufacturing.html.

28.   Harold L. Sirkin, Michael Zinser, and Justin Rose, "Why Advanced Manufacturing Will Boost Productivity," January 30, 2015, https://www.bcgperspectives.com/content/articles/lean_and_manufacturing_production_why_advanced_manufacturing_boost_productivity/?utm_source=201609EPINATED&utm_medium=Email&utm_campaign=otr.

29.   Arindam Bhattacharya, Hans-Paul Bürkner, and Aparna Bijapurkar, "What You Need to Know About Globalization's Radical New Phase," July 20, 2016. https://www.bcgperspectives.com/content/articles/globalization-growth-what-need-know-globalization-radical-new-phase/?utm_source=201609EPINATED&utm_medium=Email&utm_campaign=otr.

30.   Robert W. McChesney and John Nichols, *People Get Ready: The Fight Against a Jobless Economy and a Citizenless Democracy* (New York: Nation Books, 2016).

31.   Ohio Center for History, Art and Technology, "Where in the World Is Licking County? Globalization on a Local Level," 2016, http://www.attheworks.org/files/documents/Globalization%20Teacher%20Packet.pdf.

32.   Oxfam Canada, "Lesson Plans," 2017, https://www.oxfam.ca/our-work/publications/educational-resources/lesson-plans.

33.   Western Michigan University, "Cultural Connections: From Senegal and West Africa to Your Classroom," 2011, http://www.cultureconnections.org/index.html.

34.   Western Michigan University, "Globalization: An Introduction," 2011, http://www.cultureconnections.org/resources/curriculum-artifact-boxes/globalization-an-introduction/unit-01/lesson-plans/activities-03.html.

35.   Michael Gonchar and Tom Marshall, "Corporate Irresponsibility? Fashion's Hidden Cost in Bangladesh's Garment Industry," *New York Times*, May 14, 2013, https://learning.blogs.nytimes.com/2013/05/14/corporate-irresponsibility-fashions-hidden-cost-in-bangladeshs-garment-industry/.

36.   Bigelow and Peterson, *Rethinking Globalization*.

37.   Bill Bigelow and Tim Swinehart, eds., *A People's Curriculum for the Earth: Teaching Climate Change and the Environmental Crisis* (Milwaukee, WI: Rethinking Schools, 2015).

38.   Noam Chomsky, *Who Rules the World?* (New York: Metropolitan, 2016).

39.   Cindy Long, "Let's Work Together to Educate Our Children: National Teacher of the Year Speaks Out," http://neatoday.org/2016/10/11/teacher-of-the-year-jahana-hayes/, October 11, 2016.

40.   Phi Delta Kappan, "The 48th Annual PDK Poll of the Public's Attitudes Toward the Public School," 2016, http://pdkpoll2015.pdkintl.org/wp-content/uploads/2016/08/pdkpoll48_2016.pdf.

41. Paul Potter, "Speech at March on Washington to End the War in Vietnam Organized by Students for a Democratic Society," http://www.sdsrebels.com/potter.htm, April 17,1965.

42. Thomas Picketty, *Capital in the Twenty-First Century* (Cambridge, MA: Harvard University, 2014).

Index

Tennessee, 166–67
testing, 195
Texas, 162
The Gap (firm), 176
Tillett-Saks, Andrew, 197
toxic wastes, 106–7
Trilateral Commission, 123–24
Trumbo, Dalton, 150
Trump, Donald, 36; on corporate taxes, 183
Trump administration: educational policies of, 194–95; education funding cuts under, 36; environmental policies of, 24
Tucci, Joseph M., 19

underemployment, 74
unemployment rates, 33–34; for differing educational levels, 198; for STEM graduates, 70
UNICEF, 156
Union of Concerned Scientists (UCS), 103–4
unions: of charter school teachers, 162; corporate attacks on, 191–92; decline in membership in, 79, 199–200; at IBM, 93; outsourcing to avoid, 87; of teachers, 192–97
United Nations, on world poverty, 62
United States: academic test scores in, 31–32; attitudes toward capitalism in, 30; election of 2016 in, 197; military interventions by, 23, 50; STEM-related jobs in, 69–70
upcredentialing, 75–76
Upwork (firm), 82
Utah, 116

Venezuela, 137
Vietnam, 54
voting, 151–52

Walker, Alice, 157
Walker, Scott, 103
Walmart Family Foundation, 176–77
Walt Disney World (Florida), 80
Walton family, 176–77
War on Poverty, 7, 8
Washington (D.C.), 100
Washington (state), 161
water: access to, 139; pollution of, 107–8
Watts (Los Angeles, California), 7–9
Weil, David, 86
Weingarten, Randi, 17, 193
Weissman, Jordan, 34
West, Cornel, 21
West Point, U.S. Military Academy at, 150
Whirlpool (firm), 170
white-collar work, Taylorism in, 84–86
Whitman, Meg, 113
whole language reading, 125–26
Wilczek, Frank, 114
Wilson, Christopher, 55
winter Olympics, 112
Wisconsin, 88–89, 160
women: in Bangladesh garment industry, 53–54; child labor by girls, 60–61
World Bank: poverty line used by, 61–63; in South Africa, 138–39
World War I, 121

Yates, Michael, 61

Zapatistas (Mexico), 45